The Right to Memory

Worlds of Memory

Editors:
Jeffrey Olick, University of Virginia
Aline Sierp, Maastricht University
Jenny Wüstenberg, Nottingham Trent University

Published in collaboration with the Memory Studies Association

This book series publishes innovative and rigorous scholarship in the interdisciplinary and global field of memory studies. Memory studies includes all inquiries into the ways we—both individually and collectively—are shaped by the past. How do we represent the past to ourselves and to others? How do those representations shape our actions and understandings, whether explicitly or unconsciously? The "memory" we study encompasses the near-infinitude of practices and processes humans use to engage with the past, the incredible variety of representations they produce, and the range of individuals and institutions involved in doing so.

Guided by the mandate of the Memory Studies Association to provide a forum for conversations among subfields, regions, and research traditions, Worlds of Memory focuses on cutting-edge research that pushes the boundaries of the field and can provide insights for memory scholars outside of a particular specialization. In the process, it seeks to make memory studies more accessible, diverse, and open to novel approaches.

Volume 10
The Right to Memory: History, Media, Law, and Ethics
Edited by Noam Tirosh and Anna Reading

Volume 9
Towards a Collaborative Memory: German Memory Work in Transnational Context
Sara Jones

Volume 8
Carnivalizing Reconciliation: Contemporary Australian and Canadian Literature and Film beyond the Victim Paradigm
Hanna Teichler

Volume 7
Nordic War Stories: World War II as History, Fiction, Media, and Memory
Edited by Marianne Stecher

Volume 6
The Struggle for the Past: How We Construct Social Memories
Elizabeth Jelin

Volume 5
The Mobility of Memory: Migrations and Diasporas in Europe and Beyond
Edited by Luisa Passerini, Gabriele Proglio, and Milica Trakilović

Volume 4
Agency in Transnational Memory Politics
Edited by Aline Sierp and Jenny Wüstenberg

Volume 3
Resettlers and Survivors: Bukovina and the Politics of Belonging in West Germany and Israel, 1945–89
Gaëlle Fisher

Volume 2
Velvet Retro: Postsocialist Nostalgia and the Politics of Heroism in Czech Popular Culture
Veronika Pehe

Volume 1
When Will We Talk about Hitler? German Students and the Nazi Past
Alexandra Oeser

THE RIGHT TO MEMORY

History, Media, Law, and Ethics

Edited by
Noam Tirosh and Anna Reading

berghahn
NEW YORK · OXFORD
www.berghahnbooks.com

Published in 2023 by
Berghahn Books
www.berghahnbooks.com

© 2023, 2026 Noam Tirosh and Anna Reading
First paperback edition published in 2026

All rights reserved. Except for the quotation of short passages
for the purposes of criticism and review, no part of this book
may be reproduced in any form or by any means, electronic or
mechanical, including photocopying, recording, or any information
storage and retrieval system now known or to be invented,
without written permission of the publisher.

Library of Congress Cataloging-in-Publication Data

A C.I.P. cataloging record is available from the Library of Congress
Library of Congress Cataloging in Publication Control Number: 2022045358

British Library Cataloguing in Publication Data

A catalogue record for this book is available from the British Library

EU GPSR Authorized Representative

LOGOS EUROPE, 9 rue Nicolas Poussin, 17000, LA ROCHELLE, France
Email: Contact@logoseurope.eu

ISBN 978-1-80073-857-7 hardback
ISBN 978-1-83695-372-2 paperback
ISBN 978-1-83695-373-9 epub
ISBN 978-1-80073-858-4 web pdf

https://doi.org/10.3167/9781800738577

Contents

Preface   vii
    Noam Tirosh and Anna Reading

Introduction. A Right to Memory   1
    Noam Tirosh and Anna Reading

Chapter 1. Antigone's Shadow: Human Rights, Memory, and the Two World Wars   17
    Jay Winter

Chapter 2. Framing Memory Rights in International Law   33
    Anna Reading

Chapter 3. The "Duty to Remember" and the "Right to Memory": Memory Politics and Neoliberal Logic   53
    Lea David

Chapter 4. Memory, Rights, and Sen's "Capabilities Approach"   76
    Noam Tirosh and Amit Schejter

Chapter 5. "The Memory Belongs to No One and It Belongs to Everyone": An Analysis of a Grassroots Claim to the Right to Memory   92
    Rebecca Kook

Chapter 6. Using and Abusing Memory Laws in Search of "Historical Truth": The Case of the 2018 Amendments to the Polish Institute of National Remembrance Act   112
    Aleksandra Gliszczyńska-Grabias and Grażyna Baranowska

Chapter 7. The Right to Produce Memory: Social Memory Technology as Cultural Work   132
    Karen Worcman and Joanne Garde-Hansen

Chapter 8. Beyond a Human Right to Memory   149
    Anna Reading

Conclusion 162

Index 166

Preface

Noam Tirosh and Anna Reading

Each book has its own unique (hi)story. This book's story starts in a small, crowded room at the Complutense University, Madrid. We presented some preliminary ideas about the right to memory during the Memory Studies Association Annual Conference of 2019. The temperatures in Madrid had skyrocketed, and there was no air-conditioning to chill the boiling room. Nevertheless, people packed the venue. Some of our most respected colleagues were sitting on the floor. Many people wished to hear what we had to say about the right to memory. At this moment, we realized that speaking of memory rights and the right to memory was an intriguing contribution to the field of memory studies.

Since that meeting in 2019, a few more people have joined us on our journey, and a community of scholars interested in memory rights and the right to memory has emerged. This book is the outcome of the collective efforts of this community. While the authors of this volume's chapters are positioned in different fields and address memory rights in various ways, they share the same fundamental belief that the right to memory, in particular, and memory rights, in general, are crucial components of memory processes worldwide.

As part of writing this book, we met for a one-day (virtual) workshop. The authors of this edited collection presented their work, and scholars from around the world gave comments and reflected on the ideas expressed in this book's chapters. Notably, the audience, authors, and commentators agreed that memory can and should be protected by rights and other legal mechanisms that aim to safeguard those who need such protection. The process of writing this book, our workshop, and different encounters along the way formed a community of people who support such ideas. We hope that with the publication of this edited collection, the community of people studying memory in its relation to rights, and the right to memory in particular, will grow and that discussions about such issues within memory studies and related fields will intensify.

Indeed, this book would not have been published without the help of many people. It takes a village to write a book. We first want to thank our families for their continued support in our demanding work. Our families' support allows us to dedicate our work to new ideas and the sometimes tedious task of scholarly writing. This book is dedicated to and inspired by them in many ways.

In addition, we want to use this opportunity to thank our colleagues from different universities worldwide who engaged with our ideas about the right to memory and helped us polish and reframe them in a very constructive way. We want to especially thank Prof. Kobi Kabalek of the Pennsylvania State University, who offered his support along the way, and Prof. Neve Gordon of Queen Mary University of London, who contributed to this book in ways that he is probably not aware.

We wish to express our gratitude to all of our friends and colleagues at Ben-Gurion University of the Negev and King's College, London. Through daily discussion and mundane encounters with our brilliant colleagues, we rethought our assumptions and shaped our arguments and ideas. We wish to thank also our friends and colleagues at the Humanities Institute of the Pennsylvania State University. While working on this book, one of the editors—Noam Tirosh—served as a visiting professor at the Institute. The stimulating environment of the Institute and its generous support were essential to the completion of this volume. As part of this support, we worked with soon-to-be doctor, Ms. Aaren Pastor, who helped us edit and polish each chapter of the book.

Unfortunately, as this book was finalized, war broke out in Europe. While we have always believed that memory rights and the right to memory are intriguing aspects of our societies' memory processes, we could not begin to imagine that they would turn into a matter of life and death with the illegal Russian invasion of Ukraine.

In February 2022, Vladimir Putin, the president of Russia, ordered Russian troops to brutally attack Ukraine. This attack has its own history. Only a few months beforehand, in July 2021, Putin had published a long essay on the Kremlin website titled "On the Historical Unity of Russians and Ukrainians."[1]

In this long text, Putin highlighted what he defined as the "common history" of Russia and Ukraine. According to his twisted logic, this shared past justifies keeping Ukraine under Russian control and influence. As part of this text, Putin wrote the following:

> Ukraine's ruling circles decided to justify their country's independence through the denial of its past . . . They began to mythologize and rewrite history, edit

out everything that united us, and refer to the period when Ukraine was part of the Russian Empire and the Soviet Union as an occupation. The common tragedy of collectivization and famine of the early 1930s was portrayed as the genocide of the Ukrainian people.²

This statement is a horrific example of the leader of a world superpower denying the basic memory rights of the people in a sovereign state, in this case, the Ukrainian people. Putin denies the Ukrainians' right to memory, and by doing so, he justifies the deprivation of their right to sovereignty, as well as their right to life and right to dignity. The negation of the Ukrainians' right to memory led to the brutal invasion. An invasion that has already cost the lives of thousands of innocent people and the mass destruction of Ukrainian cities. While writing these words, more than 7 million Ukrainian people have been turned into refugees and are now seeking shelter in neighboring states.³

We wish to dedicate this book to the Ukrainian people fighting at this moment to realize their right to memory. May their struggle serve as a vivid reminder of the importance of memory in our lives and the need to protect it. We hope that our book will be of even modest help to those trying to protect such noble causes.

Noam Tirosh is a senior lecturer in the department of Communication Studies at Ben-Gurion University of the Negev. His research focuses on the relationship between memory and media and their relation with democracy, justice, and human rights. He is the author of a score of journal articles and book chapters covering topics ranging from the European Right to Be Forgotten to the memory rights of the Palestinian minority in Israel, refugees and asylum seekers, and Jews deported from Arab countries.

Anna Reading (known as Amza), PhD, is Professor of Culture and Creative Industries at Kings College, University of London, UK and Honorary Visiting Professor at Western Sydney University, Australia. She is the author of *Polish Women, Solidarity and Feminism* (Springer, 1992), *The Social Inheritance of the Holocaust: Gender, Culture and Memory* (Springer, 2002), and *Gender and Memory in the Globital Age* (Palgrave Macmillan, 2016) and co-edited *Cultural Memories of Nonviolent Struggles* (Palgrave Macmillan, 2015) and *Save as . . . Digital Memories* (Palgrave 2009). She jointly edits the journal *Media, Culture, and Society* and has written seven plays performed in the UK, Finland, India, Poland, United States, and Ireland.

Notes

1. See an English translation of this text at V. V. Putin. "Article by Vladimir Putin 'On the Historical Unity of Russians and Ukrainians.'" *Boris Yeltsin Presidential Library*. Retrieved 17 July 2022 from https://www.prlib.ru/en/article-vladimir-putin-historical-unity-russians-and-ukrainians.
2. Putin, "On the Historical Unity."
3. See data available at Operational Data Portal. "Ukraine Refugee Situation." *UNHCR*. Retrieved 9 November 2022 from https://data2.unhcr.org/en/situations/ukraine.

INTRODUCTION

A Right to Memory

Noam Tirosh and Anna Reading

At the core of this edited collection stands the right to memory, its theoretical underpinnings, its different definitions, and the varied places and social realms in which actors realize it. Indeed, choosing rights discourse as the language to describe what we deem to be the needed protections to cultural and collective memory processes is not a neutral ethical and political decision.[1] Human rights, and the discourse surrounding and legitimizing them, are more than simply the "last utopia," as Samuel Moyn has stated.[2] Human rights can also serve as a powerful discursive and legal tool that enables "a broad array of relationships of subjugation characterized by the use of force and coercion."[3] Hence, we begin by initially justifying our use of rights discourse as an anchor for discussion. It is only after this that we then move forward to address what scholars in the field of memory studies have already explored in relation to a right to memory, followed by what authors in this edited collection mean when addressing this unique and important right.

This edited collection places the right to memory in particular, and memory rights in general, at the center of attention in the field of memory studies. We understand that the importance of memory transcends its ability to inform our knowledge of the past and see memory as important in terms of its ability to influence our individual, collective, and even human well-being. We embrace the ontological assumption about the right to memory as a socio-political mechanism that we should use to achieve what Paul Ricoeur defined as "a culture of just memory":[4] a culture that promotes memory for the sake of humanity and that connects ideas of human rights with visions of justice and the empowerment of the weak.[5] In the case of a right to memory, we see this as particularly important for the empowerment of the "memory-least-advantaged," or those whose stories may be forgotten or stand at the margins.

This assumption should, as explained, not be taken for granted. As human rights discourse can also create the "human right to dominate" or the "human right to kill,"[6] why should we call for the adoption of a new human right to memory that anchors and legitimizes a rights-driven discourse? Instead, we could advocate for "memory democratization," a process in which more versions of society's past are being engaged by an as-large-as-possible fraction of a given society.[7] The answer, we believe, is twofold. First, the rights-turn in memory studies is justified and needed as the "memory democratization" approach, which was part and parcel of the hype around digital media and its influence on memory processes,[8] seems to be failing. Astrid Erll, for example, has claimed that the ethical approaches to memory (among them prosthetic memory, affiliative memory, cosmopolitan memory, and multidirectional memory) represent a utopian moment in memory studies driven by the assumption that "new media memory can help create new forms of solidarity and new visions of justice."[9] Unfortunately, these new visions of social and mnemonic justice are far from shaping current world affairs.[10]

All around the world, anti-liberal leaders mobilize history and memory to promote nationalistic and chauvinistic agendas.[11] For example, Donald Trump, the former president of the United States, called to "Make America Great Again," thus promoting an uncritical, distorted view of the American past, ignoring years of racial discrimination and other injustices. One can find similar examples in Russia, Poland, Hungry, Brazil, India, and Israel, among others.[12] Digital memory, while enabling marginalized groups to engage with their forgotten past narratives,[13] does not necessarily promote more democratic societies, nor create new forms of solidarity between different groups, nor serve as the proponent of a new culture of just memory. These digital tools, helping groups to reclaim their silenced and forgotten memories, are just tools. They are not sufficient without a well-defined set of socio-legal mechanisms, what we describe as "memory rights," which can better serve those who seek memory justice.

The second argument favoring using rights to protect memory processes is the ever-growing tendency to move debates about the proper appreciation of history and public commemorations to the courts and legal sphere.[14] Here, a detailed discussion about a specific example, the deadly clashes between extreme right-wing supporters and local activists from Charlottesville, Virginia, during the notorious "Unite the Right" rally in August 2017,[15] can help us illustrate the need to define the right to memory and explore memory rights and their role in society. These clashes are, by now, an oft-cited example of the political rift in the United States and of the incompetence of former US President Donald Trump (who falsely accused "both sides" of initiating violence). Organized by US right-wing extremists from all over the country, the participants protested against the Charlottesville city council's decision to remove a statue of Robert E. Lee from "Lee Park" and to rename the park "Emancipation Park." These decisions were realized only four years after the deadly conflicts in the city, after a long phase of legal debates attempting to overturn the decisions.[16]

Indeed, the memorialization of General Lee, the commander of the Confederate States Army during the American Civil War, clashed with the city's official commitment "to reveal and tell the full story of race through [its] public spaces."[17] It was a clash between the city's local memory scape, as demonstrated by commemorating racist and bigoted individuals and ideologies, and the attempt to tell "a more complete history of race"[18] as declared by local legislators when they decided to remove the statue and change the park's name.

The tragic events in Charlottesville have been widely discussed from various perspectives, mainly focusing on the toxic political culture rampant in the United States during Trump's presidency.[19] There is, however, an additional perspective to these events that warrants attention. From a memory perspective, this example shows that memory-related processes are increasingly in the interest of advocates who turn to courts, the legal sphere, and public policy-making arenas (such as city councils) to gain protection from what they consider "memory injustices."[20] For Mr. Gathers, a commentator at one of the city council's meetings dedicated to the issue, the statue was only "a chunk of rock, plain and simple."[21] Removing a chunk of rock therefore was irrelevant and not necessary. Mr. Jefferson, another commentator in the same meeting, could not agree less. "Slavery was a criminal enterprise and a disgrace to the country," he claimed.[22] As such, he suggested taking down the statues and "moving the[m] to the University Confederate Cemetery."[23] By doing so, he hoped, a future remembrance culture that would not be offensive to the city's communities of color would prosper. Such a culture can commemorate the city's difficult past without glorifying those who committed atrocities.[24]

Enzo Traverso claimed that anti-racist movements targeted commemoration sites and monuments "that symbolize the legacy of slavery and colonialism."[25] According to him, "anti-Racism is a battle for memory."[26] In the context of this battle, Traverso observed that the attempt to change the local mnemonic culture and replace it with a different one epitomizes "a new dimension of struggle: the connection between rights and memory."[27] In their attempt to reshape the public mnemonic landscapes, local activists tried to exercise new rights that safeguard processes related to society's memory. Removing the statue of Robert E. Lee from Charlottesville's public sphere, as such, can be seen as a realization of a particular perspective about the residents' right to memory, a right that in this case was manifested in changing local commemoration culture by altering the city's mnemonic-scape.

Indeed, as shown here, despite being a contested term, there are good reasons to develop deeper discussions about "A Right to Memory." The notion of rights carries with it, at least potentially, a liberatory potential. Even Nicola Perugini and Neve Gordon, forceful critics of the human-rights lingua franca, maintain that such rights can be "redefined in a new way that mobilizes people to struggle for emancipatory projects."[28] We hope to contribute to this liberatory understanding of human rights in a number of ways. The volume seeks to contribute to a better understanding of the theoretical underpinning to memory rights and their epistemological justification. It seeks to engage with the right to memory's different definitions in an attempt to find commonalities between them, and, finally, the volume aims to provide analyses of empirical examples within a range of public arenas in which social actors are mobilizing memory rights and the right to memory.

The next section of this introduction explores how scholars in memory studies have already engaged with the right to memory. We follow this with a summary of how each chapter of this book contributes to the principle of the right to memory as a practical and theoretical tool promoting visions and actions for memory justice.

The Right to Memory in Memory Studies

Memory is a prominent issue of exploration in the humanities and social sciences. While its origins go back to the early part of the twentieth century, memory studies has evolved over the past twenty years into an established discipline of vibrant intellectual debates with its own conferences, journals, and associations.[29] In most cases, the scholarly attempt to understand memory processes in society is focused on public commemorations, everyday practices of individuals and collectives, and media practices of memory and remembrance.[30] Memory rights and their manifestations in society, however, have not been systematically explored, despite the ways struggles over memory are inherently connected to human rights and the discourses surrounding them.[31] The right to memory, we argue, suggests more than a discursive affiliation between memory and human rights. Rather, a right to memory also includes the efficacy and challenges of existing socio-legal mechanisms (such as policies and memory laws) that aim to shape memory-related issues. It also includes the need to create new socio-legal mechanisms when pre-existing ones fail or are absent.

Although the right to memory has not been extensively explored within academia, it has been discussed to some extent by scholars from various fields, such as archival science, media and communication, political science and, indeed, memory studies. For example, memory's relation to social struggles for justice led scholars to try and establish a connection between memories and rights.[32] Pierre Nora has suggested that "to claim the right to memory is to call for justice."[33] Similarly, Kobi Kabalek has noted that scholars' attention to the right to memory is led by the assumption of memory as an "important element of social justice."[34] But what exactly does a right to memory mean, and how is it related to demands for social justice or any other socio-political movements for change? Kevin Hearty has suggested that "the right to remember" is an important aspect in societies transitioning from a troubled past, manifest in the symbolic reparations that are now integral to transitional justice.[35] Henriette Dahan Kalev has claimed that infringing on the right of people to express their collective memory is to violate a fundamental human right, the right to equally take part in shaping a national collective identity.[36] Rebecca Kook has called for the generalizability of the right to memory. For her, the right to memory promotes "the idea that remembrance should be made accessible and available to everyone."[37] According to Kook, individuals and communities can realize the right to memory in varied realms such as the platforms enabling memory processes, the mnemonic content (historical narratives) mediated through these platforms, and the audience's opportunity to take an active part in constructing such content.

Interestingly, in archival science, scholars refer to the right to memory as a "right to remembered presence" manifested during conflicts over memory and remembering.[38] This understanding of the right to memory (or the right to remembered presence) leads to "acts of archival restoration and reconstruction," enabling new information about the past to become public with new actors that gain access to the newly designed archives. Addressing memory as a right in such cases "requires further archival modeling and alternative modes of representation" that will, hopefully, give voice to the "archival" silence that "surrounds suffering."[39]

In addition, some scholars have discussed memory rights and the right to memory from a perspective that focuses on the duties such rights create. Indeed, it is not enough to speak about an abstracted right to memory. Kevin Whelan has suggested that a right to memory consists of three distinctive elements. The first is the obvious idea that we own our memories, so "no one has the right to tell us to forget our memories and move on." This, he claimed, creates the second element of the right to memory that he defined as a "right of testimony." This aspect of the right to memory includes people's right to tell stories "in the forms, shapes and ways that make sense for them." The third and most crucial element of Whelan's definition is what he called "the right of audience." According to him, the right to memory is also about the "ethical duty to hear other people's stories."[40]

Anna Reading focuses on duties in her discussion of the "right to a symbolic representation of the past."[41] According to Reading, the right to memory is integrally connected to "a set of interventions and social practices."[42] These sets of interventions and practices will help materialize the right to memory in the form of a "future-oriented civic duty to remember and remind."[43]

So, what exactly are these practices? What can be considered to be an intervention when realizing the right to memory in addition to the right to have an audience? Philip Lee and Pradip Ninan Thomas have argued that information and communication technologies as well as the ability to use them are essential in realizing memory rights. According to them, the right to memory creates the duty to "[protect] 'frameworks of memory' that ensure the physical survival and moral well-being of people."[44] The media, they claim, are central actors that guarantee memory rights and realize "the right to communicate" specific memories in public.[45] Karen Worcman and Joanne Garde-Hansen contend, similarly, that the right to memory is about utilization and access. According to them, the right to memory contains two meanings. It is both the individual's right to "record their memories through the use of media of their choosing" and the right "to access cultural memories that an individual or community may need, want and/or desire." Thus, the right to memory has to be realized by upholding duties over "organizations and businesses who are custodians of that cultural memory."[46]

Attentive readers can also find the translation of memory rights into concrete duties of different actors in a few human rights-related international covenants and declarations such as the United Nations Declaration on the Rights of Indigenous Peoples (2007).[47] In 2014, the European Court of Justice ruled that Europeans have a new "right to be forgotten," a right that was later on enshrined in the European "General Data Protection Regulation" (GDPR) of 2018. The "right to be forgotten" is about individuals' rights to demand that content providers erase personal information they keep and the providers' duty to respond to such a demand when it can be justified. In line with the new "right to be forgotten," one can ask for content removal even when the personal content was shared lawfully and voluntarily.[48] Indeed, the right to be forgotten is mainly understood as an attempt to protect users' privacy in online environments. The right's critics, on the other hand, claimed that it is an infringement of freedom of expression.[49] Noam Tirosh has highlighted, however, that the right to be forgotten is actually a new memory right, helping users gain more control over their digital identities. By establishing new digital memory rights, such as the right to actively shape the digital representation of our life stories as we see fit, we gain better control over our identity-making processes. As such, Tirosh has claimed, the right to be forgotten can and should be regarded as an integral part of a future, more encompassing right to memory.[50]

While there are more examples of such attempts to protect memory processes in the international law system, the term "right to memory" is not explicitly addressed. Moreover, to the best of our knowledge, no attempt has been made to consider these different legal provisions within the prism of the idea of the right to memory.[51]

Our edited collection builds on this previous scholarship while informing the discussion regarding the right to memory. We do not offer a codification of laws, legal debates, or legal tools that are to serve, from now on, as the singular right to memory. This edited collection instead offers rich analyses of a multiplicity of case studies, ranging from historical accounts of the human rights revolution post–World War II to understanding our anthropomorphic bias when speaking of rights and memory rights. In their previous work, Worcman and Garde-Hansen have wondered "who has a right to memory, and what work do we need to do on an everyday, community level to ensure that those rights are upheld?"[52] In a way, all chapters in this edited collection try to tackle these questions. Using case studies (from various locations worldwide) alongside more theoretical arguments, the chapters in this edited collection contribute to discussions about memory rights and create a body of knowledge in a field mostly comprised of scattered work from different disciplines. In what follows, we will briefly describe each chapter and the book's structure.

The Structure of the Book

This edited collection examines memory rights and their role as guardians of the crucial components of memory processes: "the ability to create, preserve, retrieve and endow memories."[53] In the first chapter, Jay Winter focuses on "the duty to remember," which is perhaps the ethical foundation of any discussion about memory rights and the right to memory. Winter explores the human rights revolution following World War II explicitly as a memory project and as an attempt to honor the memory of the war's innocent victims. Focusing on the French jurist René Cassin, one of the authors of the Universal Declaration of the Rights of Man, Winter demonstrates how the idea behind the human rights revolution constitutes a commitment to memory and remembrance, an obligation higher than any individual's national affiliation. For Winter, there cannot be any discussion regarding the right to memory without first anchoring it within the moral duty to remember. This duty is demonstrated in Sophocles' *Antigone* who insisted on remembering and commemorating her brother, Polyneices, even when King Creon of Thebes forbade his burial in an attempt to force his oblivion.

In the following chapter, Anna Reading examines memory rights in international law. Systematically analyzing various conventions, treaties, and peace agreements, Reading explores memory rights beyond the nation-state. According to Reading, international law and protocol discursively articulate four different memory rights: the right to national memory that seeks to protect national configurations of memory; the right to world memory that aims to preserve heritage and memories of importance to humanity; the right to victims' memory that deals with memories of war victims, state violence and genocide; and the right to indigenous memory that focuses on the preservation and protection of indigenous history, culture, and identity.

Lea David critically addresses the current right to memory discourse in the third chapter. There is a tension between David's and Winter's and Reading's chapters in this volume. In most cases, memory rights are articulated as universal rights enforced in international charters and organizations. However, David shows that merging the duty to remember and the right to memory creates a false belief in a future protected from repeating atrocities that we are now obliged to commemorate. According to David, this neo-liberal logic, in which monetary value is being imposed on human suffering, only deepens inequalities and creates new ones.

Noam Tirosh and Amit Schejter, in the fourth chapter, address the right to memory from a perspective that recognizes the centrality of media in the memory-making process. They capitalize on Amartya Sen's capabilities approach, a right-based theory that places well-being at its center, to promote a right to memory that provides individuals with mechanisms that will allow them to have better control over their memory processes. They claim that the right to memory ensures access to tools people use when constructing stories about their past. In our hyper-connected societies, these mechanisms are digital media. Tirosh and Schejter call for the realization of memory rights in contemporary media and communication law and policies.

Rebecca Kook, in the following chapter, analyzes the right to memory from a unique grassroots perspective. Kook offers insights into how an Israeli memory initiative, named "memory in the living room," materializes the right to memory. Kook demonstrates how in some cases, the right to memory is not related to narratives and perceptions of the past but instead is about equal participation in social, cultural, and political mnemonic activities and about the ability to devise, promote and disseminate platforms of memorial practices. According to her, we cannot understand the right to memory as external to the struggle for democratic inclusion and equal participation in all spheres of social action and interaction.

Memory rights and the clash between the right to memory, the right to truth, and the attempt to manipulate history for the sake of the regime are all put forward in Aleksandra Gliszczyńska-Grabias and Grażyna Baranowska's chapter. This chapter highlights current legal debates in Poland, especially in regards to Holocaust memory and commemoration. The authors demonstrate how misusing memory-rights discourse by claiming that a false historical narrative is entitled to protection from the "right to historical truth" can endanger human rights standards. Distorting history in the name of the right to historical truth, they claim, is an infringement of the right to memory, as it denies people genuine engagement with their history. This is risky when the past of a given nation is that of a perpetrator and collaborator.

Karen Worcman and Joanne Garde-Hansen use the Museu da Pessoa (Museum of the person) in São Paolo, Brazil, as a case study of the realization of digital memory rights. In this example, the digital museum works together with the audience to protect and materialize memory rights. According to them, the right to memory is about recognizing specific memories and life stories of individuals and communities. But no less important is the right to memory as an amalgamation of rights to produce memories, to access these memories, and to own them. From this perspective, memory is a co-creation of people and institutions, of media and their users. Memory is also a joint effort of past generations creating memories and the contemporarily remembering generation that also seeks to shape and design a future remembering generation. Memory rights and the right to memory should take into consideration these connections and relations.

The final chapter, written by Anna Reading, critiques the current discussion on memory, memory rights, and the right to memory from the perspective of the more-than-human. According to Reading, we tend to think about the right to memory from a predominantly anthropomorphic perspective rooted in Western knowledge structures that forgets and devalues all that is nonhuman. Reading asks us to think whether planet earth, mountains, water, and nonhuman species are also entitled to the right to memory? Drawing on indigenous knowledge paradigms and practices as well as the work of the environmental justice movement, Reading suggests what a more-than-human right to memory should and can include and what we are missing when we consider a right to memory solely in human terms. After all, Reading contends, if our planet is no longer livable, there will be no "remembering human individual" and no human communities to enjoy a right to memory.

Interestingly, many of the contributions to this edited collection engaged with writers, scholars, theories, and even mythological figures not commonly considered to be an integral part of the memory studies canon as innovative ways to illustrate, demonstrate, and deepen our understanding of the right to memory. Jay Winter highlights the duty to remember by focusing on Sophocles' *Antigone*; Anna Reading starts her journey in the realm of international law by using William Shakespeare's *Hamlet;* Noam Tirosh and Amit Schejter address Franz Kafka's "A Report to an Academy" to highlight the importance of one's identity construction to their well-being; Aleksandra Gliszczyńska-Grabias and Grażyna Baranowska address Václav Havel's writings to highlight the tension between freedom, rights, and history. In addition, theories and political thought that are not always part of the memory-scholarly debate also found their way into this edited collection. Lea David critiques memory rights by highlighting their connection to neo-liberalism. Rebecca Kook draws on platform theories to analyze activists' perceptions about the right to memory. Tirosh and Schejter build on Amartya Sen's capabilities approach to justify their approach to memory rights and media. At the end of this edited collection, Anna Reading builds her argument on theories taken from the environmental justice movement.

This is not surprising, since discussions concerning memory rights and the right to memory are rare in the already established field of memory studies. Our attempts to define and analyze a right to memory necessitates new tools and perspectives. It requires us to look at memory issues using the theoretical insights of those outside of the field of memory studies to help us construct and define a new right to memory. We suggest that drawing insights from outside memory studies can help create new ways to think about memory in general and be used to develop new methodologies to research memory.

Most importantly, our discussion about the right to memory will serve scholars, activists, and practitioners alike in advancing what can be seen as a just memory; a cultural understanding of the past that considers and recalls all people's contribution to the course of history. As Avishai Margalit asks in his exploration of the ethics of memory:

> Are we obligated to remember people and events from the past? If we are, what is the nature of this obligation? Are remembering and forgetting proper subjects of moral praise or blame? Who are the "we" who may be obligated to remember: the collective "we," or some distributive sense of "we" that puts the obligation to remember on each and every member of the collective?[54]

We hope that the deep conceptual work developed in this volume, as well as the very different perspectives and critiques of the right to memory, will transform memory ethics from a merely philosophical exploration to one that includes concrete articulations at the local, national, and transnational levels of memory rights, provisions, and legally binding norms.

Noam Tirosh is a senior lecturer in the department of Communication Studies at Ben-Gurion University of the Negev. His research focuses on the relationship between memory and media and their relation with democracy, justice, and human rights. He is the author of a score of journal articles and book chapters covering topics ranging from the European Right to Be Forgotten to the memory rights of the Palestinian minority in Israel, refugees and asylum seekers, and Jews deported from Arab countries.

Anna Reading (known as Amza), PhD, is Professor of Culture and Creative Industries at Kings College, University of London, UK and Honorary Visiting Professor at Western Sydney University, Australia. She is the author of *Polish Women, Solidarity and Feminism* (Springer, 1992), *The Social Inheritance of the Holocaust: Gender, Culture and Memory* (Springer, 2002), and *Gender and Memory in the Globital Age* (Palgrave Macmillan, 2016) and co-edited *Cultural Memories of Nonviolent Struggles* (Palgrave Macmillan, 2015) and *Save as . . . Digital Memories* (Palgrave 2009). She jointly edits the journal *Media, Culture, and Society* and has written seven plays performed in the UK, Finland, India, Poland, United States, and Ireland.

Notes

1. Perugini and Gordon, *Right to Dominate*.
2. Moyn, *The Last Utopia*.
3. Perugini and Gordon, *Right to Dominate*, 3.
4. Ricoeur, "Memory and Forgetting," 11.
5. Further on in this chapter, we show that such a perspective is debatable. According to Perugini and Gordon, this is part of the "hydraulic model" of human rights discourse that takes for granted the assumption that "more human rights equals less domination." Perugini and Gordon, *Right to Dominate*, 13.
6. See Perugini and Gordon, *Right to Dominate*.
7. Numerous publications deal with the connections between memory and democracy. Yet, interestingly, the term "memory democratization" is not commonly used. Most widely, memory is considered a crucial component in the process of democratizing transforming societies. See, for example, De Brito Barahona, Gonzalez, and Aguilar, *Memory and Democratization*.
8. Often, authors conclude that through the utilization of contemporary digitized media "silenced or overwritten memories can also make their sudden return." Høg Hansen, Hemer, and Tufte, *Memory on Trial*, 4. As digital media users are now able to take an active role in the process of constructing collective memory, this fundamentally changes, at least in the common perspective, who controls society's memory. See also Hoskins, "Memory of the Multitude"; Smit, Ansgard, and Broersma, "Witnessing in New Memory Ecology"; Villa-Nicholas, "Latinx Digital Memory."
9. Erll, "Media and the Dynamics of Memory," 312.
10. See also Gensburger and Lefranc, *Beyond Memory*.
11. This book's opening chapter demonstrates how Russian aggression against Ukraine is justified by a distorted version of Russia's history. Indeed, this is a terrifying reminder of the dire fact that memory rights, when used by ill-intentioned actors, can be used to politically manipulate the past. Nevertheless, we do think that while such a threat is real,

it does not necessarily mean that we should abandon our attempt to define memory rights better and turn them into tools in the hands of those who need them most.
12. An in-depth exploration of such a process in Israel can be found in Gutman and Tirosh, "Balancing Atrocities and Forced Forgetting."
13. See, for example, Yvonne Liebermann's recent study about the Black Lives Matter movement and its mnemonic technological practices. Liebermann, "Born Digital."
14. Laws, the legal sphere, and memory have always intermingled in profound ways. The following references can serve as good entry points to the discussion: Fronza, "The Punishment of Negationism"; Gutman, "Memory Laws"; Löytömäki, "Law and Collective Memory of Colonialism"; and Savelsberg and King, *American Memories*.
15. For a detailed exploration of the clashes in Charlottesville, see Katz, "Unrest in Virginia."
16. Hanna and Ellis, "Charlottesville Removes Two."
17. The city's commitment was publicly reaffirmed during the Charlottesville City Council's special meeting on 6 February 2017. The meeting's transcript is available online. "Special Meeting Charlottesville City Council."
18. See "Special Meeting Charlottesville City Council."
19. See, for example, Astor, Caron, and Victor, "A Guide to the Charlottesville Aftermath"; Matthew, "On Charlottesville."
20. An important discussion about memory policymaking can be found in Sarah Gensburger and Sandrine Lefranc's book, *Beyond Memory: Can We Really Learn from the Past?* They define memory policies as all actions aimed at mobilizing "references to the past in order to impact on society and its memory and transform them" (3). These policies are enacted in various social arenas, yet they fail to achieve their desired goals in most cases. According to such policies, we need to remember past atrocities to achieve a more peaceful and tolerant society in the present and future. Yet, while memory policies have abounded worldwide for many years, such achievement is far from a reality.
21. See "Special Meeting Charlottesville City Council."
22. "Special Meeting Charlottesville City Council."
23. "Special Meeting Charlottesville City Council."
24. According to Vered Vinitzky-Seroussi, a "difficult past" represents events constituted by moral trauma, disputes, and conflicts. See Vinitzky-Seroussi, "Commemorating a Difficult Past."
25. Traverso, "Tearing Down Statues."
26. Traverso, "Tearing Down Statues."
27. Traverso, "Tearing Down Statues."
28. Perugini and Gordon, *Right to Dominate*, 129.
29. The establishment of the Memory Studies Association (MSA) in 2016 is perhaps the most important aspect of the "fieldization" of memory studies. The MSA website is a valuable source of information for memory scholars and practitioners. See Memory Studies Association. Retrieved 23 July 2022 from https://www.memorystudiesassociation.org/.
30. Jeffrey Olick and Joyce Robbins, in their seminal text "Social Memory Studies: From 'Collective Memory' to the Historical Sociology of Mnemonic Practices," explore this argument in depth. In addition, Alon Confino's criticism from 1997 is also a very good reference for such discussion. See Confino, "Collective Memory and Cultural History."
31. See Winter, chapter 1 in this volume, as well as Huyssen, "International Human Rights"; and Levy and Sznaider, *The Holocaust and Memory*.
32. Hom and Yamamoto, in "Collective Memory, History and Social Justice," claim that a political demand for rights always starts with social and ethical struggles over what society

will remember and that group memory of injustice is actively constructed by an organized mnemonic attempt at the group level.
33. While we use this statement by Pierre Nora, as stated in "Reasons for the Current Upsurge," to indicate the close relationship between memory and rights and their connection to justice, it is important to note that, according to Nora, while memory rights aim to protect justice, in effect the contemporary obsession with memory "has often become a call to murder":
> For the real problem raised by the sacred aura with which memory has now been invested is to know how, why and at what moment the otherwise positive principle of emancipation and liberation on which it is based backfires and becomes a form of closure, a grounds for exclusion and an instrument of war. To claim the right to memory is, at bottom, to call for justice. In the effects it has had, however, it has often become a call to murder.

34. Kabalek, "Memory and Periphery," 11.
35. Hearty, "Problematizing Symbolic Reparation."
36. Dahan Kalev, "Identity, Memory and Ethnicity."
37. Kook, "Agents of Memory," 981.
38. Butler, "Othering the Archive."
39. Butler, "Othering the Archive," 68.
40. Whelan, "Rights of Memory," 19–20.
41. Reading, "European Roma," 122.
42. Reading, "Gender and the Right to Memory," 11.
43. Viejo-Rose, "Memorial Functions," 477.
44. Lee and Thomas, *Public Memory, Public Media*, 15.
45. Lee and Thomas, *Public Memory, Public Media*, 206.
46. Worcman and Garde-Hansen, *Social Memory Technology*, 9–10.
47. "United Nations Declaration on the Rights of Indigenous Peoples." See also Reading, chapter 8, in this volume.
48. More extensive discussions about the right to be forgotten can be found in Ghezzi, Pereira and Vesnic-Alujevic, *Ethics of Memory*; Carter, "Argentina's Right to be Forgotten"; Bennett, "The Right to Be Forgotten"; and Jones, *Ctrl +Z*.
49. See, for example, Kristie Byrum's analysis of the right to be forgotten in *The European Right to Be Forgotten*.
50. See Tirosh, "Reconsidering the 'Right to Be Forgotten.'"
51. Anna Reading's chapter in this volume is a valuable resource on memory rights in international law. Additional in-depth discussions about memory rights in international law can be found in Lee and Thomas, *Public Memory, Public Media*; Reading, "Identity, Memory and Cosmopolitanism"; and Lee, "Towards a Right to Memory."
52. Worcman and Garde-Hansen, *Social Memory Technology*, 8.
53. Tirosh and Schejter, "The Regulation of Archives," 248.
54. Margalit, *Ethics of Memory*, 7.

Bibliography

Astor, Maggie, Christina Caron, and Daniel Victor. "A Guide to the Charlottesville Aftermath." *The New York Times*, 13 August 2017. Retrieved 17 June 2021 from https://www.nytimes.com/2017/08/13/us/charlottesville-virginia-overview.html.

Bennett, Steven C. "The Right to Be Forgotten: Reconciling EU and US Perspectives." *Berkeley Journal of International Law* 30, no.1 (2012): 161–95.

Butler, Beverley. "Othering the Archive: From Exile to Inclusion and Heritage Dignity; The Case of Palestinian Archival Memory." *Archival Science* 9 (2009): 57–69.

Byrum, Kristie. *The European Right to be Forgotten: The First Amendment Enemy*. Lanham, MD: Lexington Books, 2018.

Carter, Edward L. "Argentina's Right to Be Forgotten." *Emory International Law Review* 27, no. 1 (2013): 23–39.

Confino, Alon. "Collective Memory and Cultural History: Problems of Method." *The American Historical Review* 102, no.5 (1997): 1386–403.

Dahan Kalev, Henriette. "Identity, Memory and Ethnicity: The Relation between Memory, Identity, Justice, Pluralism and Civil Rights." In *Between "I" and "We": The Construction of Identities and the Israeli Identity*, edited by Azmi Bishara, 61–72. [In Hebrew.] Jerusalem: Van Leer Jerusalem Institute and Tel Aviv: Hakibbutz Hameuchad Publishing House, 1999.

De Brito Barahona, Alexandra, Carmen Enriquez Gonzalez, and Paloma Aguilar. *The Politics of Memory and Democratization*. Oxford: Oxford University Press, 2001.

Erll, Astrid. "Media and the Dynamics of Memory: From Cultural Paradigms to Transcultural Premediation." In *Handbook of Culture and Memory*, edited by Brady Wagoner, 305–24. Oxford: Oxford University Press, 2018.

Fronza, Emanuela. "The Punishment of Negationism: The Difficult Dialogue Between Law and Memory." *Vermont Law Review* 30 (2006): 609–26.

Gensburger, Sarah, Lefrank, Sandrine. *Beyond Memory: Can We Really Learn from the Past?* London: Palgrave Macmillan, 2020.

Ghezzi, Alessia, Angela G. Pereira, and Lucia Vesnic-Alujevic. *The Ethics of Memory in a Digital Age: Interrogating the Right to Be Forgotten*. New York: Palgrave Macmillan, 2014.

Gutman, Yifat. "Memory Laws: An Escalation in Minority Exclusion or a Testimony to the Limits of State Power?" *Law & Society Review* 50, no. 3 (2016): 575–607.

Gutman, Yifat, and Noam Tirosh. "Balancing Atrocities and Forced Forgetting: Memory Laws as a Means of Social Control in Israel." *Law and Social Inquiry* 46, no. 3 (2021): 705–30.

Hanna, Jason, and Ralph Ellis. "Charlottesville Removes Two Confederate Statues as Onlookers Cheer." *CNN.com*, 10 July 2021. Retrieved 11 October 2021 from https://edition.cnn.com/2021/07/10/us/charlottesville-statues-coming-down/index.html.

Hearty, Kevin. "Problematizing Symbolic Reparation: 'Complex Political Victims,' 'Dead Body Politics' and the Right to Remember." *Social & Legal Studies* 29, no.3 (2020): 334–54.

Høg Hansen, Anders, Oscar Hemer, and Thomas Tufte. *Memory on Trial: Media, Citizenship and Social Justice*. Zurich: LIT Verlag, 2014.

Hom, Sharon K., and Eric K. Yamamoto. "Collective Memory, History and Social Justice." *UCLA Law Review* 47 (2000): 1748–802.

Hoskins, Andrew. "Memory of the Multitude: The End of Collective Memory." In *Digital Memory Studies: Media Pasts in Transition*, edited by Andrew Hoskins, 85–109. New York: Routledge, 2017.

Huyssen, Andreas. "International Human Rights and the Politics of Memory: Limits and Challenges." *Criticism* 53, no. 4 (2011): 607–24.

Jones, Meg L. *Ctrl +Z: The Right to Be Forgotten*. New York: NYU Press, 2016.

Kabalek, Kobi. "Memory and Periphery: An Introduction." *Hagar* 12 no. 11 (2014): 7–22.

Katz, Andrew. "Unrest in Virginia: Clashes over a Show of White Nationalism in Charlottesville Turn Deadly." *Time*. Retrieved 17 June 2021 from https://time.com/charlottesville-white-nationalist-rally-clashes/.

Kook, Rebecca. "Agents of Memory in the Post-Witness Era: Memory in the Living Room and Changing Forms of Holocaust Remembrance in Israel." *Memory Studies* 14, no. 5 (2021): 971–86.
Lee, Philip. "Towards a Right to Memory." *Media Development* 57, no. 2 (2010): 3–10.
Lee, Philip, and Pradip Ninan Thomas, *Public Memory, Public Media and the Politics of Justice*. New York: Palgrave Macmillan, 2012.
Levy, Daniel, and Natan Sznaider. T*he Holocaust and Memory in the Global Age*. Philadelphia, PA: Temple University Press, 2006.
Liebermann, Yvonne. "Born Digital: The Black Lives Matter Movement and Memory after the Digital Turn." *Memory Studies* 14, no. 4 (2021): 713–32.
Löytömäki, Stiina. "The Law and Collective Memory of Colonialism: France and the Case of 'Belated' Transitional Justice." *International Journal of Transitional Justice* 7 (2013): 205–23.
Margalit, Avishai. *The Ethics of Memory*. Cambridge, MA: Harvard University Press, 2002.
Matthew, Dayna B. "On Charlottesville." *Virginia Law Review* 105, no. 2 (2019): 269–314.
Moyn, Samuel. *The Last Utopia: Human Rights in History*. Cambridge, MA: Harvard University Press, 2012.
Nora, Pierre. "Reasons for the Current Upsurge in Memory." *Eurozine*, 19 April 2002. Retrieved 21 June 2021 from https://www.eurozine.com/reasons-for-the-current-upsurge-in-memory/.
Olick, Jeffrey K., and Joyce Robbins. "Social Memory Studies: From 'Collective Memory' to the Historical Sociology of Mnemonic Practices." *Annual Review of Sociology* 24, no. 1 (1998): 105–40.
Perugini, Nicola, and Neve Gordon. *The Human Right to Dominate*. Oxford: Oxford University Press, 2015.
Reading, Anna. "Gender and the Right to Memory." *Media Development* 2 (2010): 11–14.
———. "Identity, Memory and Cosmopolitanism: The Otherness of the Past and a Right to Memory?" *European Journal of Cultural Studies* 14 (2011): 379–94.
———. "The European Roma: An Unsettled Right to Memory." In *Public Memory, Public Media and the Politics of Justice*, edited by Phillip Lee and Pradip Ninan Thomas, 121–40. New York: Palgrave Macmillan, 2012.
Ricoeur, Paul. "Memory and Forgetting." In *Questioning Ethics: Contemporary Debates in Philosophy*, edited by Richard Kearney and Mark Dooley, 5–11. London: Routledge, 1998.
Savelsberg, Joachim J., and Ryan D. King. *American Memories: Atrocities and the Law*. New York: Russell Sage Foundation, 2011.
Smit, Rik, Heinrich Ansgard, and Marcel Broersma. "Witnessing in New Memory Ecology: Memory Construction of the Syrian Conflict on YouTube." *New Media & Society* 19, no. 2 (2017): 289–307.
"Special Meeting of the Charlottesville City Council." 6 February 2017. Retrieved 23 July 2022 from http://weblink.charlottesville.org/public/0/edoc/793605/20170206Feb6.pdf.
Tirosh, Noam. "Reconsidering the 'Right to Be Forgotten': Memory Rights and the Right to Memory in the New Media Era." *Media, Culture & Society* 39, no.5 (2016): 644–60.
Tirosh, Noam, and Amit Schejter. "The Regulation of Archives and Society's Memory: The Case of Israel." *Archival Science* 20 (2020): 245–61.
Traverso, Enzo. "Tearing Down Statues Doesn't Erase History, It Makes Us See It More Clearly." *Jacobin Magazine*, 24 June 2020. Retrieved 17 February 2021 from https://www.jacobinmag.com/2020/06/statues-removal-antiracism-columbus.
"United Nations Declaration on the Rights of Indigenous Peoples." *United Nations, Department of Economic and Social Affairs: Indigenous Peoples*, 13 September 2007. Retrieved 23 July 2022 from https://www.un.org/development/desa/indigenouspeoples/declaration-on-the-rights-of-indigenous-peoples.html.

Viejo-Rose, Dacia. "Memorial Functions: Intent, Impact and the Right to Remember." *Memory Studies* 4, no.4 (2011): 465–80.
Villa-Nicholas, Melissa. "Latinx Digital Memory: Identity Making in Real Time." *Social Media & Society* 5, no.4 (2019): 1–11.
Vinitzky-Seroussi, Vered. "Commemorating a Difficult Past: Yitzhak Rabin's Memorials." *American Sociological Review* 67, no.1 (2002): 30–51.
Whelan, Kevin. "Rights of Memory." In *Conference Report: Storytelling as the Vehicle?*, compiled by Gráinne Kelly, 11–20. Dunadry, Northern Ireland: Healing through Remembering, 2005. Retrieved 23 July 2022 from http://healingthroughremembering.org/wp-content/uploads/2015/11/Storytelling-as-the-vehicle_2005.pdf.
Worcman, Karen, and Joanne Garde-Hansen. *Social Memory Technology: Theory, Practice, Action*. New York: Routledge, 2016.

Chapter 1

ANTIGONE'S SHADOW

Human Rights, Memory, and the Two World Wars

Jay Winter

Antigone

The duty to remember is a family matter. Long before we engage in an examination of various forms of remembrance and their meaning in a democratic society, we need to attend to the intimate responsibility of children to bury their parents, or even at times, each other. That is the precise problem facing Sophocles' Antigone, whose brother Polyneices was killed in a rising against King Creon of Thebes.

Antigone is aghast at the decision of Creon to bury the loyal son, Eteocles, with all due respect, while "the hapless corpse of Polyneices" will be treated not like a human but like an animal "that none shall entomb him or mourn, but leave unwept, unsepulchred, a welcome store for the birds, as they espy him, to feast on at will." Violate this royal decree, and the consequences will be "death by stoning before all the folk."[1]

Antigone cannot obey the decree since it would mean that she would be "false" to Polyneices. Not to remember that he is her brother and that siblings bury each other is worse than treason; it is a sin against the gods themselves. Not to observe a *rite of passage* for a brother is to make a mockery of family ties, redolent with intimate memories from the earliest ages of family life.

Ismene, Antigone's sister, urges her to demure, since women should not strive against men, and in particular with powerful men, such as Creon, who in addition is the father of Antigone's betrothed, Haemon. Does not Antigone, Ismene asks, owe allegiance to her king? Antigone's answer is that of martyrs of every generation: "I owe a longer allegiance to the dead than to the living: in that world I shall abide forever."[2] Offend a king, and you risk your life; offend the gods and you risk much more than that.

The dead have claims on us. That is the essence of family piety, and that is what separates us from the animals. Even when a king forbids us to mourn our dead, we must resist because we are human. This is Antigone's message.

A soldier reports to Creon that someone has defied him. Someone unknown has juxtaposed piety to power, honoring the dead "after sprinkling thirsty dust on the flesh, with other such rites as piety enjoins." When Creon learns it was Antigone who did the deed, he confronts her directly. And she answers directly: I did not violate the laws of the immortal gods, but an unjust edict of a mortal king, unwisely trying to "override the unwritten and unfailing statutes of heaven."[3]

Mourning the dead is an expression of that love which makes us human, a love that transcends earthly authority. "Tis not my nature," Antigone says, "to join in hating but in loving."[4] That is human nature. But Creon will not have it so. A sister loves; a king kills, and then leaves his enemy's corpse to rot in the dust. Antigone's humanity requires her to defy the king and forfeit her life. In doing so, she affirms her humanity. In condemning Antigone, Creon offends the gods and brings their wrath down on his head. Why? Because remembering our brothers and sisters, our fathers and mothers, our children, when they die before us is what makes us human. As Hans Ruin put it, our relations with the dead both enable and inform our social life. Every one of us, he reminds us, lives not only with the living but also with the dead. Without such a vital web of remembrance of the dead, we are lost.[5]

A World in Mourning: 1914–1945

How many Antigones perished in the Holocaust? There was no dust to scatter on the corpses, since the dead themselves had already been turned to ashes and dust. Instead, there were myriad indirect ways of burying the unburyable. All of them entailed acts of memory.

In this chapter I want to interpret the human rights revolution of the period following World War II as an affirmation of the humanity of the innocent victims of that conflict by honoring their memory. The 6 million Jews killed in the Holocaust were by no means the only innocents consumed in the fires of the Third Reich. The new human rights instruments passed by the United Nations in 1948 were meant to underwrite a new relationship between the individual and the state. Here was a judicial response to the abomination of the Nazi regime, the Leviathan that had trampled the rights of individuals under the heel of the state.

Those who had perished and whose names were preserved were individual men and women. The survivors insisted that, contrary to Nazi dicta, these people had had rights that transcended the arbitrary authority of the state. The new human rights movement of the post-1945 period was based on providing ways of enunciating and defending those rights. Enforcing them was another matter, but the need for affirming such rights was undeniable.

The best way to understand the human rights moment of the period after 1945 was as a normative change in the way we understand nation-states and the limits on what they can do to their own citizens. It is in this sense that I want to argue that the Universal Declaration of Human Rights of 1948 is a memory document. It not only directly refers to the victims of the Nazis in its preamble, but it also affirms that the construction of a new human rights order is the only way to give meaning to the loss of so many lives. Working to establish a new balance between the state, the individual, and civil society was an act of remembrance then, and it remains so today, seventy-five years after the end of World War II.

The Universal Declaration was a document inscribed as well with the memory of those who had fought in World War I. These men were not victims of Night and Fog, of the cruelties of the Nazi police state. They were victims of a conflict in which millions fought so that war would never again come to ravage the world. That phrase "never again," so heavily associated with the Holocaust, was used initially to cry out against the cruelties the soldiers of 1914–18 had endured.

This two-part history of remembrance serves another purpose. It helps us see that it was not the Holocaust alone that led to the new human rights regime. After 1914, a new kind of war—total war—brought mass death to Europe. And after thirty years of butchery, it was time to remember the dead by affirming human rights as a barrier against the barbarities of the nation-state in both world wars.

Here we return to Antigone and to the double meaning of her sacrifice. The first meaning is that there were limits to the authority of the state in the person of King Creon. There was a law higher than the state's law that took precedence. That higher law conveyed rights—in this case the right to a human burial—that were inalienable.

The second meaning of Antigone's stand is that with rights come responsibilities. The duty to remember was one of those responsibilities, since it followed from the duty to uphold a moral order transcending the majesty of the state. Antigone did her duty to that higher law by remembering the dead and by performing her responsibilities to her brother, even at the cost of her own life.

The Generation of Fire

The major draftsman of the Universal Declaration of Human Rights was René Cassin, French jurist and *ancient combatant* of World War I.[6] In 1940, he fled defeated France for London and served as Charles de Gaulle's legal adviser. After D-day (6 June 1944), he returned to France and took up a new post as vice president (later president) of the French High Administrative Court, the Conseil d'Etat. His career as a jurist gave him the credentials needed to serve as representative of France on the United Nations Human Rights Commission. And it was in that capacity that he orchestrated and redrafted the document approved by the UN on 10 December 1948, the Universal Declaration of Human Rights.[7]

Elsewhere I have told the story of that moment in Cassin's life.[8] But for our purposes, what needs to be emphasized is the extent to which Cassin's framing of this document came directly out of his personal experience of the two world wars. Avoiding death by a hair's breadth in both wars, Cassin was a survivor. He never forgot the sheer accident of his returning from the battlefields of the two world wars, nor did he forget the men who were not as lucky as he.

In the 1960s, when he was already in his seventies, Cassin used to visit the former actress Ghislaine Bru, whom he later married. When he passed war memorials in villages in the Chartreuse, he would stop his car, get out, and stand in front of the local war memorial. In France, most of these stone memorials are placed at a crossroads, somewhere in the midst of life and not in the shadow of the local Catholic church. There Cassin would read out loud the names of every single villager who had died for his country in World War I.

He would then seek out the local *mairie*, the town hall, where he would ask to see the mayor or his secretary. More often than not, he would find a man near or at retirement age, who had fought, like him, many years before in the 1914–18 conflict. After asking about the local official's war service, he would ask him if there was a way he might help with an administrative problem, perhaps a delay in the receipt of a document from some Parisian official about the construction of a local road or a local school. There were always administrative problems like these in France (and elsewhere), and after listening and making notes on the matter, he would tell the secretary that he would look into it. Such officials were stunned when a few weeks later, the long-awaited document arrived, providing the cash needed to get the local project under way. They were surprised because Cassin did not tell them that the visitor to the town that they had met was the head of the French civil service, the vice president of the Conseil d'Etat. A phone call from Cassin had removed the bureaucratic obstacle in an instant.[9]

I call such solidarities the outcome of fictive kinship,[10] or the brotherhood of men who together went through the fire of World War I. And for Cassin, it was fire. In August 1914, René Cassin was a 26-year-old lawyer. Born in Bayonne to a prominent Jewish family living in Nice, he moved to Paris to complete his education as an academic lawyer. Living in the capital also helped him bypass his mother's objection to his fiancée, who was not Jewish. They remained unmarried.

The outbreak of war found him in Paris. He insisted that his fiancée register as his common-law wife, enabling her to receive a war pension in the event of his death. From Paris, he journeyed south to join the 311th Infantry Regiment in Aix-en-Provence. In September, he was promoted to the rank of corporal and served near Saint Mihiel in northeast France in the engagements grouped under the rubric of the "Battle of the Frontiers." He remained in this sector, where on 12 October he was ordered to take a squad of sixteen men and advance toward a German strongpoint near Chauvencourt on the outskirts of Saint Mihiel. German emplacements made such a probe suicidal. All sixteen of his men were hit by flanking fire from well-entrenched machine guns and artillery. He himself was hit in his side, his abdomen, and his left arm. Cassin knew very well that a stomach wound was almost always fatal. He refused evacuation, but asked a passing soldier to inform their commander of the strength of the German positions in his sector. In addition, he begged this man, Sergeant-Quartermaster Canestrier, to write to Cassin's father that he had died painlessly (which was a lie) and to send to his family a leather cigarette case, two gold pieces of 100 francs, and some small bills that he handed over to Canestrier. Canestrier vanished, and so did Cassin's valuables.[11]

Clearly Cassin thought he would not survive. He asked a priest if someone could say Hebrew prayers with him. The priest replied that his prayers were for everyone, and gave him the benefit of his company. Cassin survived the night and was then handed over to the French army medical services for further treatment.

The way these units were organized in the early days of the war almost killed him. The rule was that upon mobilization soldiers reported to the regiment in the region where they had done their obligatory national service. After battle, soldiers returned to *that* site, either intact, wounded, or in a coffin. Consequently, Cassin could not be treated in northeast France but only in Provence, 600 kilometers away. He was sent south, first by wagon and then by train, and after a long and bumpy journey, he arrived in the regiment's hospital in Antibes on the Mediterranean. The surgeons there were astonished to see that he was still alive, despite the wound to his abdomen. Cassin drank virtually nothing on the trip, knowing that to do otherwise likely would have been fatal. Still, they told him he might not survive more than a few hours, and they needed to operate immediately—there was no time to anesthetize him. This Cassin accepted, and he somehow endured an hour under the surgeon's knife. He later quipped he was fortunate that the operation was on a less than sensitive part of his anatomy.

He remained in convalescence for over a year. This period of hospitalization marked the beginning of his political life. Being overwhelmed by the massive casualties of the first phase of the war, medical administrators were unable to offer the hundreds of thousands of Frenchmen who were wounded in 1914 more than cursory care. The same chaos and neglect faced those who needed post-operative treatment or who were discharged as unfit for military service. Most took their fate as unalterable. Not Cassin. He was a soldier and a citizen, and he deserved better. He had entered into a contract with the state to put his life on the line. The state's part of the contract was to provide him with adequate care in the event that he was wounded. In that obligation, the state failed completely.

Here he started the first of a series of life-long campaigns not for crumbs, or for charity, but for justice and for the rights of men who had bled for their country. While still in hospital, he recruited a number of like-minded men to organize together and to put up a fight against the callous bureaucracy of the French state itself.

Cassin thus became a founder of the French veterans' movement and worked tirelessly to ensure that men who had been wounded in service to their country would have a decent pension, and that the orphans of the men who did not return would be given a start in their lives. This work brought him up against recalcitrant and indifferent authorities.[12]

Veterans' rights were earned, not only by military service and the shedding of blood but thereafter by harsh and long political struggle. French veterans, like others in Europe, were given their pensions grudgingly, not as a right but as a privilege, wrested from the hands of unfeeling administrators and the physicians who served them.[13]

This struggle for natural justice for the lame and the blind, for men who had answered their countries' call but then found that few nations were prepared to heed the voices of the wounded, created something new in European affairs—a pacifist veterans' movement. The notion of soldier pacifists may seem like a contradiction in terms, but in interwar France it was not at all an oxymoron.

French Republicans like Cassin were soldier citizens. They had earned the moral authority to demand decent medical treatment and pensions. They had the standing to ensure as well that their sons would not have to enter *la boucherie*—the slaughterhouse—of modern warfare. On Armistice Day, 11 November, they marched to the war memorials in every tiny village; they did so in civilian dress and frequently, deliberately out of step. They had been civilians in uniform, and they bore a message from their comrades who had died to the young: war must never return.

Remembering the dead at that time meant remembering the faces of those with whom they all had served; men who did not return from the front. In 1968, when Cassin received the Nobel Peace Prize, he conjured up the spirits of the men of his infantry platoon of 1914. He addressed each of them by name, by his home village, his oddities and habits that had made him who he was, and invited every one of them to stand with him at the podium to receive the prize that was as much theirs as his. They had fought for peace, not for another round of destruction. Yes, the Nazis had ruined their hopes, but that was no reason to give up the pacifist cause, a cause as Cassin said, for which he was prepared to give his life, just like his comrades of 1914. In 1968 in Paris, in his own secular language, Cassin, a non-observant Jew, said *Yizkhr*, the traditional prayer for the dead, for the men with whom he had fought fifty-four years before.[14]

Magnet for the Malice of Vichy France

René Cassin was one of those men who wore with dignity the title invented by the Polish historian Isaac Deutscher of being a "non-Jewish Jew," an assimilated and unobservant Jewish citizen of his country.[15] The French defeat in 1940 changed all that. The Nazis turned him from being a Frenchman who happened to have been born a Jew into a Jew who happened to be a Frenchman. But more important to Cassin than his Jewish identity was his French patriotism and his record of military service in the defense of his country. He left Paris after the catastrophic military defeat of May–June 1940, and traveled south. He paid his taxes and even managed to take a small vial of soil from his native village before leaving France on an Australian troop carrier, the *Ettridge*. On arrival in Britain, he joined de Gaulle's Free French movement and served as de Gaulle's legal adviser and unshakable political supporter. He was sentenced to death in absentia by Vichy and his property in France was confiscated.[16]

The cause of Free France intersected with that of the Allies in 1940 and 1941 in one particularly important way. Even before the United States had joined in the war, the opposition to the Nazis took the form of the creation of a human rights movement among exiles in London. Cassin was one of those who led this effort to define war aims in terms of a revolution in human rights. We shall turn to this matter below and link it to the long-term commitment Cassin had made to never forget the dead of World War I.

The French defeat of 1940 added a second generation of victims to those Cassin mourned. Many of them were from his own family. When he fled to Britain, he left a large family in France at the mercy of the anti-Semitic laws of Vichy and subsequent round-ups and deportations. Cassin had left behind his father and mother, his older brother Fedia and Fedia's four children, his sister Felice and her four children. He was worried, too, about his younger sister Yvonne, her husband Henri Bumsel and their daughter.

René Cassin was very attached as well to a young cousin who was married to a Polish-born tailor naturalized as a French citizen in 1910, Albert Montag. Both couples were very close. Neither had children, and they lived near one another: the Cassins at 53 boulevard Saint-Michel, and the Montags at 34 boulevard Saint-Germain. All four fled Paris together in June 1940.

During the occupation, twenty-six members of Cassin's family were murdered. It must be noted that other families, some of them less well integrated into French society, suffered as much or more. But even among these well-assimilated French Jews, persecution and the complicity of French authorities in Nazi crimes exacted a heavy toll. While the Cassin family was not destroyed, it was decimated by racial hatred.

Cassin knew that everyone in his family had to live a clandestine life in occupied France, and all faced terrifying risks on a daily basis. Cassin's mother died of natural causes on 2 April 1944 in Le Cannet near Cannes. Through a Catholic nurse and family friend, a granddaughter was able to arrange for the clandestine burial of Gabrielle Cassin according to Jewish rituals, held at night in the crypt of the nurse's family. His father was arrested, but survived, through the help of a doctor who, at considerable risk, took him to safety in an ambulance. After the deportation of his wife's parents, Cassin's brother Fedia went into hiding. He lived clandestinely near Gueret in the Creuse and dispersed his four children in the Jura and in the Alps. All survived, as did his sister Felice and her children. But René's other sister Yvonne Bumsel and her husband were arrested in Marseilles and deported to Auschwitz on 7 March 1944. The Montags, arrested at home, had been deported one month before, on 3 February. René's uncle, Abraham, was arrested despite his age—he was eighty-eight years old—and he was deported on 10 February together with one of his daughters, his son-in-law, and three other members of his family. One daughter and one son of another uncle, Rabbi Honel Meiss, were also deported with their spouses. None of these relatives returned.[17]

Cassin was profoundly shaken by these losses. He also faced the consequences of the official theft of Jewish property during the occupation. It is hardly surprising as one of France's leading civil servants in 1945, he was asked by everyone in his family to intervene to discover the fate of deported members of their families and their businesses and homes. He was at the center of a family in mourning, who were in constant search of some trace of those who had not yet returned. They were preoccupied too with restarting their lives.

For Cassin, *Yizkor* meant both remembering the dead of the family and the dead of France. The war of 1914–18 had created among the veterans bonds of solidarity Cassin still shared. The grief of those who lost loved ones in the Holocaust created a similar solidarity, rooted in family ties and losses but that went beyond them. Cassin went through this difficult reckoning after both world wars.

Human Rights as the Grammar of Commemoration

It is all too easy to forget that the human rights regime of the post-1945 years was created at a moment when more than a million Jewish people were stuck in displaced persons camps or even in the same concentration camps in which the Nazis had imprisoned them. Jewish survivors had lost their families and were firmly opposed to returning to their countries of origin.[18] The rights of the survivors to have a new lease on life meant rethinking the limits on the authority of the state over its own citizens.[19]

That reassessment of the theory of state sovereignty was a direct response to the criminal nature of the Nazi regime. But for Cassin and many others, the law provided a framework for remembering the dead of both world wars. This is the essential link between the soldiers' pacifism of the 1914–18 conflict and the commitment to establish a Universal Declaration of Human Rights after World War II. Both conflicts showed the need to rein in the authority of the nation-state so that the bloodbath of war between 1914 and 1945 would never recur.[20]

There were two principal domains in which this reassessment of the limits of state sovereignty took place. The first was the prosecution of war criminals, henceforth unable to claim that obedience to the state justified the commission of crimes in the name of the state. The second was the enunciation of principles of human rights to serve as the foundation of a new international era.

World War II had shown what absolute state sovereignty meant. Cassin had represented France Libre at the St. James conference of the anti-Axis alliance in September 1941 in London. He signed the document that agreed Nazi crimes against civilians would be prosecuted after the war. A further step toward a judicial reckoning took place four months later in London. Now with the United States at war, the newly formed United Nations declared that they "place amongst their principal war aims punishment through the channel of organized justice of those guilty and responsible for these crimes, whether they have ordered them, perpetrated them or in any way participated in them."[21]

Framing a new human rights regime was the second, and perhaps more long-range, commemorative project to emerge out of World War II. It shifted attention from war crimes, which were already subject to humanitarian law codified through the Geneva Conventions, to the violation of human rights and the rights of civilians in peacetime.

We can see the parallel development of these two projects in the work of émigré lawyers like Cassin in London in 1943 and 1944. On 7 October 1942, Lord Simon, the Lord Chancellor, and chief legal officer in Britain, announced to the House of Lords that the Allies had formed an international commission to find the appropriate form to bring to justice war criminals "irrespective of rank."[22] The same day, US President Roosevelt stated that there would be trials of a relatively small number of people, those he termed "the ringleaders responsible for the organized murder of thousands of persons and the commission of atrocities which have violated every tenet of the Christian faith."[23]

On 20 October 1943, Cassin was appointed French delegate to the inter-allied commission on war crimes. On 18 January 1944, Sir Cecil Hurst, the President of the Permanent Court of Justice in The Hague, convened the commission. With new US backing from Herbert Pell, formerly US ambassador to Portugal and Hungary, three sub-committees were formed. The first committee, chaired by the Belgian jurist Marcel de Baer, addressed dossiers on war crimes presented by individual nations. Between 9 and 16 February 1944, they examined the first sixteen dossiers presented by France. Several were deemed sufficiently complete to present to the whole commission, which could name individuals to be handed over to Allied authorities for trial. By May 1944 about a hundred such individuals were on this list.

The second sub-committee was chaired by Ambassador Pell and examined procedural questions. He probed national differences in the definition of war crimes and their handling by civil or military courts as well as the politically charged question of the character of an international criminal court. The third sub-committee, headed by the Polish jurist Stephan Glaser, dealt with difficulties in legal thinking on collective responsibility for crimes, as well as the viability of the defense of innocence on the grounds of following higher orders.[24]

In the following months, Cassin assembled and framed numerous reports for the commission on crimes committed in France and against French citizens.[25] These included maltreatment of French prisoners of war, black and white, in Germany; the machine gunning of civilians during the *exode* of 1940; and the role of German soldiers and the Gestapo in the transit camp of Drancy, from which French Jews and other Jews found in France were deported to Auschwitz.[26] Above all, he pressed the commission, and succeeded in persuading them, that they had a responsibility to act on behalf of millions still suffering Nazi persecution, who awaited the day of their liberation as the first day of judgment.

On 4 April 1944, the commission received from the constituent member states lists of all men in the SS, the Gestapo, the army, or in other leadership positions in each occupied nation, with the intention of seeing who among them would stand trial for war crimes.[27] This was the key step before setting up trials of those whom the Germans had to hand over to Allied authorities at the Armistice, as suspects in war crimes prosecutions.

What Cassin had helped accomplish here was important in both the French and the international realms. For the Comité Français de la Libération Nationale, on which Cassin served, here was one means to reestablish the republican judicial order and limit the role of *l'Epuration sauvage* or local vigilante justice. For the Allies as a whole, here was one way to approach the transnational character of crimes without precedent.[28] What mattered was to see a pattern at the core of the Nazi order, one that used terror and murder to execute a plan of domination of Europe and beyond. Their crimes arose out of the German idea that there were no laws of war but only the rule of force. Even if they were to lose the war, their crimes will have so weakened the countries they conquered, they reasoned, that Germany could prepare for the next war from a favorable position even when defeated.

There was injury to the international order to repair as well. To reach that goal, the Allies had to consider drafting a transnational legal code,[29] stating what the laws of humanity are, and how nations that, like Hitler's Germany, systematically violate these laws domestically are a threat to international peace. Here is the link between war talk and rights talk, between protests against the inhumanity of the Nazis and the construction of a transnational code of behavior limiting not only what states can do against other states but also what states can do against their own citizens. René Cassin was one of many activists whose remembrance of the civilian victims of the Nazis was evident in every step he took in the drafting of postwar transnational human rights instruments.

After the War

The story of the emergence of human rights thinking in the early days of the United Nations is complex and cannot be treated in extenso here. The important point is that there were many voices in this debate, some imperialist, some simply chauvinist, and others committed to a new regime of human rights. The UN in its infancy was a house of many mansions, certainly no magic palace, but it gave room to those who believed that the defense of human rights was the foundation of peace. That argument is an ongoing one.[30]

René Cassin and other London exiles—veterans of the Blitz and the preparatory work for war crimes trials—were there in San Francisco, in Geneva, in Lake Success, and in Paris, where the work of establishing a new human rights regime was done. Cassin's standing in France Libre was enhanced by his being named head of the French High Administrative Court—the Conseil d'Etat in 1944 by de Gaulle. As the head of the French civil service, he was responsible for removing collaborators and the regulations they had introduced during the four-year rule of Vichy.[31]

Cassin's standing at the UN was as a leading *Résistant* and jurist who championed a revision of the theory of absolute state sovereignty. There was a higher law than that of the state, he argued, and to prevent repetitions of the Nazi nightmare, Cassin worked with Eleanor Roosevelt, Charles Malik, John Humphreys, and others in the United Nations Human Rights Commission in drafting the Universal Declaration of Human Rights in the period 1945–48. He wrote the preamble himself, and it was Cassin who made the final changes and read out the document to the United Nations assembled in Paris on 10 December 1948. Here is how he presented the proposal to the delegates at the Palais de Chaillot: "I have the honor," he began, "to report the firm support of France" for the Declaration, which:

> 100 years after the Revolution of 1848 and the abolition of slavery on all French territory, constitutes a global step in the long struggle for the rights of man. Our declaration represents the most vigorous, the most essential protest of humanity against the atrocities and the oppression of which millions of human beings suffered through the centuries and in particular during and after the two world wars ... In the midst of the struggle, heads of state, President Roosevelt and President Beneš, two great men recently departed, proclaimed the meaning of this crusade: and in the name of France, then imprisoned and unable to speak freely, I had the honor at the St James conference of 24 September 1941 to join my voice to theirs, in proclaiming that the practical recognition of the essential liberties of man was indispensable to the establishment of a durable international peace.[32]

Cassin asked the delegates to note the difference in the title of the declaration. It was not a matter between states, an international declaration, but among the peoples of the world, on whose fundamental rights no state could trample with impunity. The Universal Declaration was a normative document, one setting standards against which the behavior of all states would be measured.

Conclusion: In the Shadow of Antigone

One way of understanding the evolution of international law in the 1940s is as a form of judicial memory, an inscription in international law of the names of the millions of innocent victims of the Nazi regime. Here was a commemorative moment on which the Allies who won the war could agree.

To be sure, that moment was short-lived. The opening of the Cold War at the very same time made it impossible for the Universal Declaration to be translated into law that an international criminal court could enforce. Consequently, Cassin and others transferred their efforts to creating an institution higher than that of state sovereignty within the project of European unification. In 1950, a European Convention on Human Rights was passed, and it had teeth.[33] It was the document every country had to sign and respect in order to join the nascent European community. It still is. To enforce the Convention, a new European Court of Human Rights was created. In 1958, that court opened in Strasbourg, and Cassin was first vice president (associate justice) and then in 1965 president (chief justice) of the European Court of Human Rights. On his retirement from that post in 1968, he was awarded the Nobel Peace Prize.

The Nobel committee was especially sensitive to the fact that Cassin had lost many members of his family in the Holocaust. They understood that his work for human rights was the most powerful way he could remember the dead, not only the Jewish victims of the Nazis, but the nearly 50 million people who were killed in World War II. The human rights achievements of Cassin's generation were limited, to be sure. But they constituted a form of commemoration—judicial commemoration—which is an important legacy of World War II.[34]

A final word on Antigone. Her insistence on the duty to remember the dead set a precedent many men and women have followed. In creating legal norms and barriers to the arrogance of the nation-state and its leaders, René Cassin, Eleanor Roosevelt, and their colleagues who together drafted the Universal Declaration of Human Rights, found a legal and moral framework in which to set Antigone's message. As Antigone knew, remembering the dead is not a choice; it is an essential affirmation of life itself.[35]

Jay Winter is the Charles J. Stille Professor of History Emeritus at Yale University. He is a historian of World War I and the author of *Sites of Memory, Sites of Mourning: The Great War in European Cultural History* (1995), editor of *America and the Armenian Genocide* (2008), and editor-in-chief of the three-volume *Cambridge History of the First World War* (2014, in English, French, and 2015, in Chinese). He has received honorary doctorates from the University of Graz, the Katholic University of Leuven, and the University of Paris—VIII. In 2017, he received the Victor Adler Prize of the Austrian government for a lifetime of work in history.

Notes

1. Sophocles, *Antigone*, 2.
2. Sophocles, *Antigone*, 3.
3. Sophocles, *Antigone*, 9.
4. Sophocles, *Antigone*, 11.
5. Ruin, *Being with the Dead*, 2–8. I am grateful to Astrid Erll for bringing this reference to my attention.
6. Agi, *René Cassin;* Cassin, *Les hommes partis de rien*.
7. See Morsink, *Universal Declaration of Human Rights* and Glendon, *A World Made New*.
8. Winter and Prost, *René Cassin and Human Rights*.
9. Many thanks are due to Professor Chantal Connachie, daughter of Ghislaine Bru, for this insight into Cassin's visits to the local war memorials in the Chartreuse.
10. See Winter, "Forms of Kinship" and Winter, "Human Rights as Lived Experience," 151–77.
11. Winter and Prost, *René Cassin and Human Rights*, 19–24.
12. See the classic three-volume study by Prost, *Les anciens combattants*.
13. Winter, "Veterans, Human Rights," 121–38.
14. A full recording of Cassin's Nobel Peace Prize acceptance speech is held by the Nobel Institute, Oslo.
15. Deutscher, *The Non-Jewish Jew*.
16. Winter and Prost, *René Cassin and Human Rights*, 109–20.
17. On Cassin's family under Vichy, see Winter and Prost, *René Cassin and Human Rights*, 303–9. We were very fortunate to have interviewed Cassin's nieces Suzie Abram and Josette Cassin on family matters.
18. Nasaw, *The Last Million*.
19. Sinti and Roma refugees were also targeted for extermination by the Nazis. Their post-1945 story is very different from that of Jewish survivors. See Joskowicz, "Romani Refugees," 760–87.
20. On this point, see Reading, "Gender and the Right to Memory," 11–15, and Reading, *Gender and Memory*.
21. 'Allies in Conference', *The Times*, 14 Jan. 1942, p. 5.
22. *Hansard's Parliamentary Debates, Lords*, vo. 124, col. 583, 7 Oct. 1942. Available: https://api.parliament.uk/historic-hansard/lords/1942/oct/07/punishment-of-war-criminals#column_583 [Last retrieved: 21.8.2022]
23. Kochavi, *Prelude to Nuremberg*, 28–32.
24. Winter and Prost, *René Cassin and Human Rights*, 231–40.
25. Archives nationales de France, Pierrefitte. Fonds Cassin, 382AP175, Crimes de guerre, 4–5.
26. Fonds Cassin, Crimes de guerre, 6.
27. Fonds Cassin, Crimes de guerre, 7.
28. Cooper, *Raphael Lemkin*, 24–47.
29. Fonds Cassin, Crimes de guerre, 45.
30. Mazower, *No Magic Palace*.
31. Winter and Prost, *René Cassin and Human Rights*, 168–90.
32. 382AP/128, dossier 3, 'Discours de René Cassin, Délégué de la France à l'Assemblée Générale des Nations Unies à Paris', 9 Déc. 1948.
33. Duranti, *The Conservative Human Rights Revolution* and Duranti, "The Holocaust"

34. For a different interpretation, see David, *The Past Can't Heal Us*.
35. Ruin, *Being with the Dead*, 37.

Bibliography

Agi, Marc. *René Cassin, prix Nobel de la paix, 1887–1976, père de la 'Déclaration universelle des droits de l'homme'* [René Cassin, Nobel Peace Prize, 1887–1976, father of the "Universal Declaration of Human Rights"]. Paris: Perrin, 1998.
Anon, "Allies in Conference," *The Times*, 14 Jan. 1942, p. 5.
Cassin, René. *Les hommes partis de rien: Le réveil de la France abattue, 1940–41* [The men started from nothing: The awakening of defeated France, 1940–41]. Paris: Plon, 1975.
Cooper, John. *Raphael Lemkin and the Struggle for the Genocide Convention*. London: Palgrave Macmillan, 2008.
David, Lea. *The Past Can't Heal Us: The Dangers of Mandating Memory in the Name of Human Rights*. Cambridge: Cambridge University Press, 2020.
Deutscher, Isaac. *The Non-Jewish Jew: and Other Essays*. London: Verso Books, 2017.
Duranti, Marco. *The Conservative Human Rights Revolution: European Identity, Transnational Politics, and the Origins of the European Convention*. New York: Oxford University Press, 2017.
———. "The Holocaust, the Legacy of 1789 and the Birth of International Human Rights Law: Revisiting the Foundation Myth." *Journal of Genocide Research* 14, no. 12 (2012): 159–86.
Fonds René Cassin. Archives Nationales de France, Pierrefitte, Fonds Privées, 382AP.
Glendon, Mary Ann. *A World Made New: Eleanor Roosevelt and the Universal Declaration of Human Rights*. New York: Random House, 2001.
Hansard's Parliamentary Debates, Lords, vo. 124, col. 583, 7 Oct. 1942.
Joskowicz, Ari. "Romani Refugees and the Postwar Order." *Journal of Contemporary History* 51, no. 4 (October 2016): 760–87.
Kochavi, Arieh J. *Prelude to Nuremberg: Allied War Crimes Policy and the Question of Punishment*. Chapel Hill: University of North Carolina Press, 2000.
Mazower, Mark. *No Magic Palace*. Princeton, NJ: Princeton University Press, 2009.
Morsink, Johannes. *Universal Declaration of Human Rights: Origins, Drafting, and Intent*. Philadelphia: University of Pennsylvania Press, 1999.
Nasaw, David. *The Last Million: Europe's Displaced Persons from World War to Cold War*. New York: Penguin, 2020.
Porsdam, Helle, ed. *Civil Religion, Human Rights and International Relations*. Cheltenham: Edward Elgar, 2012.
Prost, Antoine. *Les anciens combattants et la société française, 1914–1939* [Veterans and French society, 1914–1939]. Paris: Presses de la FNSP, 1977.
Reading, Anna. *Gender and Memory in the Globital Age*. London: Palgrave Macmillan, 2016.
———. "Gender and the Right to Memory." *Media Development* 57, no. 2 (2010): 11–15.
Ruin, Hans. *Being with the Dead: Burial, Ancestral Politics, and the Roots of Historical Consciousness*. Stanford, CA: Stanford University Press, 2018.
Sophocles, *Antigone*, http://classics.mit.edu/Sophocles/antigone.html.
Winter, Jay. "Forms of Kinship and Remembrance in the Aftermath of the Great War." In *War and Remembrance in the Twentieth Century*, edited by Jay Winter and Emmanuel Sivan, 40–60. Cambridge: Cambridge University Press, 1998.

———. "Human Rights as Lived Experience: Kinship, Fictive Kinship, and Human Rights Among Trans-National Migrants." In *Civil religion, human rights and international relations*, edited by Helle Porsdam, 151–77. Cheltenham: Edward Elgar, 2012.

———. "Veterans, Human Rights, and the Transformation of European Democracy." In *In War's Wake: International Conflict and the Fate of Liberal Democracy*, edited by Elizabeth Kier and Ronald R. Krebs, 121–38. Cambridge: Cambridge University Press, 2012.

Winter, Jay, and Antoine Prost. *René Cassin and Human Rights: From the Great War to the Universal Declaration*. Cambridge: Cambridge University Press, 2013.

Chapter 2

FRAMING MEMORY RIGHTS IN INTERNATIONAL LAW

Anna Reading

Introduction

In William Shakespeare's *Hamlet,* the character of Hamlet struggles with memory and identity, while the character Fortinbras, in the middle of murder and mayhem, also claims to have "some rights of memory in this Kingdom," meaning his claim to disputed lands.[1] Noting this, Kevin Whelan argues that a right to memory includes the right of the individual to remember, the right to give testimony, and the right to have an audience for those memories.[2] Yet four hundred years (and many performances of *Hamlet*) later, there are still no rights to memory explicitly enshrined in international law. Rather, what we find is a concern with memory rights that is expressed legally in the international domain in various direct and indirect ways that then may be said to shape human rights to how the past and history are mediated, preserved, and passed on to future generations.

In this chapter, I conduct an analysis of how a right to memory is mediated through the discourses of international law, suggesting that memory rights are framed internationally in four ways. First, international law discursively seeks to protect and preserve stories and narratives related to national identity, particularly in terms of those arising from warfare and genocide. I term this a right to national memory. Second, international law seeks discursively to support and protect those who have been subjected to violence by the state in what I term the right of victim memory. Third, international law shows a concern with memory by seeking to preserve and protect heritage and intangible heritage that gives access to the past of the world or what may be termed the right of humanity to world memory. Finally, there is discursive concern with providing for the rights of indigenous people through what may be termed autochthonous or the right of indigenous memory. The chapter concludes by considering the gaps in international legal discourse that point to remaining challenges for a right to memory at the international level.

First though, let us be clear: there is no explicit "right to memory" in international law but there are conventions, protocols, and declarations that discursively express a concern for the protection of different kinds of public pasts and forms of heritage. Implicated somewhere between memory and identities is something that we might determine as a nascent right to memory. In an earlier article in 2011 when this topic was emerging within memory studies, I suggested that a right to memory constituted "an acknowledgement of the otherness of the past made present and future through various symbolic and cultural acts, gestures, utterances and expressions."[3] This chapter builds on that earlier research that examined how mediated identities stretch memory beyond the nation-state to create cosmopolitan conventions for the protection of the past in the present.[4] It also builds on subsequent work that addressed how we might understand the intersectionality of identities and memory rights, particularly in terms of how gender and a right to memory are articulated in international conventions.[5]

Although the law and a right to memory has been explored relatively infrequently within the field of memory studies, it has, nonetheless, featured in latent ways within the thinking of key memory scholars. In Jan Assman's classic text "Communicative and Cultural Memory," he reminds us that ancient texts included some of the earliest notions of the relationship between the law and memory. Further, Western cultural memory according to Assman is not only informed by its biblical canon but also by ideas of memory within Greek and Latin literature.[6] Importantly, Assman makes the distinction between communicative memory and cultural memory. The former concerns memories embodied in our brains and bodies transmitted through interactive communication between people over no more than eighty years or three generations apart. The latter Assman conceives of as disembodied, objectified, and embedded in cultural institutions. The institutional in Assman's view is absent from communicative memory and is a key dynamic in "the transition from autobiographical and communicative memory into cultural memory."[7] Yet, what Assman's conceptualization misses is how the law might reach between the two, shaping both personal remembering and witnessing and cultural and publicly articulated memory. A right to memory, then, in this regard might be said to involve legal protection or a codicil for the transformation and the transition of communicative memory into mediated and/

or cultural memory and its ongoing protection so that cultural memory does not slip into obscurity.

Indeed, a concern with a right to memory in international law, as we shall see, may be that which seeks in various ways to protect and support the "remembering mind and reminding objects"[8] and includes the embodied memories of the individual as well as the disembodied and objectified and embedded cultural memories of institutions in terms of identity. Further, although this may include a concern with national memories, reflecting in many ways memory studies' methodological nationalism, memory is now studied in terms of its movement with recognition for the ways in which memory flows across borders in ways that are transcultural, cosmopolitan, and globalized.[9] This in turn suggests the importance of the focus in this chapter on understanding how memory rights are currently being framed and constructed at the international and transnational levels. Before addressing the different ways international law has a concern for a right to memory within and beyond national territories, I first establish how international law relates more broadly to questions of memory.

Rights, the Law, and Memory

Before we discuss how memory relates to the law and to international legal frameworks, it is important to understand the distinction between rights and law. The two terms, although connected, are not interchangeable. Rights may be understood as normative rules for what is allowed and may be social, ethical, or "natural," and may not necessarily be formally supported by human-made legal structures, although rights may also be supported by legal rights. Legal structures and the law, on the other hand, are those rules that are made by humans—which may indeed support rights or may go against them. The law at the international level, which is the focus of this chapter, involves human-made rules agreed between two or more nations which are then used to frame and govern the relations of people beyond and between nations.[10] Our focus here is a consideration of the ways international laws frame and construct questions of memory and the past in ways that offer clarity or complicate our understanding of a right to memory.

The law, according to Andreas Huyssen, has long been entwined with memory, with Greek tragedy providing evidence of "the links between memory, justice and law."[11] However, "the current international human rights movement and the transnational flows of memory politics since the 1990s represent a fundamentally new conjuncture."[12] The advent of the combination of globalization and digitization have contributed to the transnational flows of both rights discourses and memory flows through the "globital memory field."[13] The United Nations has been the key body since World War II developing international law consistent with its role in "promoting economic and social development, as well as to advancing international peace and security."[14]

Over the past decade the world itself has changed significantly in terms of how collective memory is articulated because of connectivity and digitization. How we remember individually, locally, nationally, and transnationally has been transformed with several developments within international law, protocol, and convention that reflect this. Noam Tirosh notes that digitization has impacted the development of discourse relating to ideas of the right to construct one's own narrative as articulated through the Court of Justice of the European Union establishment in 2014 of the "Right to Be Forgotten" (RtBF).[15] The COVID-19 pandemic in 2020–21 also had a major impact in this regard, as it amplified and raised important questions about digital memory rights, such as the right not to be recorded through video calls. In addition, the climate emergency along with the strengthening of indigenous knowledge making inside and outside of the academy raises questions about the significance of non-human memory.

So, how might we understand the relationship between memory and the law? Joachim J. Salvesberg and Ryan D. King argue that "law and collective memory are reciprocally associated" with law steering collective memory "directly but selectively, as trials produce images of the past through the production and presentation of evidence in ritual practices and public discourses."[16] Kirsten Campbell suggests that within this, memory is constituted through the law in three ways: the justiciable, the procedural, and the evidential.[17] Law steers collective memory through its regulation of the production, accessibility, and dissemination of the past, which will vary according to both the "legal environment" and the "political regime in which the law is embedded."[18] The political regime includes not only differences regarding national contexts but also institutional and symbolic differences in power relations, which then challenge any normative right to memory.[19] Sexual bias in the legal construction of memory, for example, results in a gendered constitution of the concept of memory in law.[20] The law, Campbell explains, is not "reducible to the formal or substantive expression of principles in legal instruments and judgements" but is also expressed through its application and practice.[21] Importantly, Campbell's work recalls intersectional biases that will impact the way memory is understood within law, particularly in terms of who is justiciable and what is evidential.

At the international level debates concerning what we might call a right to mediated or cultural memory build on ideas concerning a right to communicate that were critical internationally in the 1970s and that sought to strengthen and extend Article 19 of the Universal Declaration of Human

Rights 1949. This states that "regardless of frontiers" and through any media, "everyone has the right to freedom of opinion and expression. To hold opinions without interference and to seek, receive and impart information."[22] Jean D'Arcy in the UN Office of Publication in 1969 argued that it was not enough to simply provide for people's right to access information, but that people needed the capacity to be able to express it and to be heard.[23] It was not until the late 2000s, however, that this debate was revived to include questions of a right to memory.[24] At the same time, the World Association for Christian Communication published its special issue on a "Right to Memory" that included examples of how memory rights were articulated in different largely national contexts. What is clear in these debates, as Philip Lee admitted, was that "The notion of a right to memory is, therefore, fraught with difficulty. Whose memories are being sought/ how are they to be (re) constructed? How can their veracity, integrity and credibility be guaranteed?"[25] As Paul Ricoeur reminds us, "the duty of memory is the duty to do justice, through memories, to an other than the self."[26] This, as Jay Winter reminds us in this volume, then relates to what he terms a duty to remember. Yet, as Judith Vidal-Hall argues, perhaps what we need is also a right to forget since "all too often it is memory that stands in the way of reconciliation."[27] Debates have thus wrestled with the tension between international accountability and the often swift moves toward national impunity and forgetting in post-conflict or post-dictatorship societies with much of these debates at the international level deriving from a concern with how the past is dealt with when states transition to democracy from former dictatorships or forms of authoritarianism.[28]

Most of the laws at an international and intergovernmental level that discursively invoke, imply, or show a concern with a right to memory are predominantly those concerned with human rights and transitional justice and the ways media, culture, and heritage are critical to establishing transitions after genocide, violence, or authoritarianism.[29] However, there are some important exceptions. Lucy Hilderbrand notes that copyright laws form an important part of shaping and providing our access to mediated memories. Taking the example of YouTube, she argues that the digital platform effectively provides a vast archive of moving images from television, film, and advertisements, as well as personal memories such as wedding videos, all of which introduce "a new model of media access and amateur historiography" that is nonetheless regulated by copyright laws.[30] The 1998 Digital Millennium Copyright Act (DMCA) allows for "offended parties to demand that on-line content be taken off-line without due process to provide infringement."[31] This, in turn, might be said to restrict the individual's right to share mediated personal memories: amateur wedding videos including copyrighted music as a soundtrack, for example, may be removed from the public domain.³² Indeed, copyright laws directly shape the ways writers and artists can adapt and reuse literature and the arts. As Colin B. Harvey notes, "law can have a direct as well as an indirect impact on cultural memory, simultaneously rendering some kinds of storytelling legitimate and others illegitimate."³³

A Typology of Memory in International Law

The law, as Maurice Halbwachs argues, may be understood as a key framework for memory that at the international level may then discursively influence and shape—or not—transnational, national, and local debates and practices relating to memory rights.³⁴ The 1948 Universal Declaration of Human Rights implies a concern with memory and access to collective memory, as do the International Covenant of Economic, Social and Cultural Rights (1966), The Declaration of Social Progress and Development (1969), and The Declaration on the Right to Development 1986.³⁵ I examined these plus other legal instruments available on the UN portal, available in the UNESCO legal instrument portal, and in International Peace Treaties available in the UN Peacemaker Database.³⁶ I identified how they sought discursively to articulate a concern with a right to memory. This involved an initial content search through databases followed by a systematic discourse analysis of the ways in which international legal instruments articulated memory directly or indirectly. Using an earlier scaffold, a typology grounded in this empirical research is built into a four-part framework for understanding a right to memory in international law.³⁷

In the UN Treaty series, memory figures explicitly only twice while heritage is mentioned thirty-eight times. Most treaties are bilateral agreements between two nations such as the 2005 agreement between the government of the United States and Ukraine on the protection and preservation of cultural heritage. Several treaties are multilateral and regional such as the European Convention on the Protection of Archaeological Heritage, and a few involve the world, such as the Convention for the Safeguarding of Intangible Cultural Heritage or the Protocol to the European Convention for the Protection of the Audio-Visual Heritage on the Protection of Television Productions 2016, submitted by the Council of Europe.

The UNESCO Constitution (16 November 1945) frames the importance of memory to signatories by aiming to increase and diffuse knowledge "by assuring the conservation and protection of the world's inheritance of books, works of art and monuments of history and science."³⁸ UNESCO has twenty-two legal instruments in total that directly or indirectly relate to public memory institutions in the form of museums and collections. Over the past ten years there has been greater concern for the preservation and access to diverse human and natural cultures. This includes the establishment of international norms with expectations that these should be passed down to future generations managed at the level of nation states.

A search of a thousand peace agreements showed that "memory" is present in only 8 agreements and 24 paragraphs, while the word "future" is present in 172 agreements and 859 paragraphs. "Heritage" is present in 37 peace agreements and 257 paragraphs. Overall, in the study's corpus there were four different discursive articulations of memory: those seeking to discursively protect national configurations of memory; those seeking to protect heritage and memories of importance to humanity and the world; those preserving memories of victims of war, state violence, and genocide; and those preserving indigenous history, culture, and identity. In what follows, I begin with a diagrammatic summary of this typology before providing a more detailed discussion with examples of the ways international declarations, conventions, and agreements show concern with the right to memory (see table 2.1).

National Memory

Andreas Huyssen has noted how, in the American and French Revolutions, memory and rights were "umbilically linked" with the law connecting state, nation, and citizenship in "the invention of national traditions."[39] Within international law, the right to the protection of national memories is formulated through a recognition of the need to protect and preserve national memories as a human right. It is not that the law seeks to uphold the right to national memories to promote territorial boundaries or is concerned with the promotion of nationalism, but rather there is a concern with upholding the rights of people to have collective memories in relation to national identities. For example, the Recommendation Concerning the Protection, at National Level, of the Cultural and Natural Heritage (1972) outlines a framework for the preservation of collective memories relating to national pasts that includes elements of special value, buildings, topographical features, and monuments. This is expanded upon in the Recommendation Concerning the Safeguarding and Contemporary Role of Historic Areas (1976) with particular emphasis on historic areas and "immovable heritage."

It is unsurprising that international laws frame concerns regarding memory rights in terms of national identities, given the methodological nationalism of knowledge making.[40] This is not entirely the case however, as a study of the European Memory Project by Ann Rigney objects to methodological nationalism, arguing that the knowledge agenda in the case of Europe, including

Table 2.1. A Right to Memory in International Law

Memory rights: scope of concern	Key features	Example 1	Example 2
National	Recognizes and seeks to protect the importance of national pasts to human identity (rather than promoting the idea of memories rooted to national territory)	Recommendation Concerning the Protection, at National Level, of the Cultural and Natural Heritage (1972)	Recommendation Concerning the Safeguarding and Contemporary Role of Historic Areas (1976)
World	Recognizes and seeks to protect some heritage and cultural pasts that are universally shared and of value to all of humankind. Emblem of special protection: A pointed shield of blue and white used to protect public memory institutions during conflict, for example	Convention for the Protection of Cultural Property in the Event of Armed Conflict (1954); Declaration Concerning the Intentional Destruction of Cultural Heritage	Convention for the Safeguarding of Intangible Cultural Heritage. Declaration on the Responsibilities of the Present Generations towards Future Generations (article 7 and article 8)
Victims	Recognizes and seeks to provide mechanisms such as Truth and Reconciliation Commissions to redress legacies of atrocity, state terror, and genocides; states to ensure victims' memories are preserved through commemorations, street names, school text books etc.	Report by Louis Joinet, "Question of Impunity of Perpetrators of Human Rights Violations (Civil and Political)" (1996)	Promotion and Protection of Human Rights. Impunity. Report of the independent expert to update the set of principles to combat impunity, Diane Orentlicher. Economic and Social Council. E/CN.4/2005/102/Add.1 8 Feb 2005. United Nations
Indigenous	Recognizes and seeks to protect indigenous peoples' heritage to ensure future cultural diversity; Protects cultural memory rights of particular groups who were the first inhabitants of a territory	Convention on the Protection and Promotion of Cultural Expressions (2005)	Declaration on the Rights of Indigenous People's (2007) Article 11 and 13. And 31.

memory, has been shaped by transnational regulation from Brussels, which shapes how we conceive of memory and ourselves. Rigney's work suggest the importance of "in-betweenness" in memory work, tracing how European regulation framework programs since the Amsterdam Treaty of 1997 have been strongly concerned with memory and furthering European integration "by creating a shared view of the past."[41]

More recent conventions and recommendations also suggest a productive dialogue between what I show here to be national and world memory—such as the 2015 Recommendation Concerning the Preservation of, and Access to, Documentary Heritage including in Digital Form. This states that the preservation of documentary heritage:

> Involves identification, preservation, access of documentary heritage supported by national legislation. Access should be provided through member states supporting "outreach programmes, including exhibitions, travelling presentations, radio and television programmes, publications, consumer products, on-line streaming, social media, lectures, educational programmes, special events and the digitisation of content for downloading."[42]

Timothy Snyder argues that "the question of the importance of national sovereignty to collective memory, and the possibility of gaining sovereignty over memory by way of national policy" involves several conceptual difficulties.[43] These include distinguishing "history from memory" and the need to distinguish between "mass personal memory" and the "organizational principle that nationally conscious individuals use to organize national history."[44] To illustrate the power of transnational ideologies over national historiography, Snyder pinpoints communism but we could add other ideologies including the ideology of human rights itself and the problem of balancing political leadership with free politics. His work highlights the Gordian knot of irredentism and memory—the idea that part of a cultural and ethnic national may remain unredeemed or outside of a nation-state—and how this in turn can lead to revanchism or policies that seek to retaliate to recover lost territory. Through this he then highlights the idea that national memory can also involve memories of victims at the hands of a neighboring people or state.[45] His work suggests that the strength of international ideologies such as communism in the case of memories of Lithuanians, Poles, and Ukrainians can shape memories by emphasizing "primitive ethnic nationalism" that results in the isolation of nationals that block out "rival conceptions of nationality."[46] The problem, however, is that such protections fail to acknowledge the contradictions between national memory and minority ethnic groups long established on particular territories but who have no recognized "nation"-state and who are also not recognized in terms of being part of an indigenous population. Such groups include the Romany communities of different European countries, the Kurds who have no national homeland, and the Bedouin whose struggle for recognition of their unrecognized villages in the Egyptian Sinai and the Israeli Negev continues.

World Heritage and Human Memory

The rights of memory for national identities are to be distinguished from an evident discursive concern within several international conventions and declarations with a right to world cultural memory and world heritage. This makes clear that the value of cultural memory and particular kinds of heritage is not limited to people's experiences within territories but rather extends to elements of the past and heritage that belong to and benefit the future of the whole of humanity. The earliest of these developed by the UN was the Convention for the Protection of Cultural Property in the Event of Armed Conflict (1954). While this was built on the Convention of The Hague 1899 and 1907, as well as the Washington Pact of 1935, the UN Convention was inspired by the realization that total war and the damage inflicted on civilians and their shared cultural heritage caused irrevocable loss to the whole of humanity. Thus the 1954 Convention established a system of protection used to this day for the identification of public memory institutions and heritage sites that includes a blue and white pointed shield that can be seen from the air during warfare and by invading troops.

After the Taliban deliberately destroyed the sixth-century Buddhist statues of the Bamiyan in Afghanistan, the UN went further to protect cultural heritage with the Declaration Concerning the Intentional Destruction of Cultural Heritage in 2003. This links the deliberate destruction of public memory sites with human rights violations and seeks to provide protection within international law. During the same year, the UN also passed its Convention for the Safeguarding of Intangible Cultural Heritage, which has been crucial in seeking to provide generalized recognition of the value of "practices, representations, expressions, knowledge and skills—as well as instruments, objects, artefacts and cultural spaces individuals recognize as part of their cultural heritage."[47] What is also significant to the framing of a concern with memory is the recognition of the importance of how memories and heritage are passed down across generations as well as how memories are produced through connections with wider history and the natural world: "This intangible cultural heritage, transmitted from generation to generation [in dialogue] with their environment, their interaction with nature and their history."[48] Article 12 states that this promotes both continuity but also "cultural diversity and human creativity."[49]

Nonetheless, it is important to emphasize that despite this evident concern with memory practices and heritage, there is no direct reference to memory. The only place memory is explicitly referenced in relation to world heritage and human memory is Part III on the Safeguarding of Intangible Heritage at National Level (Article 14c) in which it is a requirement that states "promote . . . places of memory whose existence is necessary for expressing the intangible heritage."[50]

The key challenge with the concerns expressed relating to world heritage and a universal human memory, as Asbjorn Eide notes, is the challenge of bridging the particular and the general.[51] As Sally Engle Merry notes, the result is a set of contradictions between situated practices within locations and more lofty general principles and ideals.[52]

Victim Memory

The biblical book of Deuteronomy is a text that lays down how to preserve the memory of Jewish people victimized by Egyptian rulers after they fled Egyptian slavery—effectively articulating an early example of Victim/State Memory. The biblical text states not just what to remember but importantly how to remember. As Assman notes, "Moses outlines a full-fledged mnemotechnique of individual and collective remembering."[53]

There is a distinct discursive formulation within international conventions and practices that evidences a concern with victims' memories of atrocities within the public sphere.[54] It is also generally agreed that within transitional justice, a concern with memory arose out of the framework proposed by UN special rapporteur Louis Joinet in 1996.[55] His final report, "Question of the Impunity of Perpetrators of Human Rights Violations (Civil and Political)," builds on ideas of memory rights that emerged in the 1970s, which sought to provide amnesty for political rights activists struggling against dictatorships mostly in the Southern Cone but which were then twisted by the military dictatorships to provide impunity for themselves. This was accelerated in 1989 with the end of the Cold War that amplified the movement to provide victims of communist regimes with the right to remember the past to seek justice.[56] Louis Joinet's subsequent report sought to provide the basis for a right to memory in relation to individuals but also state targeted groups. Thus, the document states that there is a collective right to know that enables groups to draw "upon history to prevent violations from recurring in the future" with a "duty to remember" being part of the responsibility of the state. The report details a large range of measures that states should use to ensure mnemonic reparation. Annex I "The Duty to Remember" and "Measures for the Preservation of Archives" detail the following:

a) Public recognition of the state's responsibility
b) Official declarations of rehabilitating victims
c) Commemorative ceremonies, naming of public thoroughfares, monuments
d) Periodic tribute to the victims
e) Acknowledgement in history textbooks and human rights training manuals of a faithful account of exceptionally serious violations[57]

An updated set of principles to combat impunity was subsequently published by the Economic and Social Council of the United Nations.[58] Based on this, the Swiss Peace Foundation (SPF) has summarized that there are four pillars for dealing with the past: "the right to know, the right to justice, the right to reparations and the guarantee of non-recurrence."[59] A concern with memory, memorialization, and commemoration of victims falls mainly into a right to know (truth commissions, documentation, archives, history books) and a right to reparations (restitution, memorials, public apologies, commemorations, and educational material). Examples cited by the SPF include the digitization of the entire Guatemalan police archives and accessibility for the public, with security copies held by the Swiss Federal Archive, Chile's Museum of Remembrance to remind Chilean people of the "injustices suffered under the military regime," and Argentina's *Memoria Abierta*, which includes the CONADEP (Comisión Nacional sobre la Desaparición de Personas; National Commission on the Disappearance of Persons) archives of photos and written documents.[60]

Many of the debates internationally that have emerged from the examples of post-genocide and post-conflict societies include a concern with how to articulate difficult memories of communities subjected to traumatic experiences by the state. Yet, as Victor Igreja points out, this involves a process of mnemonic preservation and suppression and "this process of discriminating is politically controversial and a source of great division in society."[61] Many of the rights accorded around victim memory were conceived within a framework of transitional justice: this has been challenged latterly by those working in transformative justice that seek to transform the structures and conditions that caused injustices.[62]

Indigenous Memory

Within several conventions, a concern developed with regard to protecting the memories and heritage of indigenous peoples. The Convention on the Protection and Promotion of the Diversity of Cultural Expressions formulated a link between the cultural heritages of indigenous people to preserve their future identities. Philip Lee has gone so far as to claim that The Declaration on the Rights of Indigenous Peoples (2007) constitutes the basis for an international right to memory within Article 11: "Indigenous peoples have the right to practice and revitalize their cultural traditions and customs. This includes the right to maintain, protect and develop the past, present, and future manifestations of their cultures, such as the archaeological and historical sites, artifacts, designs, ceremonies, technologies and visual and performing arts and literature."[63] Article 11 and Article 31 protect indigenous cultural heritage.[64] In addition, Article 13 states that indigenous peoples have the right to: "Revitalize, use, develop and transmit to future generations their histories, languages, oral traditions, philosophies, writing systems and literatures, and to designate and retain their own names for communities, places, and persons."[65]

Integral to autochthonous or indigenous memory rights articulated here is the precept that these cultural memories, heritage, and traditions belong to particular groups while also recognizing that memories and traditions also change and indeed need to be allowed to be dynamic in order not to die out. Within these protocols then there is a tension between what we might see as the valence between traditions, people, and place and the impact of forced movement as a result of Western invasion and colonization, as well as the subsequent dynamics of memories on the move as in the twenty-first century through the movements of people, data, and things.

Conclusion: Challenges for a Right to Memory in International Law

This chapter proposes a typology for understanding how a right to memory is discursively articulated within an international context, drawing on an empirical analysis of international laws, protocols, and conventions. Deepening and extending my study from ten years ago,[66] the analysis for this chapter has considered the ways memory rights are articulated within international law by using a content search and discourse analysis of hundreds of legal instruments available on the UN portal, UNESCO legal instrument portal, and the UN Peacemaker Database. The research revealed that at the international level, a right to memory, although not explicitly articulated, safeguards memory-related issues in four domains: national memory, world heritage and human memory, victim memory, and indigenous memory.

Despite a seemingly neat typology, my categorization is itself in danger of obfuscating several challenges in terms of how a right to memory is or should be articulated within international law. Ann Rigney's work on European memory agendas raises the question of the differential and powerful role of languages and translation in protecting memory. Building on this we might add that any articulation of memory rights at the international or transnational level needs to include recognition of the crucial conduit and practice of language and translation.

In addition, the question remains of whether international law is really the place to protect something so complex as memory rights. Naomi Roht-Ariazza and Javier Curreva have argued that the problem with loading the responsibility for everything onto the law and legal protocol is that this may then give too little recognition to the power and agency of educational initiatives and the work of memory in culture.[67] Rigney argues that top-down approaches to memory, including the imposition of the law, can be counterproductive since they may lack the mobility and agility of the arts to articulate the past. Thus, any law that seeks to enshrine as part of any restitution process the right to remember victims through street names, history books, and commemorations needs to include the bottom-up power of the imaginative arts "providing a conduit for bringing into play new perspectives and unfamiliar voices that fall outside of dominant discourses."[68] Indeed, the knotty problem then remains of whether international law can and indeed should regulate dialogical memory rights that enable the protection of both shared and divided memories.[69]

It has also been evident for several decades that the framing of human rights within international law is biased toward Western knowledge structures and temporalities that place the individual human at its center while marginalizing non-human entities.[70] Such an approach may deny a right to memory or marginalize particular kinds of memory. Developing a right to memory internationally may require a more polyvalent understanding of time with room for different conceptions of temporality beyond the modernist view of past, present, and future that is prevalent within Western legal traditions.[71] Western androcentric legal jurisdictions may serve to exclude particular conceptions of memory within non-Western cultures. In an interview on the role of film in repatriation and reparation with indigenous people, Mark Inkamala, an Arrarta traditional owner, reminds us that to indigenous people in Central Australia "Culture is passed from generation to generation—don't need memory—don't need to dream this."[72]

The question of repatriation of objects of remembrance may also not necessarily fit with Western models of archive and preservation. Traditional owner Hermann Malbunke secured a VHS video of a ceremony "belonging" to him (in that it referred to the group of people that were his kinsmen) on his property in the manner of other important and restricted objects. He indicated he would place the video in a rock encasing and bury it deeply on his property. He would retrieve it once his son became of age to show him as part of his coming into "law" (initiation).[73]

We also see how different regimes historically de-legitimize non-Western forms and practices of remembering. Hence, the re-emergence of shamanism after the collapse of the Soviet Union in Mongolia signals not just a suppression of the Mongolian past but the cultural forms and practices through which the past was allowed to be remembered.[74]

Importantly, non-Western modalities, forms, practices, and methods can provide for ways of remembering that heal societies after conflict with the use of indigenous cultural techniques that include perpetrators and bystanders as well as witnesses and victims.[75] These can include approaches that incorporate the embodied rituals and dances of traditional healers to remind communities of the humanity of those made outsiders through acts of violence that can enable such perpetrators to be reintegrated into communities. One element to consider in the crafting of any future rights within international law then is to be mindful of how international law may de-legitimize modalities and media of memory that do not fit Western models. In addition, within the international framework there needs to be room for local models and practices that may be performative and embodied.[76] In the future, international law may need to include recognition of cultural variation of the articulation of memories in relation to a right to memory as well as the different understandings of what constitutes the past. Finally, there is the question of whether a right to memory is something that should only be afforded to human beings and whether in the future we also need to include memory rights that go beyond human memory.[77]

Anna Reading (known as Amza), PhD, is Professor of Culture and Creative Industries at Kings College, University of London, UK and Honorary Visiting Professor at Western Sydney University, Australia. She is the author of *Polish Women, Solidarity and Feminism* (Springer, 1992), *The Social Inheritance of the Holocaust: Gender, Culture and Memory* (Springer, 2002), and *Gender and Memory in the Globital Age* (Palgrave Macmillan, 2016) and co-edited *Cultural Memories of Nonviolent Struggles* (Palgrave Macmillan, 2015) and *Save as . . . Digital Memories* (Palgrave 2009). She jointly edits the journal *Media, Culture, and Society* and has written seven plays performed in the UK, Finland, India, Poland, United States, and Ireland.

Notes

1. FORTINBRAS (to Horatio)
   Let us haste to hear it,
   And call the noblest to the audience.
   For me, with sorrow I embrace my fortune.
   I have some rights of memory in this kingdom,
   Which now to claim my vantage doth invite me.
   William Shakespeare. *Hamlet*. Act Five, Scene Two

2. Whelan, "Rights of Memory,".
3. Reading, "Identity, Memory and Cosmopolitanism," 380.
4. Reading, "Identity, Memory and Cosmopolitanism," 380.
5. Reading, "Gender and a Right to Memory" and "The European Roma."
6. Assman, "Communicative and Cultural Memory."
7. Asmann, "Communicative and Cultural Memory," 39.
8. Assman, "Communicative and Cultural Memory," 37.
9. Nora, *Realms of Memory*; Erll, "Travelling Memory"; Bond and Rapson, *The Transcultural Turn*; Levy and Sznaider, *The Holocaust and Memory*; and Assman and Conrad, *Memory in a Global Age*.
10. Wenar, "Rights."
11. Huyssen, "International Human Rights," 607.
12. Huyssen, "International Human Rights," 607.
13. Reading, *Gender and Memory*.
14. In United Nations practice there are conventions, recommendations, and declarations. A "Declaration" is a solemn instrument resorted to only in very rare cases relating to matters of major and lasting importance where maximum compliance is expected. See the Report of the Commission on Human Rights, paragraph 105, eighteenth session, Economic and Social Council, 19 March–14 April 1962. "Recommendations" are instruments in which "the General Conference formulates principles and norms for the international regulation of any question and invites Member States to take whatever legislative or other steps may be required in conformity with the constitutional practice of each State and the nature of the question under consideration to apply the principles and norms aforesaid within their respective territories" (Article 1 [b]). "Conventions" are International Conventions subject to ratification, acceptance, or accession by States. They define rules with which the signatory states undertake to comply. See the Rules of Procedure concerning Recommendations to Member States and International Conventions covered by the terms of Article IV, paragraph 4, of the Constitution. Retrieved 28 August 2022 from https://unesdoc.unesco.org/ark:/48223/pf0000372956/PDF/372956eng.pdf.multi#page=110.
15. Tirosh, "Reconsidering the 'Right to be Forgotten.'"
16. Salvesberg and King, "Law and Collective Memory."
17. Campbell, "Legal Memories."
18. Salvesberg and King, "Law and Collective Memory," 199.
19. Salvesberg and King, "Law and Collective Memory," 197; Campbell, "Legal Memories," 151.
20. Campbell, "Legal Memories," 151.
21. Campbell, "Legal Memories," 155.
22. "Universal Declaration of Human Rights." *United Nations*. Retrieved 23 July 2022 from https://www.un.org/en/about-us/universal-declaration-of-human-rights.
23. D'Arcy, "Direct Broadcast Satellites," 118.
24. At the international level, the term was used within several reports and projects, including Elizabeth Mary Sweet's undergraduate thesis "The Right to Memory and to Truth: Brazil's Transitional Justice Policy and its Consequences," and Kevin Whelan's "Rights of Memory."
25. Lee, "Towards a Right," 3.
26. Ricœur, *Memory History Forgetting*, 89.
27. Vidal-Hall, "Memory and Forgetting," 18.
28. See, for example, Brody, "The Prosecution of Hissène Habré"; De Brito, Gonzalez Enriquez, and Aguilar, *The Politics of Memory*.
29. Lee, "Towards a Right," 3–10.

30. Hilderbrand, "You Tube," 54.
31. Hilderbrand, "You Tube," 55.
32. My own wedding video, shared through *YouTube*, was removed for several years because the film included a music compilation played after the ceremony that included copyrighted material. See GerbyTheGerbil. "Anna and Colin Wedding version 1." *Youtube*, 1 August 2008. Retrieved 23 July 2022 from https://www.youtube.com/watch?v=Oy2GOzh_dBI.
33. Harvey, *Fantastic Transmedia*, 184.
34. Halbwachs, *On Collective Memory*.
35. Lee, "Towards a Right."
36. The relevant legal instruments are available through the following open access digital archives: United Nations Treaty Collection (retrieved 23 July 2022 from https://treaties.un.org/Pages/UNTSOnline.aspx?id=2&clang=_en); United Nations Peacemaker (retrieved 23 July 2022 from http://www.languageofpeace.org), and UNESCO Legal Instruments (retrieved 23 July 2022 from http://portal.unesco.org/en/ev.php-URL_ID=12025&URL_DO=DO_TOPIC&URL_SECTION=-471.html).
37. Reading, "Identity, Memory and Cosmopolitanism."
38. "Universal Declaration of Human Rights," Article 19.
39. Huyssen, "International Human Rights."
40. Wimmer and Schiller, "Methodological Nationalism."
41. Rigney, "Transforming Memory," 608.
42. There are eight UNESCO Conventions and Recommendations relating to the protection of documentary heritage, starting with the Convention for the Protection of Cultural Property in the Event of Armed Conflict (1954) up to the 2015 Recommendation Concerning the Preservation of, and Access to, Documentary Heritage Including in Digital Form. In addition, there are six Declarations and other documents relating to documentary heritage and three International Treaties. These include the Berne Convention for the Protection of Literary and Artistic Works (last amended in 1979), Universal Copyright Convention (1952), and International Convention for the Protection of Performers, Producers of Phonograms and Broadcasting Organizations (1961). Refer to the website for the full text. Retrieved 28 August 2022 from http://unesdoc.unesco.org/images/0024/002446/244675e.pdf#page=5.
43. Snyder, "Memory of Sovereignty."
44. Snyder, "Memory of Sovereignty," 39.
45. Snyder, "Memory of Sovereignty," 49.
46. Snyder, "Memory of Sovereignty."
47. The 2003 Convention for the Safeguarding of the intangible Cultural heritage, Article 21. *UNESCO*. Retrieved 28 August 2022 from https://ich.unesco.org/doc/src/2003_Convention_Basic_Texts-_2020_version-EN.pdf.
48. "Convention for the Safeguarding, Article 12."
49. "Convention for the Safeguarding, Article 12."
50. "Convention for the Safeguarding, Article 14c."
51. Eide, *Economic, Social and Cultural Rights*.
52. Merry, *Human Rights and Gender Violence*.
53. Assman, "Communicative and Cultural Memory," 40.
54. See Bevernage, "Writing the Past out of the Present"; De Brito et al., *The Politics of Memory*; Haynor, *Unspeakable Truths*; Roht-Arriaza and Mariezcurrena, *Transitional Justice*; Sorensen, *Media, Memory and Human Rights*.
55. Haynor, *Unspeakable Truths*, 184.
56. Haynor, *Unspeakable Truths*, 184.
57. Joinet, "Question of the Impunity."

58. Orentlicher, "Promotion and Protection of Human Rights."
59. Swiss Peace, "A Conceptual Framework."
60. Swiss Peace, "A Conceptual Framework," 8, 10.
61. Igreja, "Memories of Violence."
62. Jelin, "Memory and Democracy."
63. The 2007 UN declaration on the rights of indigenous peoples, Article 11. Retrieved 28 August 2022 from https://www.ohchr.org/sites/default/files/Documents/Publications/Declaration_indigenous_en.pdf.
64. Lee, "Towards a Right to Memory," 9.
65. "The rights of indigenous peoples", Article 13."
66. Reading, "Identity, Memory and Cosmopolitanism."
67. Roht-Arriazza and Mariezcurrena, *Transitional Justice*.
68. Rigney, "Transforming Memory," 621.
69. Rigney, "Transforming Memory," 620.
70. Jelin, "Politics of Memory."
71. For a discussion of the politics of time in relation to rights, see Bevernage, "Writing the Past."
72. Inkamala cited in Cohen, "Film as Cultural Memory," 95.
73. Cohen, "Film as Cultural Memory," 94.
74. See Buyandelger, *Tragic Spirits*.
75. Jelin, "Politics of Memory."
76. Cubilie, *Women Witnessing Terror*.
77. The final chapter of this book, "Beyond a Human Right to Memory," discusses these issues further.

Bibliography

Assman, Jan. "Communicative and Cultural Memory." In *The Theoretical Foundations of Hungarian 'Lieux De Mémoire' Studies*, edited by Pál S. Varga, Karl Katschthaler, Donald E. Morse, Miklós Takács, 36–43. Debrecen: Debrecen University Press, 2013.

Assman, Jan, and Stephen Conrad, eds. *Memory in a Global Age: Discourses, Practices and Trajectories*. Basingstoke: Palgrave, 2010.

Bevernage, Berber. "Writing the Past out of the Present: History and Politics of Time in Transitional Justice." *History Workshop Journal* 69, no.1 (2010): 111–31.

Bond, Lucy, and Jessica Rapson. *The Transcultural Turn: Interrogating Memory between and beyond Borders*. Berlin: De Gruyter, 2014.

Brody, Reed. "The Prosecution of Hissène Habré: International Accountability, National Impunity." In *Transitional Justice in the 21st century: Truth Versus Justice*, edited by Naomi Roht-Arriaza and Javier Mariezcurrena, 278–300. Cambridge: Cambridge University Press, 2006.

Buyandelger, Manduhai. *Tragic Spirits: Shamanism, Memory and Gender in Contemporary Mongolia*. Chicago: University of Chicago Press, 2013.

Campbell, Kirsten. "Legal Memories: Sexual Assault, Memory and International Humanitarian Law." *Signs: Journal of Women in Culture and Society* 28, no. 1 (2002):149–77.

Cohen, Hart. "Film as Cultural Memory: The Struggle for Repatriation and Restitution of Cultural Property in Central Australia." In *Cultural Memories of Nonviolent Struggles. Pow-*

erful Times, edited by Anna Reading and Tamar Katriel, 91–110. Basingstoke: Palgrave, 2015.
Cubilié, Anne. *Women Witnessing Terror: Testimony and the Cultural Politics of Human Rights.* New York: Fordham University Press, 2005.
D'Arcy, Jean. "Direct Broadcast Satellites and the Right to Communicate." *European Broadcasting Union Review* 118 (1969): 14–18.
De Brito, Alexandra Barahona, Carmen Gonzalez Enriquez, and Paloma Aguilar. *The Politics of Memory: Transitional Justice in Democratising Societies.* Oxford: Oxford University Press, 2001.
Eide, Asbjorn. *Economic, Social and Cultural Rights.* n.p.: American Education, 2010.
Erll, Astrid. "Travelling Memory." *Parallax* 17, no.4 (2011): 4–18.
Halbwachs, Maurice. *On Collective Memory*, edited and translated by Lewis A. Coser. Chicago: University of Chicago Press,1992.
Harvey, Colin B. *Fantastic Transmedia: Narrative, Play and Memory across Science Fiction and Fantasy Storyworlds.* Basingstoke: Palgrave, 2015.
Haynor, Priscilla B. *Unspeakable Truths: Facing the Challenge of Truth Commissions.* London: Routledge, 2002.
Hilderbrand, Lucy. "You Tube: Where Cultural Memory and Copyright Converge." *Film Quarterly* 61, no. 1 (2007): 48–57.
Huyssen, Andreas. "International Human Rights and the Politics of Memory: Limits and Challenges." *Criticism* 53, no. 4 (2011): 607–24.
Igreja, Victor. "Memories of Violence in Mozambique." *Media Development* 2 (2010): 33–38.
Jelin, Elizabeth. "Memory and Democracy." In *From Transitional to Transformative Justice*, edited by Paul Gready and Simon Robins, 172–88. Cambridge: Cambridge University Press, 2019.
———. "The Politics of Memory: The Human Rights Movement and the Construction of Democracy in Argentina." *Latin American Perspectives* 21, no. 38 (1994): 1–22.
Joinet, Louis. "Question of the Impunity of Perpetrators of Human Rights Violations (Civil and Political): Final Report/Prepared by Mr Joinet Pursuant to Sub-Commission Decision 1996/119." United Nations Digital Library. Retrieved 12 April 2022 from https://digitallibrary.un.org/record/240943?ln=en.
Lee, Philip. "Towards a Right to Memory." *Media Development* 57, no.2 (2010): 3–10.
Levy, Daniel, and Natan Sznaider. *The Holocaust and Memory in the Globital Age.* Philadelphia, PA: Temple University Press, 2006.
Merry, Sally Engle. *Human Rights and Gender Violence: Translating International Law into Local Justice.* Chicago: University of Chicago Press, 2006.
Nora, Pierre. *Realms of Memory: The Constructions of the French Past.* New York: Columbia University Press, 1998.
Orentlicher, Diane. "Promotion and Protection of Human Rights: Impunity." *United Nations Economic and Social Council*, 8 February 2005. Retrieved 23 July 2022 from https://www.swisspeace.ch/fileadmin/user_upload/Media/Topics/Dealing_with_the_Past/Resources/Orentlicher__Diane__E_CN4_2005_102_add1.pdf.
Roht-Arriazza, Naomi, and Mariezcurrena, Javier, eds. *Transitional Justice in the Twenty-First Century.* Cambridge: Cambridge University Press, 2006.
Ricoeur, Paul. *Memory, History, Forgetting.* Chicago: University of Chicago Press, 2004.
Rigney, Ann. "Transforming Memory and the European Project." *New Literary History* 43, no. 4 (2012): 607–28.
Reading, Anna. "Gender and a Right to Memory." *Media Development* 57, no. 2 (2010): 11–15.

———. "The European Roma: An Unsettled Right to Memory." In *Public Memory, Public Media, and the Politics of Justice*, edited by Philip Lee and Pradip Ninan Thomas, 121–40. Basingstoke: Palgrave Macmillan, 2012.

———. "Identity, Memory and Cosmopolitanism: The Otherness of the Past and a Right to Memory." *European Journal of Cultural Studies* 14, no. 4 (2011): 379–94.

———. *Gender and Memory in the Globital Age*. Basingstoke: Palgrave, 2016.

Salvesberg, Joachim J., and Ryan D. King. "Law and Collective Memory." *Annual Review of Law and Social Science* 3 (2007): 189–211.

Shakespeare, William. *Hamlet*. London: Wordsworth Editions, 1992.

Snyder, Timothy. "Memory of Sovereignty and Sovereignty over Memory: Poland, Lithuania and Ukraine, 1939–1999." In *Memory and Power in Post War Europe*, 39–58. Cambridge: Cambridge University Press, 2002.

Sorensen, Kristin. *Media, Memory and Human Rights in Chile*. Basingstoke: Palgrave, 2009.

Sweet, Elizabeth Mary. "The Right to Memory and to Truth: Brazil's Transitional Justice Policy and Its Consequences." *Middlebury Digital Collections*. Retrieved 23 July 2022 from https://repository.middlebury.edu/islandora/object/scholarship%3A1417?solr_nav%5Bid%5D=b9da5ec99f8053f2adad&solr_nav%5Bpage%5D=0&solr_nav%5Boffset%5D=5.

Swiss Peace. "A Conceptual Framework for Dealing with the Past." Bern: Swiss Peace, 2016. Retrieved 23 July 2022 from https://www.swisspeace.ch/assets/publications/downloads/Essentials/7bdf9265 17/A-Conceptual-Framework-for-Dealing-with-the-Past-Essential-16-swisspeace.pdf.

Tirosh, Noam. "Reconsidering the 'Right to be Forgotten': Memory Rights and the Right to Memory in the New Media Era." *Media Culture and Society* 39, no. 5 (2017): 644–60.

Vidal-Hall, Judith. "Memory and Forgetting" *Media Development* 2 (2010): 18–22.

Wenar, Leif. "Rights." In *The Stanford Encyclopedia of Philosophy* (Spring 2021 Edition), edited by Edward N. Zalta. Retrieved 23 July 2022 from https://plato.stanford.edu/entries/rights/.

Whelan, Kevin. "Rights of Memory." In *Conference Report: Storytelling as the Vehicle?*, compiled by Gráinne Kelly, 11–20. Dunadry, Northern Ireland: Healing through Remembering. Retrieved 23 July 2022 from http://healingthroughremembering.org/wp-content/uploads/2015/11/Storytelling-as-the-vehicle_2005.pdf.

Wimmer, Andreas, and Nina Glick Schiller. "Methodological Nationalism and Beyond: Nation-State Building, Migration and the Social Sciences." *Global Networks: A Journal of Transnational Affairs* 2, no. 4 (2002): 301–34.

Chapter 3

THE "DUTY TO REMEMBER" AND THE "RIGHT TO MEMORY"

Memory Politics and Neoliberal Logic

Lea David

Introduction

Every attempt to pose the question of how we should remember—what, whom, and in which way—already conceals an agenda with presupposed assumptions suggesting that there is a proper, or at least better, morally correct way to remember the past. In fact, we, as a society, as citizens or even as memory scholars, are trapped in notions of morality and ethics and are highly influenced by psychological concepts around the possibility of collectively healing through adoption of a "proper" way of remembering.[1] There is a widely accepted belief that communities, even entire societies can "heal" after grave human rights abuses. This idea is deeply anchored in a presumption held by human rights and transitional justice that a "proper memorialization" is crucial in establishing moral responsibility for past atrocities and consequently, human rights values in conflict and post-conflict settings.[2] This prevailing presumption relies on a three-pronged reasoning. The first, borrowed from individual psychology, is that working through the past is necessary for healing, forgiveness, and reconciliation.[3] The second, a political position, argues that accountability fosters democracy and promotes peace and human rights, while the third ethical presumption posits processes of dealing with the past as a moral duty, to remember the victims and acknowledge their trauma.[4]

Hence, as a consequence, the right to memory is situated and well embedded at the center of the "healing" process, where memory is directly linked to healing, reconciliation, and human rights.

Those presumptions are dubious on a number of grounds,[5] but they inevitably imply that social memory has to be managed, navigated, and framed in a particular way as insurance for both the non-repetition of the crime and a better appreciation of human rights and democracy.[6] This is not new. It goes without saying that there is no complete account of the past, one that embodies all—and only the true—facts. Social memory is always instrumentalized, used, and abused to different ends. If one precept is well established and documented in the field of memory studies, it is that both remembering and forgetting are selective as well as strategic in nature and are never exploited to their fullest. Whether we speak of nation-states or human rights-sponsored memorialization projects, social memory is inevitably a construct. This is not to say that social memory is either homogeneous or entirely artificial. However, it is, without exception, always manipulated to fit a certain agenda.[7] Moreover, we often take it for granted. National calendars are tailored to shape and produce temporal boundaries for any given national identity; history textbooks are clearly set to design homogenized narratives of the past in order to sketch the moral path for the future; monuments are supposed to ground particular values to guide us; commemorations, bridging temporal and spatial dimensions, are meant to further establish certain narratives of the past; museums are intended not only to customize the past but first and foremost to direct our feelings and produce a calculated outcome: to make us empathize, to recruit our sentiments in order to enforce a particular worldview.

"Duty to remember" as the public acknowledgment of grave violations of rights and "the right to remember" as both an extension of "duty to remember" and "the right to be forgotten" are embedded in the proliferation of the human rights memorialization agenda and the neoliberal turn. Those two notions share some commonalities but they also differ in their intentions. This article proceeds in four parts. I will first briefly account for the historical-societal emergence of the notions of "duty to remember" and "right to memory." Second, I will place these notions into a wider historical-sociological process that has given rise to the human rights memorialization agenda called "moral remembrance." Then, I will show how the notions of "duty to remember" and the "right to memory" rely heavily on the neoliberal logic of the monetization of human rights abuses. Finally, I will point out some undesired outcomes of the collision of the human rights memorialization agenda with neoliberal logic, showing that they often end up promoting what they initially wanted to prevent. Instead of enforcing and enabling certain rights and establishing moral guidance as a means to prevent the re-occurrence of violence, they often set the stage for increased inequalities and the further marginalization of those who have suffered massive human rights abuses.

The "Duty to Remember" and the Emergence of a Moral Road Map for Human Rights

The "duty to remember" is today recognized as one of the main principles of the human rights memorialization agenda.[8] In 1997, Louis Joinet, the former Special Rapporteur of the Sub-Commission on Prevention of Discrimination and Protection of Minorities, enumerated a "set of principles for the protection and promotion of human rights through actions to combat impunity," putting forward four pillars of transitional justice: the right to know, the right to justice, the right to reparation, and the right to guarantees of non-recurrence.[9] The notion of "the duty to remember" was placed under "the victim's right to know." Joinet introduces the "duty to remember" as a "corollary" to the "victim's right to know," a burden on the state to "be forearmed against the perversions of history that go under the names of revisionism or negationism . . . . These, then, are the main objectives of the right to know as a collective right."[10] Under principle 2 of "The Duty to Remember," he further elaborates: "[a] people's knowledge of the history of their oppression is part of their heritage and, as such, shall be preserved by appropriate measures in fulfilment of the State's duty to remember. Such measures shall be aimed at preserving the collective memory from extinction and, in particular, at guarding against the development of revisionist and negationist arguments."[11]

Joinet bases this understanding on the notion that "collectively, symbolic measures—annual homages to the victims or public recognition by the State of its responsibility, for example—besides helping to restore victims' dignity, also help to discharge the duty of remembrance."[12]

However, the notion of "duty to remember" has a much longer history. Jay Winter in his chapter in this volume rightly points out that the notion of "duty to remember" can be traced back to Rene Cassin, a wounded veteran of World War I, who inscribed the "duty to remember" in the Universal Declaration, and made human rights work a form of commemoration of the innocent victims of state violence, from the Nazis to the present. For Winter, the "duty to remember" is first and foremost a family matter, arguing that engaging in an examination of various forms of remembrance and their meaning in a democratic society, reflects the intimate responsibility of children burying their parents, or even each other. The human rights revolution of the period following World War II as an affirmation of the humanity of the innocent victims of that conflict, came only after the recognition of the "duty to remember" as an important aspect of "family" and "community" in the bereavement process.

The universalized, yet vague notion of the "duty to remember" appeared in the aftermath of World War II, with mediatized criminal proceedings, most famously during the international military tribunal in Nuremberg (1945–46), the Israeli trial of Adolf Eichmann (1961) and Ivan Demjanjuk (1986–88), and the French trial of Klaus Barbie (1987).[13] In that sense, the right to memory is largely articulated in terms of a universal right, one that demands recognition from international and transnational discourses, and the enforcement of international charters by international organizations. However, from a discursive point of view, it was not until Chancellor Helmut Schmidt's speech, delivered in a Cologne synagogue at the Kristallnacht commemoration on 9 November 1978, that this notion generated an outstanding meaning of resurrection through acknowledgment. A "duty to remember" mass crimes echoed strongly during the Historians' Debate in Germany in a way that can be read as a criticism of this culture of "Remembering to Forget and Forgetting to Remember," arguing that remembering always already entails forgetting and forgetting is possible only where there is remembering in the first place.[14]

All of this set a tone and developed a belief in redemption through memory. Since the 1980s, historians, politicians, political scientists, and human rights lawyers and activists have all advanced this idea either directly or indirectly. The question was not whether to forget but how to engrave memory into the flesh of a nation. Over the past forty years or so, "duty to remember" has come to be regarded by human rights promoters as a crucial element of progress toward a more satisfactory and more democratic political and social relationship.[15] Rebecca Kook, in her chapter in this volume, is correct when she says that the idea of a "right" is central to the concept of democracy because all members of the polity are equally deserving of the rights and benefits accrued by virtue of membership.

The seemingly simplistic but catchy phrase "duty to remember" has become both a political slogan for redemption and a panacea for digesting atrocities committed in the past, and has become widely used in a variety of often opposing and contradictory contexts. This assumption, developed mostly by human rights lawyers, activists, and political scientists, was based on an idealized view: by compelling the honoring of the memory of those who died, the "duty to remember" would serve as an insurance policy against the repetition of such crimes. However, just as Sarah Gensburger and Sandrine Lefranc demonstrated in their study and I did in mine, there is close to nothing that supports this idea.[16] In fact, memorialization policies are often counterproductive. And yet it is still one of the most deeply embedded ideas that impacts not only day-to-day politics and policy-making but, more profoundly, the meaning-making processes of selfhood and nationhood.[17]

The Right to Memory

Noam Tirosh and Anna Reading in their introduction to this volume are correct that the "right to memory" is enshrined in only a few memory rights in rights-based legal apparatuses worldwide. Most notably among these rights is the contested "right to be forgotten" that emerged as a response to the rapid digitization of memory and the collective fear from a "never-forgetting" new media. Whereas the notion of "duty to remember" as a collective moral imperative has a long trajectory and is directly connected to human rights abuses, the concept of the "right to memory" is a recent one and developed in the interplay between values of privacy and the demand for transparency. In May of 2014, the European Court of Justice ruled in *Google Spain v. Gonzalez* that, in order to protect European citizens' "right to be forgotten," search engines like Google are required to censor certain search results, and in response, Google posted a removal request form online. In addition, Article 10 guarantees all Europeans the right to receive and the right to impart information. Both of these rights are infringed upon by the right to be forgotten.[18]

Therefore, according to Eduard Fosch Villaronga, Peter Kieseberg, and Tiffany Li, the "right to memory" stands as an antidote to "the right to be forgotten" that eminently brings to the fore the antagonism between the values of privacy and transparency under the current EU privacy law that was designed to better our understanding on whether and how the law should address the "right to be forgotten" in a post-artificial intelligence (AI) world.[19] However, Noam Tirosh offers another interpretation. He suggests that "the right to be forgotten" actually reflects the right to construct one's narrative.[20] Those two rights developed in the context of advanced technology and media, artificial intelligence with its learning capabilities, and were, in their inception, broadly understood in terms of human rights values.

Apart from this technological development related mostly to media, the "right to memory" has another route of development that is managed through the process of juridification—the transformation of political and ethical questions into legal ones. The question, raised in relation to individual health and ethics, tries to define when and under what conditions the use of memory-altering substances or tools is beneficial for an individual. This issue has been regulated by different legal provisions. Mental health, as a human right under the European Convention of Human Rights, affords citizens claims against states to refrain from actions that inflict mental harm and to protect them against such actions by private parties. Christoph Bublitz and Martin Dresler rightly point out that from the perspective of neuroscience, some aspects of memory concern issues of identity and personhood and may therefore relate to human dignity. Therefore, according to them, memory as such deserves heightened legal protection.[21] Persons compose stories about themselves, woven from various sources such as their recollections, beliefs, self-image, how others perceive them, and expectations and aspirations for the future.[22] On a basic level, this implies that we should be entitled to the right to remember. It guarantees that persons are entitled to use their powers of memory at will. This right corresponds with the duty of others to refrain from interfering with memory. In that context, Adam Kolber has proposed acknowledging a novel right, "freedom of memory," which he described as a "poorly defined bundle of rights to control what happens to our memories."[23]

Though at its core "the right to memory" is not directly connected to the notion of "duty to remember" and was deeply embedded in individual rights to preserve or eliminate memory, these notions often tend to overlap. Anna Reading describes at length in her chapter in this volume, "Framing Memory Rights in International Law," the different ways these articulate, in the past and today, what might be termed a "right to memory." She demonstrates that when it comes to international law the right to memory is expressed in one of four ways: (1) to protect and preserve national memory, i.e., stories and narratives related to national identity particularly in terms of those arising from warfare and genocide; (2) to support and protect the rights of victim memories, i.e., those who have been subjected to state violence; (3) to preserve and protect the right of humanity to world memory, i.e., heritage that gives access to the past of the world; and (4) to protect the right of indigenous memory, i.e., particular rights of indigenous people. The prevalence of legal language and ideas that have been downloaded from international discourse have infiltrated memorial practice with claims of memorial rights. Francisco J Ferrándiz, on the other hand, identifies three different claims: the "right to be remembered," the "duty to remember," and the "freedom to mourn."[24] Hence, we see how the notion of "right to memory" is understood and promoted in three ways: as an individual right connected to the preservation/removal of the content from different media platforms, as a health issue with ethical and legal implications, and as a collective right to address past historical injustices and human rights violations.

Moral Remembrance

To understand how "duty to remember" and "right to memory" started to overlap, and more importantly, what the outcomes of such a collision are, we need to briefly examine the intersection between the rise of the human rights memorialization agenda, for which I have coined the term "moral remembrance,"[25] and its entanglement with neoliberal values.

Moral remembrance prescribes standards for a "proper method of remembrance" with which states are expected to comply when dealing with legacies of mass human rights abuses. It refers to a standardized, isomorphic set of norms and is based on normative worldviews of human rights that promote "facing the past," "duty to remember," and "victim-centered" approaches as its pillars. Moral remembrance points to the current worldwide preference for memory standardization, institutional homogenization, and norm imitation. It provides a technocratic-like set of policies and a tool kit of practices that aims to advance a human rights vision of memorialization processes in order to promote democratic human rights values across the globe. Moral remembrance, as the human rights memorialization agenda, offers a variety of memorialization practices, such as public expressions of emotions and the performance of guilt, shame and remorse that include actions such as public apologies, truth telling, models of reconciliation, the erection of monuments and museums, and legal, penal or financial measures such as reparations and restitution, as well as the formation of international domestic and hybrid courts and passage of memory laws. Moral remembrance also fosters educational and artistic projects, dialogue groups, memory activism, historical justice claims, and peacebuilding memorialization activities. The vast diversity of moral remembrance practices should be understood against the background of a number of historical-sociological processes in which different paradigms collided and overlapped to forge the "sacred" pillars of facing the past, the duty to remember (and recently the right to memory), and a victim-centered approach to justice and memorialization.

The institutionalization of the human rights memorialization agenda started with the adoption by the UN, on 10 December 1948, of the Universal Declaration of Human Rights (UDHR).[26] The UDHR has no legal force, and was not tailored to address memory issues per se, but as the single most important statement of ethics, its authority is unparalleled even for memorialization processes. However, at the beginning, the human rights understanding of memorialization processes was developed on the fringes of the core human rights agenda. World War II and the Holocaust led to a whole range of normative and institutional changes that primarily focused on preventing human suffering as a result of war and political persecution that took memory for granted. The importance of memory surfaced only gradually in the years that followed.

I have written elsewhere at length about these historical trajectories, but what is important to stress here is that the rapid growth of memorialization across the globe during the 1980s and 1990s might be explained by the fact that memorialization became a crucial representation of the struggle over identity politics.[27] The politics of recognition developed in the past two centuries as a political tool to achieve social and justice claims. Charged with an emancipatory promise to bring normative change and the adoption of a human rights worldview, as well as putting an emphasis on the recognition of distinctive perspectives when it comes to ethnic, racial, and sexual minorities and gender differences,[28] at the turn of the twenty-first century, issues of recognition and identity became even more central. In particular from the 1980s onward, and even more so since the 1990s, when identity politics established the importance of witnesses after the Soviet Union collapsed in 1989,[29] it became clear to all parties involved in the process of memory construction that memory is not a guaranteed right but a privilege. In other words, one has to fight for it as it is not naturally given. With the demise of communism and the surge of free-market ideology, together with identity politics fueled by a universalist morality of justice, the focus gradually shifted from "blaming and shaming" governments to a "justice for victims" approach as a prime category of the human rights activist struggle.[30] The increasing importance of memory also has to do with developments in information technology. In that sense, it is essential that when discussing memory rights, the focus should also be on information and communication technologies and their role as memory enablers as well as on the normative underpinnings of media regulations that will anchor and protect this role.[31]

Additionally, these processes coincided with the dilemmas experienced in the 1980s by human rights activists, lawyers and legal scholars, policymakers, journalists, donors, and comparative politics experts in relation to places such as Korea, Chile, South Africa, Brazil, the Philippines, Uruguay, Guatemala, Haiti, Poland, and Czechoslovakia, to mention but a few, concerned with the transition from conflicts and dictatorships to democracies.[32] A new sort of human rights activity was generated, called "transitional justice," defined as "the full range of processes and mechanisms associated with a society's attempt to come to terms with a legacy of large-scale past abuses, in order to ensure accountability, serve justice and achieve reconciliation."[33] It includes criminal prosecutions, truth commissions, reparations programs, and various kinds of institutional reforms. The paradigm of transitional justice, which included not only juridical but also political and social mechanisms (with a strong focus on memorialization), was intensively promoted from the late 1980s on and has become the main ideological force behind the human rights memorialization agenda. Facilitating transitions from authoritarian regimes to stable democratic governance has come to involve cosmopolitan imperatives commanding a narrative that acknowledges past injustices.[34]

However, the appearance of transitional justice was followed by a broader spectrum of ideas, concepts, and practices that only gradually defined the memorialization agenda clearly.[35] Together with the principles of reparations, drafted by the Special Rapporteurs Theo van Boven and Cherif Bassiouni and adopted by the UN General Assembly in 2005, the principles of memorialization standards were discussed at length as pillars of the broader issue of reparations, arguing that these principles may bring about reconciliation in divided societies and are to be considered the best roadmap for memorialization processes. Two important reports, one on history textbooks and the second on memorialization standards, were presented at the UN General Assembly as part of dealing with the promotion and protection of human rights. Attempts to incorporate memorialization processes as an integral part of transitional justice mechanisms and to move from "duty to remember" as a moral instance to the policy-oriented and prescribed "duty to remember in a proper way" are designed and envisioned through the standardization of memory. According to Pierre Hazan, one of the main composers of the UN report on "Memorialization Standards," "memorialization has become a core principle and has developed as a set of policies for combating injustice and promoting reconciliation."[36] Further, the UN adoption of "memorialization standards" is explained as "Western memorial models commemorating the victims of Nazism, while not always the most adequate or appropriate, have become a template or at least a political and aesthetic inspiration for the representation of past tragedies or mass crimes."[37]

Between 2013 and 2014 memorialization became mainstream within the field of cultural rights, and "duty to remember" and "right to memory" became a standard framework for addressing past human rights abuses. Through a policy-oriented framework, standardization became a crucial feature of the process of the emergence of moral remembrance. This exposed both the cumulative and coercive bureaucratic nature of the human rights regime, which tries to homogenize and monopolize the way we are supposed to frame and remember our past and the deep embedment of its logic into neoliberal discourse. The Holocaust turned into something resembling a template for many other processes of, and pleas for, dealing with the past, informing human rights thinking and placing reparation and compensation processes at the heart of it.

The impact of this shift is far reaching. For example, recent developments in EU law indicate the substantial evolution of activist citizenship discourse on historic memory, from "invitation to remember" to "duty to remember."[38] In a similar trend, Jenna Thompson claims that citizens are obliged to remember the deeds of their predecessors and to apologize and make recompense for historical injustices.[39] Those claims are important as they reflect the overreaching practical implication of this deeply embedded notion of "duty to remember" and its shift toward ethics of moral remembrance. However, it also set the groundwork for placing a capitalist value on human suffering by applying symbolic or real monetary values on it.

Neoliberal Imprint on Moral Remembrance

Since the end of the 1970s, generally speaking, we have seen increasing linkages between the memorialization agenda of human rights and the global ascension of neoliberalism. One of the defining features of the international human rights movement has become this new concern for the suffering of specific others in distant lands—an agenda that, to some extent, displaces those earlier, very nation-specific struggles, even in the same places. To this end, certain necessary historical and social conditions had to take place to bring about the rise of the moral state of compassion, defined by Natan Sznaider as an active moral demand to address the suffering of others.[40] The moral demand to act in order to lessen the suffering of others, across spatial and temporal dimensions, became possible only at the intersection between "humanitarianism" and the emergence of liberal society, with its distinctive features of capitalism (the market) and democracy (civic equality and citizenship).[41] On the one hand, through democratization and the lessening of profoundly categorical and corporate social distinctions, compassion became more socially desired and widespread value.

On the other hand, the emergence of the market society widened the scope of exchange and unintentionally extended the public scope of compassion.[42] Further, through the institutionalization of memories of human rights abuses in international conventions, cruelty became understood as the infliction of unwarranted suffering and compassion as a public response to this evil.[43] Such developments enabled human rights to become an effective strategy for framing grievances because human rights enjoy widespread legitimacy. Framing grievances as human rights has been a transformative process that has given voice to and empowered previously marginalized populations. The popularization of human rights as a vernacular for framing grievances has resulted in "rights inflation," which is the tendency to frame any grievance as a rights violation.

Both Costas Douzinas and Mary Nolan stressed that the human rights project became a complementary force to neoliberalism, effectively showing the ways that those two agendas go hand in hand.[44] The intimate connection between human rights and neoliberalism points to the hidden links between human rights and moral remembrance, with neoliberalism and the power of the Global North intentionally or unintentionally aimed at colonializing and imposing an ideological set of beliefs and values worldwide. The clashes between different sets of values have real implications for the ways people on the ground perceive human rights in general and moral remembrance in particular, as they also largely disable culturally specific ways of remembering.[45]

More specifically, Cristian Cercel rightly spots the entanglement of the human rights memorialization agenda with neoliberal discourse, often expressed through "corporativist-marketizing-neoliberal jargon."[46] Though the processes by which individuals and groups remember or forget the past has been a concern for centuries, the rapid growth of memorialization across the globe during the 1980s and 1990s, and the obsession that shifted from commemorating specific victories to commemorating massive past human rights abuses in general, might be explained by the fact that memorialization became a key to personal, social, and cultural identities and a crucial representation of the identity politics struggle.[47] A person or entity who has control over memory is entitled to financial, political, and social resources within society. This control over resources in relation to memory is often visible in the vocabulary used, for instance when we talk of "memory markets,"[48] "management of the past,"[49] "mnemonic/memory entrepreneurs,"[50] or "memory stakeholders."[51] I myself have written on "memory trade," which refers to the process in which memory content is treated as a trading currency in order to gain particular tangible or symbolic means, similar to the process where memory is understood as marketized and consumed.[52] Jay Winter rightly pointed out that, in the West, one important precondition of the "memory boom" has been affluence. He stressed the fact that "rising real incomes and increased expenditure on education since the Second World War have helped shift to the right the demand curve for cultural commodities."[53] This is important as it goes hand in hand with the acceptance of the notion of post-traumatic stress disorder (PTSD), previously termed "shell shock" or "combat fatigue," into medical diagnostic classification in the 1980s. Once accepted as a syndrome, PTSD validated various forms of entitlements, not only to pensions, medical care, and public sympathy, but also the right to "proper" commemorations.[54] However, it is important to stress that not all voices are heard equally, as they always reflect their positioning in social structures of power. Further down the road of a neoliberalist approach to memorialization, we see that only during the 1990s, and only after learning about the mistreatment of victims in Bosnia by the state but also by the ICTY (International Criminal Tribunal for the Former Yugoslavia) where they experienced re-traumatization, did human rights NGOs (non-governmental organizations) succeed in lobbying to redirect the focus from crimes to victims. Introducing terms with legal ramifications such as "remedy," "compensation," and "reparations" gave victims a platform for the acknowledgment of their sufferings but also the leeway to claim tangible compensation. The use of neoliberal language reflects the way the memorialization agenda is both declarative and points to a deeper connection to the imagined solution—that it is possible to measure human suffering and to adequately put a price on it.

This trajectory, where certain memories can be translated into commodities or benefits, plays a crucial role for both the "duty to remember" and the "right to memory," and is a testimony to the "uncontested triumph of liberal democracy (that) has been accompanied by an increase in the interest in memory issues and in processes of dealing and coming to terms with the past, and by the intensified dissemination and institutionalization of neoliberal ideas and practices in the political and economic realms."[55] Therefore, over the past four decades, memory politics and neoliberalism have become deeply interconnected, if not always visibly so, in hegemonic discourses, practices, and politics.

Consequently, the analytical vocabulary frequently employed when researching and discussing issues related to past human rights abuses is imbued with expressions that largely pertain to "corporativist-marketizing-neoliberal jargon."[56] This speaks loudly about how framing a grievance as a human rights issue shapes the way people understand both the problem and the solution. By appropriating the language of neoliberalism, it also shows the limits of framing social problems as rights violations.[57] In a way, whereas human rights have become an effective strategy for framing grievances (often through appealing to international human rights treaties), the increasing interconnectedness of rights-talk with neoliberal discourses to frame any and all grievances and past human rights abuses, effectively undermines attempts to successfully address systemic social problems. This is because it displaces grievances from their social realm to the sphere of economics and politics. Under the pretense of "duty to remember" and "right to memory" as means of eventually achieving reconciliation and implementing human rights values, the burning questions of entitlement to benefits and privileges and the division of scarce resources lurk underneath.

Memorialization Agenda of Human Rights, Neoliberal Solutions, and the Day-to-Day Politics of Victimhood

When "duty to remember" and "right to memory," with their toolkits of practices and discourses, become embedded into the performative and operative vocabulary in local (often post-conflict) communities, they disclose the gap between desired visions of the future and on-the-ground day-to-day politics. Once those who suffered or lost their loved ones to human rights abuses manage to claim their victim status, they often become consumed in promoting the principle of "duty to remember" as the way to advance the public and official recognition of their suffering and grievances. At the same time, as an antidote, groups labeled "perpetrators," adopt the principle of the "right to memory," through which they can claim the right to their own narrative.[58] Both notions of "duty to remember" and "right to memory" become indispensable tools in the struggle of different parties for their own public recognition. This is because the logic of these two principles enables everyone to posit their own memories as deserving of recognition. This means that the emergence of the right of remembrance owed to certain parties must be balanced and countered by the right of acknowledgment owed to the opposing constituencies.[59]

To further comprehend how this discourse becomes monetized and ends up creating new social inequalities, one must understand the dynamics of day-to-day politics in post-conflict settings in which this vocabulary of rights and duties operates. To start with, we need to understand the elusive role of human rights NGOs operating on the ground. Human rights (I)NGOs (international non-governmental organizations) are deeply embedded in the structures and processes of the neoliberal architecture of the aid system.[60] Human rights (I)NGOs run in the moral sphere of "doing good" and helping those who are deprived of their rights by their advocacy, mobilization or channeling of resources that support their moral stance. (I)NGOs are also part of the civilizing crusade project, backed by interventions that grant legitimacy to the art of governing behavior and shaping subjectivities. In most for-profit or strictly economic markets, the formation of monopolies—the exclusive control of the supply or trade of a commodity or, in this case, a service—is usually discouraged by governmental policies and reforms.[61] In the tertiary sector, and particularly in the human rights NGO sector, monopolization seems to be present with little effort and too few regulations.[62] This means that bigger and better-established (I)NGOs will oversee the tone and the direction of what is to be funded and why. It is true that human rights are transformative because they enable an effective master frame for mobilizing public support and forging alliances, and they lend legitimacy to grievances and provide a common language to unify a diverse constituency.[63] However, the "right causes" will not be instantly recognized and promoted as such, but instead, those claims need to be reframed to fit the donor agendas. Clifford Bob, for example, showed why Tibet's quest for self-determination has roused people around the world, while simultaneously pushing aside and making other minorities invisible, such as Mongols, Zhuang, Yi, Hui, and Uighurs, all of whom suffer similar conditions as the Tibetans.[64] He brilliantly demonstrated the importance of adjusting and reframing one's agenda to that of human rights in order to achieve visibility and wide recognition. In fact, this means that an enormous number of grievance groups will stay "undiscovered," because they were "not managed properly," meaning they either lack discursive resources and proper marketing or will fail to frame their suffering to fit the budgetary agenda in order to deliver on their success.[65] Hence, within day-to-day politics, both the right to memory and duty to remember become tightly aligned to the logic of neoliberal markets, in which recognition and identity politics play a crucial part in the distribution of scarce resources. Consequently, the language of neoliberalism in memory politics limits emancipatory and transformative possibilities, as well as effective channels of political action.

Transnational-national-local linkages are mediated by power and resource disparities between both the interplay between the local groups and the international and local NGOs, and the geo-political and national political contexts in which these groups operate.[66] However, Patrice McMahon rightly pointed out that "scholars and policymakers tend to accept and even celebrate NGO involvement in post-conflict countries, but rarely do they examine what these associations do or their impact on everyday life."[67] This is evident in the creation of hierarchies of victimhood. The use of the identification of "innocent" or "real" victims within conflicts and post-conflict societies perpetuates very powerful moral conceptions of victimhood.[68] The legitimizing stamp of human rights in providing justice to innocent victims has been reduced to a simplified logic: if I am a victim, I cannot be responsible for anything, and no one can argue with me because it would be showing a lack of respect for a victim.[69] The local and international NGO selection of victims is made based on those who are perceived to be the most deserving, the most "innocent" or "pure." However, those who consider themselves, or are considered by others to be, innocent victims dispute the "deservingness" of other "bad" or "impure" victims.[70] This is the cornerstone upon which hierarchies of victimhood are constructed and sustained.[71] This means that, in fact, the memory politics of the "right to memory" and "duty to remember" are being utilized within day-to-day reality to create a trading currency in which only those with sufficient discursive and other means can gain benefits, while many others are marginalized and pushed deeper into oblivion.[72]

This struggle for victimhood appropriation is a common feature for both human rights (I)NGOs and the nation-state political apparatus. Examples of the ways the ruling political elite appropriates grievances to claim victimhood are well documented. We see, for example, that in order to consolidate power in the aftermath of violence, political elites in both Rwanda and Bosnia mobilized ethnically defined social groups and elevated certain groups as being those "most" victimized.[73] Gruia Badescu goes even further, demonstrating, in the case of postwar Sarajevo's repurposed memorials and religious buildings, how categories of victimhood are sustaining and perpetuating conflicts through processes of humiliation.[74] In Argentina, the state's solution was to produce a hierarchy of victims ranked according to their "innocence" and further correlated with their rights. Less focus has been given to the way human rights organizations and institutions enabled the rise of new social inequalities based on hierarchies of victimhood.[75] Jacques Leider convincingly showed how, in the case of Myanmar, human rights NGOs contributed significantly to creating a field of competitive victimhood between Buddhists and Muslims.[76] In Northern Ireland, concerns about hierarchies of victimhood and the legitimacy of victimhood have a very similar "inter-communal competitive dynamic" where legitimate identification as the victim may be used to attract resources and international support to the "in-group," thus strengthening in-group solidarity and moral superiority over the "out-group."[77] Jennifer Curtis similarly demonstrated how, in Northern Ireland, claims around economic inequality and welfarism structured the discourse of peace and human rights, effectively supporting Samuel Moyn's argument that human rights are concerned with status but not distributive equality.[78] Jessie Hronesova, while researching the different outcomes of claim-making by Bosnian victims of sexual violence and ex-combatants, showed likewise that while grassroots victims' associations often start as mutual support groups, they ultimately become political instruments for their members, typically in ways that are competitive with victims who have divergent identities.[79] The creation and reproduction of the hierarchies of suffering relies heavily on the idea of both the "duty to remember" and "right to memory," as those ideas are well integrated into discourses around claiming rights, recognition, and benefits.

The creation of hierarchies of victimhood by assigning different resources to different groups inevitably leads to animosities between different victim groups and organizations. The logic that the more innocent get more rights and the less innocent fewer rights is a well-established one.[80] In Serbia, different war veterans groups have been allocated distinct rights to encourage hostility between them and make them unable to unify and gain political power.[81] In Spain, a similar struggle for legitimacy has taken place, which involves legal recognition as a victim and the appropriation of the status of "ideal victim" by denying it to other groups.[82] Often, victim organizations will try to align with their governments. For example, Peruvian victim organizations became politicized in light of the government's promise to implement the individual economic reparations program.[83]

Hence, victimhood becomes a substitute for identity where both "duty to remember" and the "right to memory" end up being weapons of that struggle. In this interplay of day-to-day politics, grief and suffering become substituted with the promise of public recognition, reparations, or other symbolic or tangible benefits, which open up a stage for continuous battles and competitions that sustain and fuel disagreements and facilitate new social divisions. Consequently, struggles over victimhood are never about human rights values; rather, they arise because the human rights principles of the "duty to remember" and the "right to memory," deeply engrained in neoliberal monetized solutions to human rights problems, set a platform for addressing one's own past injustices and claiming victimhood status recognition. In fact, both the "duty to remember" and the "right to memory" demand an "activism of victimhood" that "compels the survivors to constantly reassess their victim status."[84] This effectively means that victims who carry the most physical and mental scars and remain in the moment of the atrocity even after decades, are often trapped in the role of victims,[85] trying to navigate "the moral truth in atrocity and the facts of the atrocity itself."[86]

The tension between, on the one hand, human rights ideals and the backstage politics of organizations, and on the other, the political interests of various groups behind nation-states results in very particular and often tangible trade-offs between groups affected by massive human rights abuses, national political elites, and various human rights organizations. The outcomes of such negotiations, trade-offs, transactions of real or symbolic benefit and the political struggle over scarce resources lead to new social inequalities and the marginalization of those who cannot afford (for various reasons) to participate in these mnemonic battles. In other words, new social inequalities are formed at the intersections of the human rights memorialization agenda that has adopted neoliberal discourse and the day-to-day politics of victimhood, which have enabled differential access to state power and state bureaucracy and should be seen as a foundation for the emergence of a new social class.[87]

Conclusion

In the introduction to this volume, Tirosh and Reading point out that the relationship between memory and human rights and socio-legal constructs that protect and legitimate the well-being of individuals and groups have yet to be fully explored. They argue that memory rights can serve as the guardians of the crucial components of memory processes: the ability to create, preserve, retrieve, and endow memories. However, this chapter points out some downsides and possible pitfalls of the linkages between rights and the neoliberal logic in which they are embedded. The main goal of this chapter has been to point out the historical-sociological connection between the rise of the notions of the "duty to remember" and the "right to memory" and their intersection with the neoliberal logic of monetization, which ends up creating social stratification and animosities between victim groups and organizations.

I have argued here that the direct connection between human rights and neoliberalism and the "duty to remember" and the "right to memory" derived from this linkage often end up disabling victim agency and potential channels of political action. This limits the emancipatory and transformative possibilities for those involved. The crossbreeding between moral remembrance as the human rights memorialization agenda (in which the notions of "duty to remember" and "right to memory" have become the main pillars) and neoliberal thinking brings to the fore an expected and highly disputed outcome. It actively promotes hierarchies of victimhood that, at the level of day-to-day politics, translates into an endless battle for scarce resources, various trade-offs, and competition over recognition. This is precisely why only those victims capable of framing their struggle to fit the agendas of human rights (I)NGOs and the ruling political elite gain support (financial or symbolic) while others remain unrecognized, marginalized, and voiceless. However, while pointing out the possible misuses and abuses of the concepts of the "duty to remember" and "right to memory," the research on memory and human rights through the prism of socio-legal boundaries of rights protection is nascent and deserves additional attention. In fact, the outcomes on the ground may vary significantly depending on the context, use, and application.

Lea David is an Assistant Professor and an Ad Astra Fellow at the School of Sociology, University College Dublin (UCD). She is a comparative historical sociologist with a strong interdisciplinary background in cultural anthropology and history. Previously, Lea David held several postdoctoral fellowships such as the Fulbright Fellowship, the Rabin Fellowship, the Jonathan Shapira Fellowship, the Marie Curie Research Fellowship, among others. She has published a number of peer-reviewed articles, book chapters in edited volumes, and opinion pieces in English, Hebrew, and Serbo-Croatian. Her book *The Past Can't Heal Us: The Dangers of Mandating Memory in the Name of Human Rights* that won several prizes was published in 2020 by Cambridge University Press.

Notes

1. See my previously published works "Against Standardization of Memory," *The Past Can't Heal Us*, and "Moral Remembrance."
2. See more in the "Report of the Special Rapporteur." This report summarizes and further cements the belief in "healing" societies, a debate that has historical trajectory, in both scholarly and activist circles.
3. Adorno, "What Does Coming to Terms with the Past Mean?"
4. Dragovic Soso, "Conflict, Memory, Accountability."
5. Hamber and Wilson, "Symbolic Closure," and David, *The Past Can't Heal Us*.
6. "Social memory" refers here to the dissemination of beliefs, feelings, moral values, and knowledge concerned with the past. Memory is social because it exists by means of its relation with what has been shared with others: language, symbols, events, as well as geography and mental and cultural topography. However, there are a variety of generic terms in the field of memory research such as collective, public, historical, and cultural memory or "collective remembrance," which deals with theories elucidating the context of memory construction for groups, societies, or nations.
7. For examples, see Verdery, *National Ideology under Socialism* and David, "Fragmentation."

8. David, "Against Standardization of Memory" and *The Past Can't Heal Us*.
9. Joinet, "Administration of Justice."
10. Joinet, "Administration of Justice," 253.
11. Joinet, "Administration of Justice," 265.
12. Joinet, "Administration of Justice," 258.
13. Belavusau and Gliszczyńska-Grabias, *Law and Memory*, 1–26.
14. Zehfuss, "Remembering to Forget."
15. Kabalek, "Memory and Periphery."
16. Gensburger and Lefranc, *Beyond Memory*; David, *The Emergence of*;
17. There are at least two separate problems with this assumption. First, it would need to be tested, but when is an appropriate timeframe for such a test? Ten years, a generation, a century? Further, not only are memory constructions long-term processes but remembrance is also always dynamic, in flux and steadily (but not evenly) changing. Second, once conflict emerges, it is nearly impossible to isolate processes of facing the past from wider geopolitical, economic, and societal contexts in order to test its relationship to the outbreak of conflict. It seems that the notion of facing the past for the sake of the non-recurrence of violence is just a wishful ideological construct based on false premises.
18. Article 10 of the European Convention on Human Rights provides the right to freedom of expression and information, subject to certain restrictions that are "in accordance with law" and "necessary in a democratic society." This right includes the freedom to hold opinions and to receive and impart information and ideas. European Court, *Guide on Article 10*; Wechsler, "The Right to Remember."
19. Fosch, Kieseberg and Li, "Humans Forget, Machines Remember."
20. Tirosh, "Reconsidering the 'Right to be Forgotten.'"
21. Bublitz and Dresler, "A Duty."
22. Galert and Hartmann, "Person, Personal Identity, and Personality."
23. Kolber, "Therapeutic Forgetting."
24. Viejo-Rose, "Memorial Functions."
25. David, *The Past Can't Heal Us*; David, "Moral Remembrance."
26. Although its foundations were already laid down with the establishment of the League of Nations in 1920.
27. David, "Against Standardization"; David, *The Past Can't Heal Us*; David, "Moral Remembrance."
28. Fraser and Honneth, *Redistribution and Recognition*.
29. Winter, "Generation of Memory."
30. Arthur, "How 'Transitions' Reshaped."
31. For more, see Tirosh and Schejter's chapter in this volume.
32. Arthur, "How 'Transitions' Reshaped."
33. See United Nations Regional Information Centre (UNRIC), Transitional Justice (2014). Retrieved 23 July 2022 from https://unric.org/en/unric-library-backgrounder-transitional-justice/.
34. See Levy and Sznaider, *Human Rights and Memory*.
35. Transitional justice adopted memorialization processes as part of its own agenda, which further added to its transformative potential. See Gready and Robins, *From Transitional to Transformative Justice*.
36. "Report of the Special Rapporteur," 8.
37. "Report of the Special Rapporteur," 8.
38. Fronza, "The Punishment of Negationism."
39. Thompson, "Apology."
40. Sznaider, "The Sociology of Compassion."

41. Sznaider, "The Sociology of Compassion," 118.
42. Sznaider, "The Sociology of Compassion," 119.
43. Sznaider, "Compassion, Cruelty, and Human Rights."
44. Douzinas, *The End of Human Rights*; Nolan, "Utopian Visions," 13–16.
45. See Kidron, "Alterity and the Particular Limits of Universalism"; Wikan, "Bereavement and Loss in two Muslim Communities"; and Eastmond and Mannergren-Selimović, "Silence as Possibility."
46. Cercel, "Towards a Disentanglement," 28.
47. Kenny, "A Place for Memory."
48. Huyssen, *Present Pasts*, 21.
49. Tunbridge and Ashworth, *Dissonant Heritage*.
50. Levy and Sznaider, *Human Rights and Memory*, 136. See also Jelin, *State Repression*; and Neumeyer, "Advocating for the Cause."
51. Hourcade, "Shaping Representations of the Past," 93.
52. David, "Lost in Transaction"; Brunk, Giesler, and Hartmann, "Creating a Consumable Past."
53. Winter, "Generation of Memory," 61.
54. Winter, "Generation of Memory."
55. Cercel, "Towards a Disentanglement," 28.
56. Cercel, "Towards a Disentanglement," 29.
57. Clément, "Human Rights."
58. It is worth noting that both categories are often explicitly constructed along ethnic or religious lines.
59. Hearty, "Problematising Symbolic Reparation."
60. Bernal and Grewal, *Theorizing NGOs*.
61. Which, at times, may be frowned upon but monopolistic practices abound within wider capitalism.
62. Munck and Kleibl, "NGOs and the Political Economy," 31–53.
63. Clément, "Human Rights."
64. Bob, *The Marketing of Rebellion*; Bob, "The Quest for International Affairs."
65. Bob, *The Marketing of Rebellion*.
66. Fleshe, *Social Movements and Globalization*.
67. McMahon, *The NGO Game*, 2.
68. Moffett, "A Pension for Injured Victims."
69. Franović, "Dealing with the Past," 5.
70. McEvoy and McConnachie, "Victimology in Transitional Justice."
71. Baumann, "Contested Victimhood."
72. The subject of how certain memory contents transform to become trading currencies at local, national, and international levels has not, so far, been given much attention. For some indications and mechanisms on how this may happen, see David, "Lost in Transaction."
73. Berry, "Barriers to Women's Progress," 833.
74. Badescu, "Between Repair and Humiliation."
75. On this issue, see more in David, "Moral Remembrance and New Inequalities."
76. Leider, "History and Victimhood."
77. Mac Ginty and du Toit, "A Disparity of Esteem," 14; Novick, *The Holocaust in American Life*.
78. Curtis, "Human Rights as War."; Moyn, "Philosophy of Human Rights History."
79. Hronesova, "Explaining Compensation."
80. Humphrey and Valverde, "Human Rights," 194.

81. See David, "Fragmentation as a Strategy of Silencing."
82. Druliolle, "Recovering Historical Memory."
83. de Waardt, "Are Peruvian Victims."
84. Barkan and Bacirbasic, "The Politics of Memory," 100.
85. There is a long list of literature pointing to how different categories of people became trapped in their "victim" identities. See, for example, Langer, "The Alarmed Vision"; Malkki, "Speechless Emissaries"; David, "The Holocaust and Genocide"; and Močnik, "Collective Victimhood."
86. Hopgood, *The Endtimes*, 74.
87. I have made this argument elsewhere in *The Past Can't Heal Us* and "Moral Remembrance and New Inequalities."

Bibliography

Adorno, Theodor. 1959. "What Does Coming to Terms with the Past Mean?" In *Bitburg in Moral and Political Perspective*, edited by Geoffrey Hartman, 114–29. Bloomington: Indiana University Press, 1986.

Arthur, Paige. "How 'Transitions' Reshaped Human Rights: A Conceptual History of Transitional Justice." *Human Rights Quarterly* 31, no. 2 (2009): 321–67.

Badescu, Gruia. "Between Repair and Humiliation Religious Buildings, Memorials, and Identity Politics in Post-war Sarajevo." *Journal of Religion & Society* 20 (2019):19–37.

Barkan, Elazar, and Belma Bacirbasic. "The Politics of Memory, Victimization and Activism in Post-Conflict Bosnia and Herzegovina." *Historical Justice and Memory*, edited by Klaus Neumann and Janna Thompson, 95–113. Madison: University of Wisconsin Press, 2015.

Baumann, Marcel. "Contested Victimhood in the Northern Irish Peace Process." *Peace Review* 22, no. 2 (2010): 171–77.

Belavusau, Uladzislau, and Aleksandra Gliszczyńska-Grabias, eds. *Law and Memory: Addressing Historical Injustice by Legislation and Trials*. Cambridge: Cambridge University Press, 2017.

Bernal, Victoria, and Inderpal Grewal, eds. *Theorizing NGOs: States, Feminisms, and Neoliberalism*. Durham, NC: Duke University Press, 2014.

Berry, Marie E. "Barriers to Women's Progress after Atrocity: Evidence from Rwanda and Bosnia-Herzegovina." *Gender & Society* 31, no. 6 (2017): 830–53.

Bob, Clifford. *The Marketing of Rebellion: Insurgencies, Media and International Activism*. New York: Cambridge University Press, 2005.

———. "The Quest for International Affairs." In *The Social Movement Reader: Cases and Concepts*, edited by Jeff Goodwin and James Jasper, 325–35. West Sussex: Blackwell Publishing, 2015.

Brunk, Katja H., Markus Giesler, and Benjamin J. Hartmann. "Creating a Consumable Past: How Memory Making Shapes Marketization." *Journal of Consumer Research* 44, no. 6 (2018): 1307–24.

Bublitz, Christoph, and Martin Dresler. "A Duty to Remember, a Right to Forget? Memory Manipulations and the Law." In *Handbook of Neuroethics, Springer Science & Business Media*, edited by Jens Clausen and Neil Levy, 1280–303. Dordrecht: Springer Reference, 2015.

Cercel, Cristian. "Towards a Disentanglement of the Links between the Memory Boom and the Neoliberal Turn: Intersections." *East European Journal of Society and Politics* 6, no. 1 (2020): 27–42.

Clément, Dominique. "Human Rights or Social Justice? The Problem of Rights Inflation." *The International Journal of Human Rights* 22, no. 2 (2018): 155–69.

Curtis, Jennifer. *Human rights as war by other means: Peace politics in Northern Ireland*. Pennsylvania: University of Pennsylvania Press, 2014.

David, Lea. "Fragmentation as a Strategy of Silencing: Serbian War Veterans against the State of Serbia." *Contemporary Southeastern Europe* 2, no. 1 (2015): 55–73.

———. "Against Standardization of Memory." *Human Rights Quarterly* 39, no. 2 (2017): 296–318.

———. "Lost in Transaction: Memory Content as a Trade Currency." In *Replicating Atonement: Foreign Models in the Commemoration of Atrocities*, edited by Mischa Gabowitsch, 73–97. Cham: Palgrave Macmillan, 2017.

———. "The Holocaust and Genocide Memorialization Policies in the Western Balkans and Israel and Palestine." *Peacebuilding* 5, no.1 (2017): 51–66.

———. *The Past Can't Heal Us: The Dangers of Mandating Memory in the Name of Human Rights*. Cambridge: Cambridge University Press, 2020.

———. "Moral Remembrance and New Inequalities." *Global Perspectives* 1, no. 1 (2020): 11782.

———. "The Emergence of the 'Dealing with the Past' Agenda: Sociological Thoughts on Its Negative Impact on the Ground." *Modern Languages Open* 1 (2020): 1–14.

de Waardt, Mijke. "Are Peruvian Victims Being Mocked?: Politicization of Victimhood and Victims' Motivations for Reparations." *Human Rights Quarterly* 35, no. 4 (2013): 830–49.

Douzinas, Costas. *The End of Human Rights: Critical Thought at the Turn of the Century*. Oxford: Hart Publishing, 2000.

Dragovic Soso, Jasna. "Conflict, Memory, Accountability: What Does Coming to Terms with the Past Mean?" In *Conflict and Memory: Bridging Past and Future in [South East] Europe*, edited by Wolfgang and Vedran Džihić, 163–79. Baden-Baden: Nomos Gesellschaft, 2010.

Druliolle, Vincent. "Recovering Historical Memory: A Struggle against Silence and Forgetting? The Politics of Victimhood in Spain." *International Journal of Transitional Justice* 9, no. 2 (2015): 316–35.

European Court of Human Rights. *Guide on Article 10 of the European Convention on Human Rights: Freedom of Expression*. Strasbourg: Council of Europe, 2021. Retrieved 23 July 2022 from https://www.echr.coe.int/Documents/Guide_Art_10_ENG.pdf.

Eastmond, Marita and Johanna, Mannergren-Selimović, "Silence as possibility in postwar everyday life." *International Journal of Transitional Justice* 6, no. 3(2012): 502–524.

Fosch Villaronga, Eduard, Peter Kieseberg, and Tiffany Li. "Humans Forget, Machines Remember: Artificial Intelligence and the Right to Be Forgotten." *Computer Law & Security Review* 34, no. 2 (2018): 304–13.

Franović, Ivana. "Dealing with the Past in the Context of Ethnonationalism: The Case of Bosnia Herzegovina, Croatia and Serbia." *Bergof Occasional Paper* 29 (2008): 1–59.

Fraser, Nancy, and Alex Honneth. *Redistribution and Recognition: A Political Philosophical Exchange*. Verso: London, 2004.

Fronza, Emanuela. "The Punishment of Negationism: The Difficult Dialogue between Law and Memory." *Vermont Law Review* 30 (2006): 609–26.

Galert, Thorsten and Hartmann Dirk. "Person, personal identity, and personality." *Intervening in the brain. Changing psyche and society*, edited by Reinhard Merkel et al, 189–287. Berlin/New York: Springer, 2007

Gensburger, Sarah, and Sandrine Lefranc. *Beyond Memory: Can We Really Learn from the Past?* Cham: Palgrave Pivot, 2020.

Gready, Paul, and Simon Robins, eds. *From Transitional to Transformative Justice*. Cambridge: Cambridge University Press, 2019.
Hamber, Brandon, and Richard A. Wilson. "Symbolic Closure through Memory Reparation and Revenge in Post-conflict Societies." *Journal of Human Rights* 1, no.1 (2002): 35–53.
Hearty, Kevin. "Problematising Symbolic Reparation: 'Complex Political Victims,' 'Dead Body Politics' and the Right to Remember." *Social & Legal Studies* 29, no. 3 (2020): 334–54.
Hopgood, Stephen. *The Endtimes of Human Rights*. New York: Cornell University Press, 2013.
Hourcade, Renaud. "Shaping Representations of the Past in a Former Slave-Trade Port: Slavery Remembrance Day (10 May) in Nantes." In *At the Limits of Memory: Legacies of Slavery in the Francophone World*, edited by Nicola Frith and Kate Hodgson, 90–108. Liverpool: Liverpool University Press, 2015.
Hronesova, Jessie. "Explaining Compensation in Post-war Bosnia and Herzegovina: The Case of Victims of Torture and Sexual Violence." In *The Politics of Victimhood in Post-conflict Societies: Comparative and Analytical Perspectives*, edited by Vincent Drulilolle and Roddy Brett, 161–86. Cham: Palgrave Macmillan, 2018.
Humphrey, Michael, and Estela Valverde. "Human Rights, Victimhood, and Impunity: An Anthropology of Democracy in Argentina." *Social Analysis* 51, no. 1 (2007): 179–97.
Huyssen, Andreas. *Present Pasts: Urban Palimpsests and the Politics of Memory*. Stanford, CA: Stanford University Press, 2003.
Jelin, Elizabeth. *State Repression and the Labors of Memory*, trans. Judy Rein and Marcial Godoy-Anativia. Minneapolis: University of Minnesota Press, 2003.
Joinet, Louis. "The Administration of Justice and the Human Rights of Detainees: Question of the Impunity of Perpetrators of Human Rights Violations (Civil and Political): Revised Final Report." *United Nations Digital Library*. 1997. Retrieved 31 August 2022 from https://digitallibrary.un.org/record/245520/files/E_CN.4_Sub.2_1997_20_Rev.1-EN.pdf?ln=en.
Kabalek, Kobi. "Memory and Periphery: An Introduction." *HAGAR Studies in Culture, Polity and Identities* 12 (2014): 7–22.
Kenny, Michael. "A Place for Memory: The Interface between Individual and Collective History." *Comparative Studies in Society and History* 41, no. 3 (1999): 420–37.
Kidron, Carol. "Alterity and the particular limits of universalism comparing Jewish–Israeli Holocaust and Canadian–Cambodian genocide legacies." *Current Anthropology* 53, no. 6 (2012): 723–754.
Kolber, Adam. "Therapeutic Forgetting: Legal and Ethical Implications of Memory Dampening." *Vanderbilt Law Review* 59, no. 5 (2006): 1561–626.
Langer, Lawrence. "The Alarmed Vision: Social Suffering and Holocaust Atrocity." *Social Suffering* 125, no. 1 (1996): 47–65.
Leider, Jacques P. "History and Victimhood: Engaging with Rohingya Issues." *Insight Turkey* 20, no. 1 (2018): 99–118.
Levy, Daniel, and Natan Sznaider. *Human Rights and Memory*. University Park: The Pennsylvania State University Press, 2010.
Mac Ginty, Roger, and Pierre du Toit. "A Disparity of Esteem: Relative Group Status in Northern Ireland after the Belfast Agreement." *Political Psychology* 28, no. 1 (2007): 13–31.
Malkki, Liisa. "Speechless Emissaries: Refugees, Humanitarianism, and Dehistoricization." *Cultural Anthropology* 11, no. 3 (1996): 377–404.
McEvoy, Kieran, and Kirsten McConnachie. "Victimology in Transitional Justice: Victimhood, Innocence and Hierarchy." *European Journal of Criminology* 9, no. 5 (2012): 527–38.
McMahon, Patrice. *The NGO Game: Post-Conflict Peacebuilding in the Balkans and Beyond*. Ithaca, NY: Cornell University Press, 2017.

Močnik, Nena. "Collective Victimhood of Individual Survivors: Reflecting the Uses and Impacts of Two Academic Narratives Two Decades after the War-Rapes in Bosnia-Herzegovina." *East European Politics* 35, no. 4 (2019): 457–73.

Moffett, Luke. "A Pension for Injured Victims of the Troubles: Reparations or Reifying Victim Hierarchy?" *Northern Ireland Legal Quarterly* 66, no.4 (2015): 297–319.

Moyn, Samuel. "Theses on the Philosophy of Human Rights History." *Humanity Journal Blog*, 20 April 2015. Retrieved 15 April 2021 from http://humanityjournal.org/blog/theses-on-the-philosophy-of-human-rights-history/.

Munck, Ronaldo, and Tanja Kleibl. "NGOs and the Political Economy of International Development and Development Education: An Irish Perspective." *Policy & Practice: A Development Education Review* 29 (2019): 31–53.

Neumeyer, Laure. "Advocating for the Cause of the 'Victims of Communism' in the European Political Space: Memory Entrepreneurs in Interstitial Fields." *Nationalities Papers* 45, no. 6 (2018): 992–1012.

Nolan, Mary. "Gender and Utopian Visions in a Post Utopian Era: Americanism, Human Rights, and Market Fundamentalism." *Central European History* 44, no. 1 (2011): 13–36.

Novick, Peter. *The Holocaust in American Life*. New York: Houghton, 1999.

"Report of the Special Rapporteur in the Field of Cultural Rights, Shaheed F: Memorialization Processes." United Nations General Assembly, 2014. Retrieved 28 February 2020 from https://digitallibrary.un.org/record/766862?ln=en#record-filescollapse-header.

Sznaider, Natan. "The Sociology of Compassion: A Study in the Sociology of Morals." *Journal for Cultural Research* 2, no.1 (1998): 117–39.

———. "Compassion, Cruelty, and Human Rights." In *World Suffering and Quality of Life*, edited by Ronald E. Anderson, 55–64. Dordrecht: Springer, 2015.

Tirosh, Noam. "Reconsidering the 'Right to Be Forgotten': Memory Rights and the Right to Memory in the New Media Era." *Media, Culture & Society* 39, no. 5 (2017): 644–60.

Thompson, Janna. "Apology, Historical Obligations and the Ethics of Memory." *Memory Studies* 2, no. 2 (2009): 195–210.

Tunbridge, J. E., and G. J. Ashworth. *Dissonant Heritage: The Management of the Past as a Resource in Conflict*. Chichester: Wiley,1996.

Verdery, Katherine. *National Ideology under Socialism: Identity and Cultural Politics in Ceausescu's Romania*. Berkeley: University of California Press, 1991.

Viejo-Rose, Dacia. "Memorial Functions: Intent, Impact and the Right to Remember." *Memory Studies* 4, no. 4 (2011): 465–80.

Wikan, Unni. "Bereavement and loss in two Muslim communities: Egypt and Bali compared." *Social Science & Medicine* 27, no. 5 (1988): 451–460.

Wechsler, Simon. "The Right to Remember: The European Convention on Human Rights and the Right to Be Forgotten." *Columbia Journal of Law and Social Problems* 49, no. 1 (2015): 135–65.

Winter, Jay. "The Generation of Memory: Reflections on the 'Memory Boom.'" *Contemporary Historical Studies* 10, no. 3 (2001): 57–66.

Zehfuss, Maja. "Remembering to Forget/Forgetting to Remember." *Memory Trauma and World Politics: Reflections on the Relationship between Past and Present*, edited by Duncan Bell, 213–31. New York: Palgrave Macmillan, 2006.

Chapter 4

MEMORY, RIGHTS, AND SEN'S "CAPABILITIES APPROACH"

Noam Tirosh and Amit Schejter

Introduction

There is ever-growing attention—both academically and publicly—to the importance of memory rights and the implications for recognizing these rights in society. Memory in general, and memory rights in particular, have been recognized as fundamental components of current social, national, and international conflicts, notable among them the recent racial struggle in the United States (US) and the debate surrounding the Polish compensation law.[1] In academic discourse, scholars have tried to define the right to memory and to translate it into a usable theoretical structure that can help memory actors in their mnemonic work.[2] However, despite growing attention to the concept of memory rights, there is a paucity in discourse focusing on the relationship between memory rights and media, although it is media (and, more than ever, digital media) that communicate memories in society and turn the abstracted "collective memory" into a "tangible" social construction.[3]

Recognizing the centrality of media in memory processes implies that when discussing memory rights, we should also be speaking about information and communication technologies and their role as memory enablers as well as about the normative underpinnings of media regulations that will anchor and protect this role. In other words, "if public or collective memory is inherently mediated, there is an urgent need for some rules of the game, ethical principles that guarantee that [memory remains] highly visible and collectable."[4] In this chapter, we will propose a link between memory and media, and how they relate to rights, utilizing Amartya Sen's capabilities approach. Suggesting that memory is a "capability," we offer a new way to justify memory rights. Not only are memory rights needed because "memory is important," but also because people cannot live a meaningful life without the mechanisms that will allow their engagement with narratives about the past. Indeed, the formation of memory is a requirement for the development of the uniqueness of the individual, as it is an essential "tool" without which constructing a sense of continuity over the life span is not possible. Similarly, the social form of memory preserves the unity and continuity of groups, which vary from family and national communities to global, transnational society.[5] By considering these aspects, the capabilities approach helps us define memory as a basic element of individuals' and groups' well-being and it justifies the recognition of memory as a right and the creation of a defined set of provisions to guard it. In what follows, we discuss the capabilities approach and the way the relationship between rights and memory can be understood in its light. We then stress the importance of media in memory processes and demonstrate how the capabilities approach addresses media and communications and how different scholars tried to use the capabilities approach as a normative basis for the development of media policy. We will conclude by suggesting that the mediated mechanisms of Sen's approach, capabilities, functionings, and freedoms, can safeguard the right to memory.

The Capabilities Approach, Rights, and Memory

The capabilities approach is a rights-based theory of social justice focusing on what a person can do or be, rather than on what a person has or should have, as its goal. The capabilities approach stresses people's actual ability to make use of the goods, services, and opportunities available to them rather than on mere access to or ownership of those goods. Rooted in the writings of Amartya Sen, the theory emphasizes freedom, which Sen defines as the ability to lead the kind of lives people have reason to value, and the recognition that the goal of policy is to help people be what they value being.[6]

The theory differentiates between the "things people want to be," which are labeled "functionings," and the "tools" to make them happen, which have been termed "capabilities." The capabilities literature also differentiates between three types of capabilities: basic capabilities, which are the necessary inborn characteristics of individuals; internal capabilities, which are the circumstances in which people are situated and allow them to materialize the functions required for the exercise of the capability; and combined capabilities, which are internal capabilities joined with "suitable external conditions for the exercise of the functioning."[7] Hence, individuals may own basic capabilities, such as the capability to speak their mind, yet they may be unable to exercise them or express their thoughts and feelings when they are very young and have not obtained the necessary vocabulary. In order for internal capabilities to emerge, personal development is needed. This can be achieved through education or natural growth, for example, or through obtaining the knowledge to utilize technologies that make it possible. However, external conditions are often needed for individuals to be able to realize their internal capabilities. For example, a functioning democratic regime that allows the exercise of internal capabilities as well as access to media technologies and knowledge of how to operate them are required for people to exercise their capability to speak out. Martha Nussbaum posits that "[t]he aim of public policy is the production of combined capabilities."[8] Indeed, in order to reach this state, the recognition of rights and their safeguarding are required.

Sen states that "[t]he capability to function is the thing that comes closest to the notion of positive freedom."[9] "Positive" freedom is the "freedom to," meaning that it exists when an individual may do things, pursue goals, and achieve objectives. Oftentimes, in order to reach that ability, it is not enough that they are not obstructed from doing the things they wish to do (which is the narrow, "negative" form of freedom), but rather that they have a right to be provided with the tools to do so (which requires a "positive" notion of freedom). Utilitarianism, the accepted philosophy guiding public policy in Western thought, focuses more on "freedom from," which identifies freedom when individuals are not hindered or prevented by others to act. The difference between negative and positive approaches to freedom lies in the fact that "positive" freedom concentrates on what a person may choose to do or achieve, while the negative focuses on the absence of restraints preventing people from doing the things they wish to do.[10] Nussbaum has suggested that rights can be realized through capabilities. According to her, in order to secure rights, we need "to put them in a position of capability."[11] For her, the role of public policy is to transform internal capabilities to combined capabilities. In order to do so, policymakers should recognize that to attain rights, it is not enough to abstain from limiting them, but rather that society may at times have an obligation to proactively enable them. In other words, to speak about the capabilities approach as a guiding principle of public policies is to speak about the need to recognize that enablement of rights may require legal mechanisms that facilitate individual capabilities.

Based on previous studies, we contend here that incorporating capabilities within the discussion regarding rights in general and memory rights in particular, can help us translate the amorphic notion of memory rights into concrete policy tools and provisions.[12] This will be made possible if we establish a deeper connection between the capabilities approach and memory. Memory processes, or the active engagement with perceptions of the past that are aimed at the narrativization of individual and group "life-stories," are a crucial aspect of the formation of individual and group identities.[13] In order to be active in the ongoing project of identity making, people need to have the ability to control certain aspects of their memory-making processes.[14] This idea, we think, justifies our attempt to connect between memory, capabilities, and rights.

As explained, the capabilities approach is aimed at enabling people to be what they value being.[15] Capabilities, as such, are the "range of options of being . . . a person has available."[16] The notion of "being" can be addressed from various philosophical perspectives that cannot be addressed in this chapter. Yet, we understand Sen's notion of being as focusing on the way people want to live their life according to their own self-perceptions about what a "good life" is, and most importantly, with the sense of understanding the self based on being at ease with their individual and collective identities. Memory, thus, is central to this sense of being.

A human being is a "storytelling animal."[17] Telling stories about our lives, in a variety of opportunities along our life span, is a way of providing meaning to ourselves. This is also true when it comes to different groups that create collective mechanisms of telling, and ever-repeating, stories about a shared past.[18] By telling stories we turn contingent life events into an imagined, yet coherent, story, which is the cornerstone of our identity, both individual and collective.[19] These stories are not mere fictions we invent, nor are they comprised of scattered anecdotes from past experiences. Rather, as we tell stories, we specifically select events that we choose, we revise and reinterpret these events on different occasions and for varied reasons, and by doing so, we turn "memories" into meaning-carrying narratives.[20] In the process of narrativizing, memories of our past become relevant to "a particular 'here' and 'now,' a particular audience, and a particular set of interactional concerns and interpersonal issues."[21] Individuals, and groups of individuals, act as the narrators or editors-in-chief, and the heroes of their life stories. This process is defined as our "mnemonic imagination": "The ways in which we continuously qualify, adapt, refine and re-synthesize past experience, our own and that of others, into qualitatively new understandings of ourselves and other people, including those to whom we stand in immediate or proximate relation, and those from whom we are more distant."[22] Within the context of the capabilities approach, we contend that in order for individuals to be what they value being, they should have the ability to choose which stories they want to tell, to whom and with what consequences; they should be able to control the processes of remembering and forgetting, of selecting and re-evaluating, and of highlighting certain aspects over others.

A literary example of an application of this definition can be found in Franz Kafka's memorable short story "A Report to an Academy." Kafka offers in most of his writings a unique and thorough exploration of memory.[23] In this short story, he describes an ape that became human and was asked by the "esteemed gentlemen of the academy" to "submit a report about his previous life as an ape," and so share his memories with them.[24] Yet, the ape finds this task impossible, explaining that: "Almost five years separate me from my existence as an ape, a short time perhaps when measured by the calendar, but endlessly long to gallop through, as I have done . . . . This achievement would have been impossible if I had stubbornly wished to hold on to my origin, onto the memories of my youth."[25] Perceiving itself as "a free ape," the former ape decides to give up his memories and forget his past. His rationalization of the choice he made is that "my memories for their part constantly closed themselves off against me."[26]

Kafka's now-human ape's experience and rationalization demonstrate how the construction of one's identity, and moreover, the performance of humanity, require deliberate processes of remembering and forgetting. In order for apes to be free, some control over the narrative they create for themselves is required. As Kafka brilliantly highlights, people should have the ability to choose which stories they want to tell, to whom, and with what consequences. To limit this ability is to infringe on our freedom to be what we value being, which is the core idea behind the capabilities approach.

Indeed, the capability to function in a specific way can only be realized if a person is free to perform that function. As already discussed, the safeguarding of freedoms requires the assurance of a set of appropriate rights. As such, if we understand memory as a "capability," and "capabilities" as performable only when individuals are free to perform them, we also need to identify the corresponding set of rights, which ensure these freedoms. Thus, in order to be able to choose the stories we wish to tell, in order to control the circumstances of performances of "telling," in other words, in order to safeguard our memory processes, we need a specific set or bouquet of rights that enable the articulation of the "right to memory" to be recognized.

In the next section of this chapter, we demonstrate how in contemporary societies, the most crucial mechanism through which individual and collective memories are being processed, constructed, disseminated, and worked through are contemporary media. As such, in order to materialize the right to memory, we claim we should think of media and communications and the rights associated with their free and deliberate use by individuals, in relation to memory and capabilities.

Memory, Media, and Rights

To discuss memory in relation to capabilities is to realize that providing individuals with mechanisms that will allow them to have better control over their memory processes should be a goal of a rights-based regime. These mechanisms, we contend, are contemporary media. Indeed, memory is a mediated phenomenon,[27] and it is "transferable through time and space with the help of different types of semiotic representations and communication technologies."[28] These are the media that create a tangible record of a selected version of society's cultural memory, turning the abstracted concept of cultural memory into a concrete product to which people can react to and engage with.[29] According to Joanne Garde-Hansen, we understand our individual, familial, and collective past "through media discourses, forms, technologies and practices."[30] Through these mediated processes individuals and groups explore their unique identities.[31] It is clear that society's media and communication technologies, and their constant transformations, shape memory processes. Indeed, "how that past is and is not recorded, archived, accessed, retrieved, and represented is entangled with the nature, forms and control of the technologies, media and institutions of the day."[32]

In the mass media era, newspapers, radio, and television were considered prominent public spaces in which society's cultural memory was constructed, evaluated, and reconstructed.[33] However, media are changing and "new media" alter the way we engage with the past and perceive the meaning of memory, remembering, and forgetting.[34] Contemporary media are constituted of a "global web of horizontal communication networks that include the multimodal exchange of interactive messages from many to many, both synchronous and asynchronous."[35] From the perspective of their users, contemporary digital media have four novel characteristics: they are mobile, and thus not bounded to a specific location; they offer an abundance of channels through which data can travel and multiple connected storage spaces in which information can be stored; they are interactive, as individuals can tailor the mediated environments they use based on their own needs and preferences; they allow multi-mediality and transmediality, as a plethora of adaptable means are used to convey messages.[36]

These new or enhanced characteristics have led scholars to suggest that contemporary memory is also changing. New media's mobility, for example, was described as creating a "lived and embodied memory" that is both publicly available and easily transferable to "the domain of the private individual."[37] Others claim that new communication technologies are "shifting the power base of social history and taking it away from the traditional and institutional producers of media."[38] More recently, Hoskins suggested that contemporary media created a new form of society's memory: "the memory of the multitude."[39] If, in the mediated environment of the past, we discussed a collective "cultural memory,"[40] of which a shared understanding of the past shaped individual and collective identities, in the memory of the multitude era the parameters of "who, what, when and why of remembering"[41] have changed, thus complicating the relationship between memory and identity.

However, regardless of the varied ways contemporary media has changed individual and social memory processes, it is clear that by using new means of communications, different actors are now able to "generate new ways of remembering."[42] It is through new media that we "tell ourselves" to others. Our identity is constantly projected by means of communications in which we socialize and interact with others. These new opportunities, and the attempt to capitalize on these new opportunities when engaging with memory and past narratives, connect the discussions about media and memory back to the realm of rights and capabilities. Philip Lee and Pradip Ninan Thomas contend that the media "should play a political, social, and cultural role that guarantees the right to memory and—equally important—the right to communicate that memory in public."[43] Similarly, Karen Worcman and Joanne Garde-Hansen suggest that a right to memory is an individual's right to record memories through the use of media and to access "the cultural memories that an individual or community may need, want and/or desire or that are the past mnemonic tools through which they have constructed their identity."[44]

The much-debated "right to be forgotten" (RTBF), first suggested by the European Court of Justice in 2014 and materialized in the European General Data Protection Regulation (GDPR) in 2018, is perhaps the most advanced attempt to address memory-related concerns in the form of individual rights and in the realm of media policy. According to the GDPR,[45] individuals ("data subjects") now have the right to demand from data controllers the erasure of personal data and private information. This right created an equal duty on data controllers to erase such information when the request is justified. While not always understood as such, the new RTBF is actually about the process of individual memory constructions and the attempt to have better control over our online identity.[46] However, memory construction processes for both individuals and collectives are more complicated and comprised of delicate tensions between remembering and forgetting. As such, the RTBF is only a starting point for a much wider understanding of the right to memory.

Moreover, there are instances in which technological progress is used by different authorities to deny memory rights. Thus in 2018, the Israeli Ministry of Defense tried to deny entry to Israel to West Bank Palestinians who had been invited to participate in a commemoration ceremony organized by two NGOs: Combatants for Peace and the Israeli Palestinian Bereaved Families for Peace.[47] For more than a decade, the two organizations have been hosting a commemoration ceremony that aims to "remember and acknowledge the pain of both sides of the [Israeli-Palestinian] conflict, and to remind that wars are not an eternal fate."[48] The commemoration ceremony is presented as an alternative to Israel's annual official commemoration day for fallen soldiers—Memorial Day—that, as dictated by law, takes place every year on the day before Israel's Independence Day. As the alternative commemoration ceremony has grown ever more popular, so have the criticisms against it and the attempts to prevent it. In 2018, these obstructionist efforts were stepped up when the Ministry of Defense tried to prevent the ceremony by denying West Bank Palestinians the ability to enter Israel and participate in the ceremony. Among other justifications, the Ministry of Defense claimed that there are new "technological means that will allow Palestinians to participate [in the ceremony] from a distance."[49] Hence the security measures that are enhanced around Independence Day and include a blockade on travel between the occupied West Bank and Israel-proper should not be compromised. While Israel's Supreme Court ruled against the state's position and ordered the Ministry of Defense to allow entrance to the West Bank Palestinians who wished to participate in the alternative commemoration event, this example proves that not only is technological progress alone insufficient to ensure protection of memory rights, it can even be used in some cases as the reasoning for obstructing the realization of the right to memory. Indeed, the new technological advancement was used as yet another form of control and suppression that aims to prevent alternative remembrance and commemoration.

In order to regulate new technological progress in a way that will contribute to the protection of the right to memory, the capabilities approach and the way media are addressed within the discourse of this rights-based approach need to be bridged. This will help us advance the discussion of memory rights and the right to memory in the new media environment.

Media and Capabilities

Sen's approach is highly relevant to our understanding of contemporary media, yet it has been scarcely addressed within the discipline of media and communication studies.[50] In order to link media and the capabilities approach, focusing on the approach's main tenet—individual freedom is the goal of a just society—is required. It thus calls for identifying the freedom-enhancing characteristics of media and their contribution to individual and social well-being.

Sen's work identifies the value of a free media for a functioning democratic society and as a necessary component in ensuring the provision of the most basic needs of humans. In his early work, he saw the free and adversarial role of media in India as the critical element in making its battle against famine more successful than China's, whose media's freedom is limited.[51] In his later work, he listed a number of justifications for a free press, among them the contribution of free speech in general, and press freedom in particular, to the quality of our lives.[52] He found the informational role of the press and the media's role in protecting the "neglected and disadvantaged" by providing them with a voice essential in a democracy and claimed that "a well-functioning media can play a critically important role in facilitating public reasoning in general."[53]

Scholars who applied the capabilities approach to the media submit that mass media, in particular television, are capable of contributing to well-being and the quality of life.[54] However, the capabilities approach developed in a media world dominated by traditional, unidirectional, and limited (in both space and speed) apparatuses owned and run by large corporations or states. Contemporary media, as noted, is different.[55] Media technologies have changed dramatically since the beginning of the century, and the revolutionary transition requires looking at the media-capabilities connection through both angles, that of mass media and that of their contemporary heirs. The commonality between these two viewpoints is the centrality of freedom of expression and of the media, among the liberties cherished by free societies, a liberty whose realization contemporarily is dependent in large part on the availability, as well as on the ability to utilize information and communication technologies.

Among the most notable capabilities the media can potentially enable, is voice. To voice, according to Nick Couldry, is to be capable of giving "an account of one's life and its conditions."[56] However, the ability to speak is insufficient to enable voice, as one also needs to be heard. A voice is not a capability if there is no enabling of mechanisms on the receiving end. In Sen's words, it is about "enhancing the hearing that people get in expressing and supporting their claims," and allowing them to "learn from one another."[57]

Policies regulating media that developed in the twentieth century concomitant with the development of traditional mass media were oblivious to capability-oriented questions. Capabilities are questions of a second order, as they focus not on problems emanating from the mere access to media technologies, but rather from the way these media serve the needs of individuals. In addition to ensuring access, media policies rooted in the capabilities philosophy should pay equal attention to the distribution of resources that enable the usability of such access. What really matters is whether opportunities are available, if capabilities can be utilized and if functionings are realized.[58] In other words, media policies should focus on the "freedom that citizens have to choose among preferred development options [and] individual identity options."[59] These take place "in the personal, the social, the economic and the political sphere."[60] The capabilities angle takes us away from focusing on access to focusing on the ability to put technology to use and, further, enables users to choose what exactly they wish to do with it.

At the same time, the media-capabilities nexus lies in recognizing that contemporary media are personalizable. Indeed, a society that sees individual freedom as a fundamental value whose realization should be among its goals, and recognizes that current media can assist in achieving that goal, should make them both accessible and usable to all, putting media to use in order to materialize freedom. Technical objects, while not having a life of their own (yet) "have a 'transformative dimension' through which other inputs are affected in the attainment of valued capabilities."[61]

If memory is indeed an important capability, and if it is through media that the capability of memory can materialize, it seems to us that safeguarding memory rights, and the right to memory in particular, is needed.

The Right to Memory

The capabilities approach helps us to understand memory as central to our being. Memory rights, and specifically, the right to memory, should safeguard individual and collective memory processes. Addressing the capabilities approach when discussing memory rights is actually a conversation focusing on turning the stories we choose to tell about ourselves—constructing our identity—into protectable elements of a rights-based regime. Since memory is a mediated phenomenon, the right to memory is actually about protecting memory capabilities with rights and provisions that emanate from the realm of media and communication policies.

Recently, Worcman and Garde-Hansen suggested that a right to memory should pay attention to institutional "gatekeeping mechanisms" such as "copyright, storage location, data protection, intellectual research only, privacy, property rights, pay per view, entrance fees, as well as the preservation, transfer and access costs of material" that are at play when memory constructions are taking place.[62]

Using the capabilities approach allows us to expand our understanding of the right to memory and its relation to media. From this unique perspective, the right to memory should aim to protect our access to all available mechanisms we may use to tell and construct stories about our past. Furthermore, when the right to memory evolves from the capabilities approach's understanding of media, policies that focus merely on provision of access to such mechanisms should not suffice, but rather the focus should be also on the attempt to make these mechanisms available and useful at each individual's choice.

The combination of access to media, the ability to capitalize on various media, and the understanding of media as enablers of memory processes that are integral to our sense of being and living a worthy life are the main contributions of the capabilities approach to the discussion regarding the right to memory. In this chapter, we offered a novel argumentation, or justification, for the protection of memory with rights. We also highlighted that a right to memory should offer and develop legislative and policy tools that will utilize significant and meaningful access to contemporary media as an integral part of individual and social memory processes.

Noam Tirosh is a senior lecturer in the department of Communication Studies at Ben-Gurion University of the Negev. His research focuses on the relationship between memory and media and their relation with democracy, justice, and human rights. He is the author of a score of journal articles and book chapters covering topics ranging from the European Right to Be Forgotten to the memory rights of the Palestinian minority in Israel, refugees and asylum seekers, and Jews deported from Arab countries.

Amit M. Schejter is professor of communication studies at Ben-Gurion University of the Negev, currently serving as President of Oranim College in the north of Israel. He serves as a visiting professor at Penn State University, as well as co-director of the Institute for Information Policy and is founding co-editor of the Journal of Information Policy. Author or editor of eight books and more than seventy journal articles, law reviews, and book chapters, his research focuses on the relationship between media and justice. Schejter serves on the boards of various civil society organizations focusing on human rights and shared society.

Notes

1. See, for example, Enzo Traverso's recent discussion about the "statue debates" in the United States, "Tearing Down Statues"; see, also, the framing of reactions to the law as cited in Wanat, "Poland's Restitution Law."
2. It is important to note here that agency in memory studies is a contested topic. Yifat Gutman and Jenny Wüstenberg defined "memory activists" as both individual or collective actors "who engage in the strategic commemoration of the past in order to achieve or prevent change in public memory by working outside state channels." Gutman and Wüstenberg, "Challenging the Meaning," 2. Broadly speaking, when we talk about memory actors, we seek to address all those human actors who try to influence memory processes within cultural, political, institutional, and social frames. A. Assmann and Shortt, *Memory and Political Change*; Anna Reading, for example, defines the right to memory as: "the right to a symbolic representation of the past embedded within a set of interventions and social practices." Reading, "Gender and the Right to Memory," 11. A more practice-oriented approach was suggested by Karen Worcman and Joanne Garde-Hansen in *Social Memory Technology: Theory, Practice, Action*. See an extended discussion about the right to memory and its varied definitions in the introduction to this volume.

3. Halbwachs, *On Collective Memory*; Olick and Robbins, "Social Memory Studies"; and Edy, "Journalistic Uses of Collective Memory."
4. Lee and Thomas, *Public Memory, Public Media*, 206.
5. See J. Assmann and Czaplicka, "Collective Memory and Cultural Identity"; Olick and Robbins, "Social Memory Studies"; and for a more detailed discussion about the transnational turn in memory studies, Erll, "Travelling Memory."
6. Sen, *Resources*.
7. Nussbaum, "Capabilities and Human Rights," 290.
8. Nussbaum, "Capabilities and Human Rights," 290.
9. Sen, *Resources*, 316.
10. Sen, "Freedom of Choice."
11. Nussbaum, "Capabilities and Human Rights," 293.
12. Shomron and Tirosh, "Contemporary Migrants and Media Capabilities."
13. See Assmann and Czaplicka, "Collective Memory and Cultural Identity"; Klar, Schori-Eyal and Klar, "The 'Never Again' State of Israel"; and Ariely, "National Days, National Identity, and Collective Memory."
14. Bruner, "Life as Narrative."
15. Garnham, "Amartya Sen's 'Capabilities' Approach."
16. Garnham, "Amartya Sen's 'Capabilities' Approach," 34.
17. This definition is suggested by the Scottish philosopher Alasdair MacIntyre in "The Virtues."
18. A noted example of such mechanisms is Jewish ceremonies and religious rituals. See Yerushalmi, *Zakhor*.
19. Kerby, *Narrative and the Self*; Schiffrin, "Narrative as Self-Portrait"; McAdams, *Power, Intimacy and the Life Story*.
20. Keightley and Pickering, *The Mnemonic Imagination*.
21. Schiffrin, "Narrative as Self-Portrait," 168.
22. Keightley and Pickering, *The Mnemonic Imagination*, 121.
23. Noam Tirosh recently published an analysis of Kafka stories from a memory-driven perspective, "The Dialectics of Forgetting in Kafka's Writings and Will."
24. The full text is available from the valuable website Franz Kafka Online. Quotes hereafter are taken from this website. Kafka, "A Report."
25. Kafka, "A Report."
26. Kafka, "A Report."
27. See Hoskins, "Anachronisms of media," and Neiger, Meyers, and Zandberg, *On Media Memory*.
28. Pentzold, Lohmeier, and Hajek, "Remembering and Reviving," 4.
29. Edy, "Journalistic Uses of Collective Memory."
30. Garde-Hansen, *Media and Memory*, 6.
31. Olick, "Collective Memory: The Two Cultures."
32. Hoskins, "The Mediatisation of Memory," 27.
33. Pogacar, "(New) Media and Representations of the Past"; Roediger and Wertsch, "Creating a New Discipline."
34. Reading, "Memory and Digital Media."
35. Castells, "Communication, Power and Counter-Power," 246.
36. A detailed discussion about contemporary media's unique characteristics can be found in Schejter and Tirosh, *A Justice-Based Approach to New Media Policy*.
37. Reading, "Memobilia," 91.
38. Garde-Hansen, "Introduction," 7.
39. Hoskins, "Memory of the Multitude."

40. J. Assmann and Czaplicka, "Collective Memory and Cultural Identity."
41. Hoskins, "Memory of the Multitude," 89.
42. Garde-Hansen, "Introduction," 18.
43. Lee and Thomas, *Public Memory, Public Media*, 206.
44. Worcman and Garde-Hansen, *Social Memory Technology*, 9.
45. The GDPR full legislation is available from European Parliament, "Regulation (EU) 2016/679."
46. Tirosh, "Reconsidering the 'Right to Be Forgotten.'"
47. See the *The Times of Israel* article "Defense Ministry Denies Entry to Palestinians for Joint Memorial Day Ceremony."
48. See an entry about the ceremony in the Israeli Palestinians Bereaved Families for Peace website. "The Joint Memorial Day Ceremony." *Israeli Palestinians Bereaved Families for Peace*. Retrieved 26 July 2022 from https://www.theparentscircle.org/en/pcff-activities_eng/memorial-ceremony_eng/.
49. This quote is translated from Hebrew and was part of the Ministry of Defense Response to the legal appeal by the two NGOs.
50. Hesmondhalgh, "Capitalism and the Media"; Rao, "Amartya Sen's Value"; Rao and Malik, "Conversing Ethics."
51. Dreze and Sen, *Hunger and Public Action*.
52. Sen, *The Idea of Justice*, 335.
53. Sen, *The Idea of Justice*, 337.
54. Hesmondhalgh, *Television, Quality of Life*.
55. Schejter and Tirosh, *A Justice-Based Approach*.
56. Couldry, *Why Voice Matters*, 7.
57. Sen, *Development as Freedom*, 10.
58. Garnham, "Amartya Sen's 'Capabilities' Approach."
59. Jacobson and Chang, "Sen's Capabilities Approach," 111.
60. Kleine, "ICT4WHAT?," 676.
61. Haenssgen and Proochista, "The Place of Technology," 99.
62. Worcman and Garde-Hansen, *Social Memory Technology*, 10.

Bibliography

Ariely, Gal. "National Days, National Identity, and Collective Memory: Exploring the Impact of Holocaust Day in Israel." *Political Psychology* 40 (2019): 1391–406.

Assmann, Jan, and John Czaplicka. "Collective Memory and Cultural Identity." *New German Critique* 65 (1995): 125–33.

Assmann, Aleida, and Linda Shortt. *Memory and Political Change*. New York: Palgrave Macmillan, 2012.

Bruner, Jerome. "Life as Narrative." *Social Research* 71, no. 3 (2004): 691–710.

Castells, Manuel. "Communication, Power and Counter-Power in the Network Society." *International Journal of Communication* 1 (2007): 238–66.

Couldry, Nick. *Why Voice Matters: Culture and Politics after Neoliberalism*. London: Sage Publishing, 2010.

Dreze, Jean, and Amartya Sen. *Hunger and Public Action*. Oxford: Clarendon Press, 1989.

Edy, A. Jill. "Journalistic Uses of Collective Memory." *Journal of Communication* 49, no. 2 (1999): 71–85.

Erll, Astrid. "Travelling Memory." *Parallax* 17, no.4 (2011): 4–18.
European Parliament, Council of the European Union. "Regulation (EU) 2016/679 of the European Parliament and of the Council of 27 April 2016 on the Protection of Natural Persons with Regard to the Processing of Personal Data and on the Free Movement of Such Data, and Repealing Directive 95/46/EC (General Data Protection Regulation)." *Eur-Lex*, 27 April 2016. Retrieved 26 July 2022 from https://eur-lex.europa.eu/eli/reg/2016/679/oj.
Garde-Hansen, Joanne. "Introduction." In *Save as . . . Digital Memories*, edited by Joanne Garde-Hansen, Andrew Hoskins, and Anna Reading, 1–21. New York: Palgrave-Macmillan, 2009.
———. *Media and Memory*. Edinburgh: Edinburgh University Press, 2011.
Garnham, Nicholas. "Amartya Sen's 'Capabilities' Approach to the Evaluation of Welfare: Its Application to Communications." *Javnost [The Public]* 4, no. 4 (1997): 25–34.
Gutman, Yifat, and Jenny Wüstenberg. "Challenging the Meaning of the Past from Below: A Typology for Comparative Research on Memory Activists." *Memory Studies* (2021): 1–17.
Haenssgen, J. Marco, and Ariana Proochista. "The Place of Technology in the Capability Approach." *Oxford Development Studies* 46, no.1 (2018): 98–112.
Halbwachs, Maurice. 1925. *On Collective Memory*. Chicago: University of Chicago Press, 1992.
Hesmondhalgh, David. *Television, Quality of Life and the Value of Culture*. Submission to the Puttnam Inquiry on Public Service for the Twenty-First Century, 2016.
———. "Capitalism and the Media: Moral Economy, Well-Being and Capabilities." *Media, Culture & Society* 39, no. 2 (2017): 202–18.
Hoskins, Andrew. "The Mediatisation of Memory." In *Save as . . . Digital Memories*, edited by Joanne Garde-Hansen, Andrew Hoskins, and Anna Reading, 27–43. New York: Palgrave-Macmillan, 2009.
———. "Anachronisms of Media, Anachronisms of Memory: From Collective Memory to a New Memory Ecology." In *On Media Memory: Collective Memory in a New Media Age*, edited by Neiger Motti, Oren Meyers, and Eyal Zandberg, 278–89. New York: Palgrave Macmillan, 2011.
———. "Memory of the Multitude: The End of Collective Memory." In *Digital Memory Studies: Media Pasts in Transition*, edited by Andrew Hoskins, 85–109. Routledge, 2017.
Jacobson, Tom, and Leanne Chang. "Sen's Capabilities Approach and the Measurement of Communication Outcomes." *Journal of Information Policy* 9 (2019) 111–31.
Kafka, Franz. "A Report for an Academy." Translated by Ian Johnston. *Franz Kafka Online*. Retrieved 26 July 2022 from https://www.kafka-online.info/a-report-for-an-academy.html.
Keightley, Emily, and Michael Pickering. *The Mnemonic Imagination: Remembering as Creative Practice*. New York: Palgrave Macmillan, 2012.
Kerby, Anthony Paul. *Narrative and the Self*. Indianapolis: Indiana University Press, 1991.
Klar, Yechiel, Noa Schori-Eyal, and Yonat Klar. "The 'Never Again' State of Israel: The Emergence of the Holocaust as a Core Feature of Israeli Identity and Its Four Incongruent Voices." *Journal of Social Issues* 69, no. 1 (2013): 125–43.
Kleine, Dorothea. "ICT4WHAT?: Using the Choice Framework to Operationalize the Capability Approach to Development." *Journal of International Development* 22, no. 5 (2010): 674–92.
Lee, Philip, and Pradip Ninan Thomas. *Public Memory, Public Media and the Politics of Justice*. New York: Palgrave Macmillan, 2012.
MacIntyre, Alasdair. "The Virtues, the Unity of Human Life, and the Concept of a Tradition." In *Liberalism and Its Critics*, edited by Michael L. Sandel, 125–48. New York: New York University Press, 1984.

McAdams, Dan. *Power, Intimacy and the Life Story: Personological Inquiries into Identity.* Homewood, IL: Dorsey Press, 1985.

Neiger, Motti, Oren Meyers, and Eyal Zandberg. *On Media Memory: Collective Memory in a New Media Age.* New York: Palgrave Macmillan, 2011.

Nussbaum, Martha C. "Capabilities and Human Rights." *Fordham Law Review* 66 (1997): 273–300.

Olick, Jeffrey K. "Collective Memory: The Two Cultures." *Sociological Theory* 17, no. 3(1999): 333–48.

Olick, Jeffrey K., and Joyce Robbins. "Social Memory Studies: From Collective Memory to the Historical Sociology of Mnemonic Practices." *Annual Review of Sociology* 24, no. 1 (1998): 105–40.

Pentzold, Christian, Christine Lohmeier, and Andrea Hajek. "Remembering and Reviving in States of Flux." In *Memory in a Mediated World: Remembrance and Reconstruction*, edited by Andrea Hajek, Christine Lohmeier, and Christian Pentzold, 1–13. New York: Palgrave Macmillan, 2016.

Pogacar, Martin. "(New) Media and Representations of the Past." In *Digital Memories: Exploring Critical Issues*, edited by Anna Maj and Daniel Riha, 23–31. Oxford: Inter-Disciplinary Press, 2009.

Rao, Shakuntala. "Amartya Sen's Value to Media Scholars." *Media Asia* 40, no. 3 (2013): 215–18.

Rao, Shakuntala, and Malik Kanchan. "Conversing Ethics in India's News Media." *Journalism Practice* 13, no.4 (2019): 509–23.

Reading, Anna. "Memobilia: The Mobile Phone and the Emergence of Wearable Memories." In *Save as . . . Digital Memories*, edited by Joanne Garde-Hansen, Andrew Hoskins, and Anna Reading, 81–95. New York: Palgrave-Macmillan, 2009.

———. "Gender and the Right to Memory." *Media Development*, 2 (2010): 11–14.

———. "Memory and Digital Media: Six Dynamics of the Globital Memoryfield." In *On Media Memory*, edited by Motti Neiger, Oren Meyers and Eyal Zandberg, 241–52. London: Palgrave Macmillan, 2011.

Roediger, Henry L., and James V. Wertsch. "Creating a New Discipline of Memory Studies." *Memory Studies* 1, no. 1 (2008): 9–22.

Schiffrin, Deborah. "Narrative as Self-Portrait: Sociolinguistic Constructions of Identity." *Language in Society* 25, no. 2 (1996): 167–203.

Schejter, Amit, and Noam Tirosh. *A Justice-Based Approach to New Media Policy: "In the Paths of Righteousness."* New York: Palgrave MacMillan, 2016.

Sen, Amartya. *Resources, Values and Development.* Oxford: Basil Blackwell, 1984.

———. *Development as Freedom.* Oxford: Oxford University Press, 1999.

———. "Freedom of Choice: Concept and Content." The Alfred Marshall Lecture presented at the annual meeting of the European Economic Association, Copenhagen, 22 August 1987.

———. *The Idea of Justice.* Cambridge: The Belknap Press, 2009.

Shomron, Baruch, and Noam Tirosh. "Contemporary Migrants and Media Capabilities: Understanding Communication Rights in International Migration Policies." *Journal of Ethnic and Migration Studies*, 2020. https://doi.org.10.1080/1369183X.2020.1758553.

The Times of Israel. "Defense Ministry Denies Entry to Palestinians for Joint Memorial Day Ceremony." *The Times of Israel*, 2 May 2019. Retrieved 26 July 2022 from https://www.timesofisrael.com/defense-ministry-denies-entry-to-palestinians-for-joint-memorial-day-ceremony/.

Tirosh, Noam. "Reconsidering the 'Right to Be Forgotten': Memory Rights and the Right to Memory in the New Media Era." *Media, Culture & Society* 39, no. 5 (2017): 644–60.

———. "The Dialectics of Forgetting in Kafka's Writings and Will." *Memory Studies* (2019). https://doi.org/10.1177/1750698019894689.
Traverso, Enzo. "Tearing Down Statues Doesn't Erase History, It Makes Us See It More Clearly." *Jacobin Magazine*, 24 June 2020. Retrieved 17 February 2021 from https://www.jacobinmag.com/2020/06/statues-removal-antiracism-columbus.
Wanat, Zosia. "Poland's Restitution Law Sparks Row with Israel and the US." *Politico*, 12 August 2021. Retrieved 26 July 2022 from https://www.politico.eu/article/poland-parliament-restitution-law-property-compensation-nazi-communists/.
Worcman, Karen, and Joanne Garde-Hansen. *Social Memory Technology: Theory, Practice, Action*. New York: Routledge, 2016.
Yerushalmi, Yosef H. *Zakhor, Jewish History and Jewish Memory*. Seattle: University of Washington Press, 1982.

Chapter 5

"THE MEMORY BELONGS TO NO ONE AND IT BELONGS TO EVERYONE"

An Analysis of a Grassroots Claim to the Right to Memory

Rebecca Kook

Introduction

The concept of "rights" is central to the idea of democracy; and while the democratic ideal posits an equal and universal distribution of rights among all members, the history of democracy is a history of uneven development laden with struggles by excluded groups for eligibility for basic rights and protections and thus for full membership.[1] Similarly, contemporary memory discourse, with its articulation of the notion of the right to memory, is largely conceived of as a universal right. Tracing its origins to post–World War II international charters and the emergence of a universal human rights discourse and regime,[2] the discourse surrounding the right to memory largely engages with the capacity—not always implemented—of international charters and organizations to universally enforce this right. Nonetheless, on the ground, the politics surrounding the right to memory—like the politics surrounding other democratic rights—follows an uneven path, and often takes place in conjunction with local struggles for increased accessibility to rights enforcement, participation, and civic equality.

In this chapter I examine the discourse surrounding the right to memory in the context of research that I conducted from 2017 to 2020 on a grassroots Holocaust remembrance initiative based in Israel called Zikaron Basalon (remembrance in the living room). Founded in 2010, by the year 2020 the initiative boasted 1.5 million participants, making it one of the main forms of Holocaust remembrance in Israel.[3] Based on my research, I suggest three directions that may contribute to our thinking regarding the right to memory. First, claims to the right to memory often emerge on the ground—rising from the bottom up—and are informed by grassroots demands for increased democratic inclusivity and equality. Thus, an analysis of the claims to the right to memory should attend to the wider context of similar, yet distinct claims for accessibility to other democratic rights. Second, the right to memory manifests itself not only in terms of narrative, but also in terms of demands for equal access to practices of remembrance. Third, the development of local discourse regarding the right memory, like the discourse surrounding other rights, usually reflects a distinct conception of personhood/identity that seeks to concretize the capacity of individuals to reflect historically on their relationship to their community. An analysis of these memory claims can help us identify and examine the particular role remembrance plays in the historical construction of national and local identities.

The Emergence of the Right to Memory

Remembrance is most commonly premised on the assumption that we—either as a society or as individuals—have an obligation to remember the past, and that current generations have an essential debt to their predecessors;[4] as Jay Winter notes in his contribution to this volume, "The dead have claims on us." While such a commitment to remember the past has been a constant characteristic of human society, both the motivations behind this and the general role of remembrance have shifted over time. Historically, remembrance of the past was rooted in religious injunctions, in the veneration of family ancestors, and the glorification of military victories.[5] With the advent of modernity and the rise of nationalism, obligation to remembrance of the past shifted to focus on the constituting of myths of national origins and the forging of national narratives.[6] National remembrance emerged as a central vehicle of both historical and ethical knowledge, with national narratives constituting the basis of collective identities and national solidarity.[7]

World War II, in general, and the horror of the Holocaust in particular, had a radical impact on the nature of the obligation to remember. With the passing of the International Charters of Human Rights and the Convention on the Prevention of Genocide in 1948,[8] remembrance of the past became indelibly linked to the memory of the victims of violence and to aspirations to end global conflict. Hence, increasingly, remembrance became tied to global understandings of human rights and the ways people think of justice and reconciliation.[9] Indeed, it is largely seen as a particular characteristic of modern notions of remembrance that the obligation to remember is an act due to the victims, and hence memory is now often framed as an ethical duty.[10] In the words of Paul Ricoeur, "We must remember because remembering is a moral duty. We owe a debt to the victims . . . By remembering and telling, we . . . prevent forgetfulness from killing the victims twice."[11] This ethical and moral link forged between the remembrance of past violence, the dignity of the victims, and the ability to prevent future violence is at the basis of many remembrance and human rights practices that have emerged since the end of the twentieth century. These practices include truth and reconciliation commissions,[12] the passing of local and international memory laws,[13] and other transnational remembrance projects including international commemorative days.[14] It is within this context, which links remembrance and human rights, that the discourse about the right to memory has emerged.

The right to memory, as the editors of this volume explain in the introduction, is seen as an ethical right which "promotes memory for the sake of humanity and that connects ideas of human rights with visions of justice and the empowerment of the weak." The right to memory is linked in a basic way to the human right we all have to lead healthy and stable physical and emotional lives. The right to recall past injuries, to confront our perpetrators in words if not in person, is considered by many a fundamental component of how we think societies (and individuals) can and should work through traumatic pasts. This claim is not, however, uncontested, as is evident in Lea David's insightful observation and argument in her contribution to this volume, that this right constitutes a moral and ethical "trap" that serves to lock people into false cognitive frames.[15]

Two main lines of research can be identified within the larger research agenda aimed at exploring the idea of the right to memory, even though some do not explicitly employ this term. The first investigates the ways socio-legal constructs, mainly on the global and international level, have worked and can work to protect and legitimate the right of individuals and groups to remember the past. This research contextualizes the right to memory within the larger discourse of basic civic universal rights.[16] Recent contributions within this line of research highlight the diverse role played by social media in the promotion of the right to memory, enabling access to a diverse set of narratives of the past, while at times privileging certain narratives of the past;[17] the ways globalized platforms of communication have influenced and in many cases facilitated the ability of individuals to exercise their right to memory through the promotion of individual and personal stories that can then contribute to larger narratives;[18] and the ways international organizations often impose standardized modes of commemoration.[19]

Another line of research explores the right to memory in the face of political and politicized efforts at either erasing memory or prohibiting counter-memories, thus imposing official or hegemonic narratives.[20] As efforts to silence counter-memories often target minority groups, significant research has recently highlighted the ways cultural and political minorities engage in their struggles against dominant majorities invoking their right to memory as a signifier and representation of their right to identity and culture within the arena of commemoration.[21] Research on these struggles highlights the centrality of contested narratives of the past and looks at the ability of these narratives to serve as both mechanisms of political inclusion and exclusion. Memory activism as a central type of remembrance activity has emerged largely in this context.[22] The ability to retrieve, maintain, and promote memories of difficult pasts serves as both a condition for and a result of human rights struggles.

Hence, what both of these research agendas seem to share is their focus on the issue of narrative, locating and articulating the right to memory as the right to include previously contested, denied, or erased narratives within the larger national or social-historical memory. In some cases, this involves shifting the victims from the background to the foreground of the story; in other cases, it involves retelling the story entirely, while shifting the chronology of major events. In this chapter I suggest a third line of research about the right to memory. I argue that in some cases, the right to memory is invoked not in the context of narrative at all but rather as a generalized right to participate equally in social, cultural, and political activity, i.e., to be recognized, through access to a remembrance activity, as an equal and active member of society. More often than not, this particular articulation of the right to memory emerges within grassroots or vernacular commemorative projects with the aim being not to promote forgotten or suppressed narratives or memories but rather to devise, promote, and disseminate platforms whose purpose is to expand access to memorial practices for populations, communities, and groups whose ability to participate effectively in standard commemorative activities is limited. Hence, the right to memory is articulated as the right to equal participation and as a pathway to democratic inclusion.

I explore this particular iteration of the right to memory within the context of a rapidly widespread commemorative project in Israel called Zikaron Basalon. Based on interviews conducted with founders and leaders of the project, and participation in leadership seminars, I examine the role the right to memory plays in the overall structure of the remembrance project. I suggest that there are three main contexts within which this project emerges: the effort to make the structure of remembrance more relevant, the effort to domesticate commemoration by redefining the home as the arena of public remembrance, and the effort to reach out to previously excluded communities.

The Emergence of Zikaron Basalon

Zikaron Basalon was established in 2011, at a time of change in the Israeli commemorative landscape.[23] Up until then, and during Israel's first fifty years, Holocaust remembrance was constituted within very strict traditional commemorative structures with most Israelis marking the day mainly by viewing the official ceremony at Yad Vashem (Israel's official Holocaust Museum and Archive), on television, or by participating in local government or school ceremonies, themselves structured along similar lines.[24] These ceremonies include what are considered paradigmatic or traditional ceremonial elements, including lowering of the flag at the start and singing of the national anthem at the end; speeches by national or local dignitaries; the recitation of prayers, and, in the case of the official main ceremony, the lighting of six beacons by survivors.[25] The audience is cordoned off and separated from the performers and hence experiences the ceremony as a spectacle whose purpose is to inspire a sense of sacredness and awe.[26]

The rise of individualism, the social and ideological fragmentation of society, and the onset of neoliberal values changed Israeli society toward the end of the twentieth century and impacted the landscape of commemoration, resulting both in an overall decline in the appeal of state-led ceremonies, and the rise in local non-state initiatives.[27] Within the increasingly varied landscape of Holocaust commemoration in Israel, Zikaron Basalon manages to stand out because of its mass appeal and relative longevity. It was founded by a group of young Israelis led by Adi Altschuler, a highly successful young Israeli entrepreneur with an impressive history of social activism, and has been taking place in ever growing numbers since 2011.[28] According to Altschuler, the initial incentive to establish Zikaron Basalon was the deep sense of alienation that she and her friends experienced while participating in the more official modes of remembrance and their growing awareness of the need for a "different way to relate to the past."[29] Altschuler organized the first gathering in 2010 in her own living room. She invited a Holocaust survivor, a friend of her mother's, along with about thirty close friends. Since then, the project has spread like wildfire. By 2019, 750,000 people are said to have participated in Zikaron Basalon gatherings,[30] and in 2020, the year of the COVID-19 pandemic, 1.5 million people are estimated to have taken part in what were mainly online gatherings.[31] Hence, while Zikaron Basalon is by no means the only form of contemporary Holocaust remembrance in Israel, it is by far the most popular and represents a significant social phenomenon. In Israel, these gatherings have also taken place in prisons, mental health facilities, and among communities of refugees and migrants. Since 2013, major online radio stations and news sites have been broadcasting survivor testimonies under the auspices of Zikaron Basalon.[32] By 2019, members of Israel's political leadership, including then President Reuven Rivlin, were hosting Zikaron Basalon gatherings as highly publicized media events, with many leaders of Israel's political parties following suit.[33] Given both the scope of participation and the high profile of many of the participants, Zikaron Basalon has emerged as the most popular form of Holocaust remembrance among younger Israelis, constituting a real challenge to the hegemonic position of the official ceremony at Yad Vashem.

Zikaron Basalon itself is a slim organization. The founding members and the current leadership belong to a similar generational cohort: young Israelis mainly in their late twenties to thirties, predominantly female, largely but not exclusively secular, largely but not exclusively Ashkenazi Jews, most of them with a strong background in social and political activism.[34] The mainstay of its activities take place on and around the official national Holocaust and Heroism Memorial Day (HHMD), and the organization relies extensively on a network of part-time volunteers. Zikaron Basalon promotes what can be defined as an informal and dispersed mode of remembrance that is based on testimony, discussion, and artistic expression. It aims to promote local, neighborhood-based gatherings in people's private homes, which bring together friends and family to listen to Holocaust testimony and talk openly and informally about related issues. Each gathering ranges from fifteen to forty-five participants. The structure of the evenings is intended to have three sections: testimony, artistic interlude, and discussion. A typical evening will always open with a testimony, which will be followed by discussion. At times an artistic interlude will separate the two parts. The testimony, however, is the heart of the event. The evenings are informal by design, with the guests sitting on sofas and chairs, sometimes on the floor. Usually, the hosts will prepare refreshments. The testimony is given either by a survivor (in person or recorded), or the child of survivors (second generation), or by an expert such as a Holocaust scholar, a journalist, or a writer. The discussion will take one of two forms: a question-and-answer session with the testimony giver, either during the testimony or afterward, or a separate discussion session on a specific topic, moderated by the host or a designated person after the testimony.

The gatherings intentionally lack any of the paradigmatic ceremonial accoutrements mentioned above: there is little if any distinction between the audience and the "performers," and there is no evident protocol in terms of the setting or the interactions. There is no rendition of the Jewish memorial prayer *Yizkor* (*yizkor*, remember, is the first word of the traditional prayer, and also represents the overall theme of the prayer for the deceased) as typical in formal events, and the national anthem is not played at the end. Hence, Zikaron Basalon offers a radically new set of practices with which to commemorate the Holocaust, practices that for many, particularly at the beginning, seemed iconoclastic.[35] These new remembrance practices were, from the outset, promoted as being more relevant to larger sections of Israeli society, and hence more inclusive. As such, the Zikaron Basalon remembrance project was articulated within a larger context of the need perceived by the founders to allow people to exercise their right to partake in Holocaust commemoration and thus to be able to share in the benefits of memory. The mnemonic gaze shifted from the national collective to the individual. There is less and less focus on what the community owes the past and more on what the past "owes" the community. Summarizing this sentiment, Altschuler noted that the purpose was to "transition the memory from a memory of survival to a memory of healing through intimate gatherings in which the participants re-connect with the memory of the Holocaust, and through this reconnection engage with themselves and with contemporary society."[36]

Exploring the Right to Memory in the Context of Zikaron Basalon

I researched Zikaron Basalon for three years, from 2017 to 2020. In the course of my research, I conducted interviews with the founding members of the project, participated in leadership workshops aimed at training and recruiting Zikaron Basalon community leaders, and participated in and hosted Zikaron Basalon gatherings. I discovered that the project, from the perspective of its founders and leaders, is defined by a relatively clear mnemonic vision and agenda.[37] Prompted mainly by what I described above as the strong sense of alienation from mainstream official Holocaust remembrance practices, Zikaron Basalon is offered as a form of relevant and inclusive remembrance, appealing to previously indifferent as well as excluded populations. Furthering agendas of social justice, which many brought with them to Zikaron Basalon, the founding members were motivated by the idea of transforming the public, official, rigid commemorative practices into intimate, engaging, unofficial, and local remembrance events, which would be easily accessible—both geographically and socially—to a wide variety of communities.

Thus, the founding members transplanted their social justice agenda of promoting equality and inclusivity within Israel to the arena of Holocaust remembrance. Their commitment to Holocaust memory, alongside their commitment to democratic activism, produced a hybrid mnemonic agenda comprised of two elements. The first was relevancy. Faced with the general social and political apathy of many of their generation, coming up with a form of commemoration that would engage younger people was an indirect way of instilling public spirit and solidarity. Relevance was sought by domesticating remembrance (bringing it into the literal living room), by localizing it (encouraging people to participate in gatherings in their own neighborhood), and by encouraging discussion and interaction. The centrality of interaction to contemporary forms of digital memory, as discussed in this volume by Noam Tirosh and Amit Schejter, is reflected in the mnemonic vision of the founders of Zikaron Basalon who aimed at activating remembrance by including discussion as a core part of the gatherings.

The second element of the agenda was inclusion and accessibility. Many of the founding members had been socially active in different initiatives aimed at the inclusion of previously excluded communities into mainstream social activities. Before founding Zikaron Basalon, Altschuler founded The Wings of Krembo, the first youth movement for children with disabilities.[38] Devising a form of remembrance that would be aimed at making remembrance practices widely accessible was both an end and a means, a way of expanding the inclusive reach of Holocaust remembrance activities while at the same time making it a means of social, cultural, and even political inclusion. This was achieved by placing emphasis on accessibility, aimed both at those communities traditionally less involved in Holocaust commemoration (mainly Jews of non-European descent such as Sepharadi or Mizrachi Jews[39]) and other Jewish minorities who had refrained from participating in commemorative events (Jews of Ethiopian descent and Jews from the Former Soviet Union),[40] while also targeting populations who are more generally disenfranchised, disabled, or in other ways disassociated from the mainstream of Israeli society. These included, as mentioned above, prisoners, mentally challenged communities, refugee and asylum seeker communities, disaffected youth, and others.

In the following analysis of the interviews I conducted, I demonstrate how it is in the larger context of relevancy and inclusivity/accessibility that the rhetoric and practice of Zikaron Basalon invokes the right to memory not as the right to promote a specific narrative, but as the equal right to partake in remembrance practices.

Making Remembrance Relevant

For the leaders of Zikaron Basalon, making Holocaust remembrance relevant was achieved by devising a set of new commemorative practices embodied and manifested in the physical space of the living room. Multiple meanings and significations became attached to the living room, rendering it a complex and nuanced site of memory. First, the living room invoked a sense of intimacy that stood in stark opposition to the sites of official commemoration. While the sites of official Holocaust commemoration events were austere and somber, the living room was promoted as intimate and inviting. Indeed, intimacy was one of the most frequent adjectives evoked by both hosts and participants when describing the experience. Since "alienation" was the word so often chosen to describe and explain the lack of engagement with existing official Holocaust commemoration, offering an intimate setting was like an antidote, a way to draw young people in both metaphorically and literally. "Open your doors and your home tonight" is one of the slogans on the Zicharon Basalon website. As Ben noted:

> To take it out of the realm of the official, the national, the public—and to bring it back into the private sphere—the home. Memory does not survive through public rituals—only through private rituals. It must be privatized in order to survive as memory.[41]

And then Ruth:

> Zikaron Basalon, historically—it is the right thing. This platform, which is so individual, at home, it is the right time for this.[42]

The architecture of the gatherings, as envisioned by the leaders, in which people literally open their homes and invite the local "public" to join them in the privacy of their living room to "remember together" is the basis for reimagining new communities. The gatherings are intended to be local, to be neighborhood based. However, while Zikaron Basalon brings commemoration from the public to the private, it is not private remembrance. It is, in fact, bringing the public into the private, creating a public site within the physical space of the home. Thus, the living room was chosen to act as an antidote not only to the malaise surrounding Holocaust memory, but to the more general sense of pervasive social and political disengagement. Opening up one's home constitutes the renegotiation of informal modes of association, of congregation, and of the possibility of solidarity.

> How do we manage to escape from a world of loneliness and alienation? . . . if we manage to bring half a million people together, in intimate settings, to talk and listen—and there is a follow up—I think we manage to create a community.[43]

Thus, the "privatization of memory" becomes the "domestication" of memory. It is not the elimination of community but rather the creation of community centered in the home. It is in this sense that the concept of the living room has become a brand name—and has, over the past decade, been adopted by countless grassroots organizations—both remembrance groups and community organizing groups. These include, to name but a few, Around the Campfire,[44] Our Brothers,[45] and Story on the Road.[46] Each one of these initiatives promotes yearly gatherings in the privacy of people's homes, with a testimony and discussion. Clearly, the notion of domesticating public activity resonated with both a desire and a need. In an interview with one of the leaders, she noted that it has been said of Zikaron Basalon that they "redefined the purview of domestic activity."[47] In the wake of Zikaron Basalon, the domestic sphere has been gradually transformed into a newly central arena for public activity and participation.

In addition, expanding and endlessly multiplying the sites of remembrance to encompass everyone's own home and thus to be potentially available to everyone, was one of the ways of concretizing the right to memory. It was not merely the multiplicity of settings that concretized the right to memory, it was the personalization invoked by hosting the event in your home, inviting your neighbors, your friends, and individualizing the commemorative practices. As Shira said:

> Zikaron Basalon is doing to memory what Google did to our email, and what Facebook did to the way we communicate. It takes this thing and personalizes it. Adjusts it just for you . . . this is why we are successful—[our generation] needs and loves things to be just right for us: our coffee, our Facebook—our memory . . . And it's amazing because it is to take something so sensitive like memory and adjust it . . . Now there is a platform that is just right for me, and I can do what I want and talk about what I choose.[48]

An additional way the founders of Zikaron Basalon sought to make Holocaust commemoration relevant was through the introduction of interaction as an inherent part of the remembrance practice. Based on their premise that discussion is an inherent characteristic of their generation, the founders of Zikaron Basalon insisted on including discussion as a core part of the gatherings. Encouraging discussion within the remembrance practice was a way of including younger generations in dominant discourses and providing a platform for their voices to be heard. The promised intimacy of the living room is enhanced by the fact that the remembrance practices are informal and encourage dialogue. This vision of remembrance practice is an active vision, one that provides a voice to those who participate and aspires to a dynamic memory that engages with the testimony and brings it into the universe of the participants. As one of the leaders noted:

> The testimony is not the most important part. For testimony you can read Anne Frank's diary and then analyze it . . . I'm not interested in that. The most important thing is that you talk. So that the memory stays alive. It stays alive when we speak about it—makes it relevant to our lives. If we close the memory away—it means that once the last survivor dies—the memory dies along with him. So what have we accomplished?[49]

Promoting this kind of active form of remembrance constitutes, for the leaders, a form of social critique and social activism. Not only is it aimed at giving a voice to those who remember, it is an open criticism of hegemonic forms of commemoration and expresses a reaffirmation of the fact that it is the right of those who participate in remembrance activities to define what is and what is not a legitimate exercise of that right:

> There is this paradigm that we are taught all our lives about how to remember and what to feel—and I say that we are not denigrating the Holocaust if we sit together, drink a beer, and talk about the Holocaust.[50]

Making Remembrance Inclusive and Accessible

Another important way the founders of Zikaron Basalon sought to make Holocaust remembrance relevant was by focusing on accessibility and inclusion. In the first iteration of relevance, expanded upon above, relevance implied intimacy and discussion and was manifested in what I have called the domestication of remembrance. In this second iteration, relevance is drawn from an agenda of social justice and social activism and is based on making remembrance practices available and accessible to different, often previously excluded, communities. Most of the founding members, as well as many of the community leaders in Zikaron Basalon came to the arena of Holocaust remembrance from the world of social activism and civil society. As noted above, Altschuler's first initiative was the founding of the world's first youth movement for children with disabilities, an initiative that won her numerous international awards and recognition.[51] Social inclusion and social equality have been an integral part of the fabric of Zikaron Basalon from day one. The goal of social inclusion and accessibility has operated on two parallel levels. The first offers an alternative to the hegemonic paradigm of Holocaust remembrance in Israel, which has been criticized for promoting the idea that the Holocaust "belongs" only to Ashkenazi Jews—i.e., Jews of European descent and whose families were, in most cases, directly affected by the Holocaust.[52] The second focuses on communities who are excluded from mainstream society and aims to promote gatherings for populations who are disenfranchised, disabled, and in other ways disassociated from cultural and social activity within Israeli society.

It was mainly through the metaphor of "platform" that the founders and leaders of Zikaron Basalon discussed the notion of accessibility. The concept of "platform" was the most commonly used in the interviews I conducted, and while it indicated the creation of face-to-face gatherings, it echoes the use of platform in the newly emergent platform studies within contemporary media studies.[53] While in these theoretical elaborations "platform" refers to the ability of social media to connect diverse actors and to highlight the accessibility of data, for the founders of Zikaron Basalon, many of whom came from the world of technology, the concept of "platform" was employed as a technology of inclusion that enabled easier access to commemorative "data" and activities. Drawing on the culture of social media, the founders of Zikaron Basalon used the concept of "platform" as a trope that underscored its flexibility, its potential for diversity, and its ability to make remembrance practices totally accessible and inclusive. As Noa noted:

> If I say that I want Zikaron Basalon to be a social platform, all of society needs to be a part of this. Up till Zikaron Basalon, most of Israeli society was excluded from the discourse on Holocaust memory . . . Mizrahim—they don't care—all special needs people—we don't talk to them . . . youth—it's too much . . . We say: from now on, everyone can partake . . . everyone has the ability—that is Zikaron Basalon.[54]

In many of the interviews, this idea of a platform as a means of promoting inclusion and democracy was linked explicitly to the idea of "the right to memory," the idea that remembrance should be made accessible and available to everyone. In response to a question regarding efforts made by Zikaron Basalon to bring the gatherings to groups of youth at risk, Michal responded:

> these kids do not have a platform to say what they really want to say . . . it is their right to also talk about things . . . It is Holocaust Memorial Day—people come together and do something—so every person has the right to do this. We give them this platform.[55]

Hence, one of the main goals of Zikaron Basalon is to provide a remedy to the alienation felt by members of younger generations from the traditional forms of Holocaust commemoration. In the following quotes, the hegemonic paradigm, which saw the memory of the Holocaust as somehow "belonging" only to Ashkenazi Jews, is confronted directly, and Zikaron Basalon is framed as a force of democratization:

> Accessibility is an integral part of creating a discourse that everyone can take part of . . . we try to bring this memory to people for whom it is not "their" trauma . . . the Holocaust created a kind of hierarchy in Israeli society and therefore you need to make the effort to bring it to everyone—all different groups . . . and if you don't make it relevant to everyone, you lose the attempt to create a different discourse in society.[56]

Moshe, a religious young man of North African origins with a strong ethnic identity, described his sense of feeling removed from Holocaust memory, feeling that it was not "his" and he had no "right" to this memory:

> All those years I felt that the Holocaust wasn't "mine." I wasn't connected. Adi told me she felt the same way . . . she has no direct family connection . . . but I celebrate Passover and my parents didn't really leave Egypt but the fact that I am a Jew—that connects me to Passover . . . So the fact that my great-grandfather didn't experience the Holocaust doesn't mean that I am not connected to it. It is part of the history of the Jews so we need to commemorate it.[57]

Although the percentage of gatherings that take place within marginal communities is relatively small, the organization focuses a lot of attention on enabling them. By the year 2020, Zikaron Basalon gatherings had taken place in every prison in Israel. Promoting these gatherings, allowing them to exercise their right to memory is seen as a fundamental part of citizenship:

> Yes—they are part of this state—they are citizens no matter where they are . . . These people have no chance to go to a ceremony . . . they will do nothing that is relevant to them—and not because they don't want to or they can't—but because it is not accessible to them . . . I was in the gathering in the Maasyahu prison—it was amazing. And today—all the prisons in Israel do Zikaron Basalon.[58]

The ability to partake in remembrance gatherings is presented as a means of fulfillment and as a path of healing. However, as opposed to the sense of healing invoked in the context of allowing victims of past violence to commemorate their trauma, in this case, the process of healing does not stem from the specific memory evoked, but rather from the opportunity to partake in the social activity of commemoration within the larger society.

Discussion and Conclusions

Based on my study of Zikaron Basalon, I draw three main conclusions regarding the right to memory. My first conclusion concerns the meaning of Holocaust memory in Israel. Within Israel, the memory of the Holocaust has, since the state's establishment in 1948, constituted one of the main pillars of its national and social identity. For many years, however, this component of national identity was seen as shared mainly and implicitly, only by those ravaged directly by the tragedy of extermination, that is, the Jewish communities of Europe. This exclusive connection to the Holocaust evolved over the years into a component of the state's claim to hegemonic power and is perceived by many as having served, historically, as a mechanism of political exclusion in the state's relationship to those who did not come "from there."[59] Specifically, this has excluded not only the Arab non-Jewish citizens of the state, but members of marginalized Jewish communities, particularly communities from northern Africa, Ethiopia, and from the Former Soviet Union (FSU).[60] These communities are peripheral communities within the larger Jewish Israeli society and occupy the lower strata of society, socially and economically. Thus, the "othering" of these communities as unconnected to the major national trauma is seen as constituting an additional and intersectional level of marginalization.[61]

The memory of the Holocaust, as Michal noted above "belongs to everyone, and belongs to no one." By articulating remembrance in terms of a universal right, and by highlighting accessibility as a main goal, Zikaron Basalon can be read as an act of political protest against the limited and exclusionary reach of belonging and membership in Israel's project of national redemption, suggesting that the right to partake in commemorative practices serves as a precondition for the more general extension of equal access in society. Thus, Zikaron Basalon does not object to the centrality of the memory of the Holocaust in Israeli identity nor does it take issue with any particular narrative approach to the history of the Holocaust. It argues for the right to partake in practices regardless of the narrative.

The study of Zikaron Basalon furthers our understanding of the ways the discourse surrounding the right to memory can benefit not only from a focus on issues of narrative, but on issues related to practices as well. Indeed, the centrality of form in the context of remembrance has been underscored and highlighted by theorists of memory ever since Maurice Halbwachs.[62] James Young, for example, demonstrates how meaning is often generated through form, not through narrative.[63] What concretizes shared memories and what extends collective remembrance beyond the reading of a historical text is not merely the story of the past that is generated, but rather the experience generated by participation in shared remembrance events. Paul Connerton, in his seminal study of commemoration echoes a similar conclusion: "To interpret ritual as an alternative symbolic medium for expressing what may be expressed in other ways . . . is to ignore what is distinctive about ritual itself."[64]

As this study has demonstrated, Zikaron Basalon does not offer an alternative mnemonic narrative, but it does offer a set of practices that aim to constitute a type of alternative mnemonic message or meaning. By focusing on the relevance of the practices, on their availability and accessibility, Zikaron Basalon rewrites our understanding of the right to memory by shifting it from a focus on the particular story that is told to a focus on the structures adopted to tell the story. The inherent inclusivity in the message of Zikaron Basalon implies that at stake is not what is remembered, but who remembers it and how.

Which leads me to my third and final conclusion. As I noted in the introduction to this chapter, the idea of rights is fundamental to democratic and liberal discourse. Inherent in this link between rights and democracy is the idea that by guaranteeing fundamental freedoms democracy constitutes a particular conception of selfhood as defined by individual, universal capacities. While classical liberal thinking imagined these capacities as primarily the capacity to rationality and productivity, contemporary democratic thinking, in its numerous variations, highlights the human capacity for sociability, for the expression of self-identity, and for the ability to thrive within culturally coherent communities.[65] I suggest that in many contexts, such as the one I discussed in this chapter, the discourse of the individual right to memory can be read within this wider context as a discourse that seeks to concretize the capacity of individuals to reflect historically on their relationship to their community by articulating memory as one more democratic and universal right.

To sum up, the central message of Zikaron Basalon is that the ability to partake in commemorative practices is a universal right, and that the set of remembrance practices that they have devised serves to guarantee that this right is indeed universally distributed. The paradigmatic, scripted, and awe-inspiring ceremonies, such as those enacted to commemorate the Holocaust in the past, served as mechanisms of exclusion by virtue of their inaccessibility and also by constituting the audience as passive subjects. Zikaron Basalon sets out to provide an accessible commemorative platform that easily adjusts to everyone's own individual needs and in this way invokes the right to memory as a way to gain a sense of belonging to the larger community and hence to the enactment and reinforcement of the citizenship of those who are or have been excluded in different ways. This research has demonstrated that the right to memory is invoked not only as a right to a particular narrative of the past but as a constitutive right of belonging to the community of citizens.

Rebecca Kook is associate professor of Politics and Government at Ben-Gurion University. She is interested in issues related to identity, solidarity, and remembrance and over the years has written over thirty articles on related topics. She is the recipient of an Israeli Ministry of Science grant (since 2019) to study the future of Holocaust remembrance in Israel and is the author most recently of *Agents of Memory in the Post-witness Era: Memory in the Living Room and Changing Forms of Holocaust Remembrance in Israel* published in *Memory Studies* (2021).

Notes

1. Cunningham, *Theories of Democracy*.
2. For an in-depth discussion of the 1948 Universal Declaration of Human Rights as a foundational memory document, see Jay Winter's chapter in this volume.
3. This is data provided by the organization. Shira, interview with the author, 29 May 2020.
4. Baines, "Duty to Remember (and Forget?)."
5. Assmann, *Cultural Memory and Early Civilization*.
6. See Smith, "Ethnic Sources of Nationalism," and Greenfeld, *Nationalism*.
7. Anderson, *Imagined Communities*.
8. "Convention on the Prevention and Punishment."
9. See Huyssen, "International Human Rights"; Huyssen, "Present Pasts"; and David, *The Past Can't Heal Us*.
10. Margalit, *The Ethics of Memory*.
11. Ricoeur, *Figuring the Sacred*, 290.
12. See Bakiner, *Truth Commissions*; and Lessa, *Memory and Transitional Justice*.
13. See Tirosh and Gutman, "On Media, Memory and Laws."
14. See Kaiser and Storeide, "International Organizations and Holocaust Remembrance."
15. In her contribution to this volume, "The 'Duty to Remember' and the 'Right to Memory': Memory Politics and Neoliberal Logic," Lea David critically assesses the implications of this deep link forged between memory and healing.
16. See Reading, "Identity, Memory and Cosmopolitanism"; Lee, "Right to Memory"; and Levy and Sznaider, *The Holocaust and Memory*.
17. See Viejo-Rose, "Memorial Functions"; and Cameron, "Communicating Cosmopolitanism."
18. See Tirosh, "iNakba, Mobile Media and Society's Memory"; and Recuber, "The Presumption of Commemoration."
19. See David, "Against Standardization of Memory."
20. See Beiner, *Forgetful Remembrance*; Jelin, *State Repression and the Labors of Memory*; and Confino, "Telling about Germany."
21. See Tirosh, "iNakba, Mobile Media and Society's Memory"; Sorek, *Palestinian Commemoration in Israel*; Wang, *Memory Politics, Identity and Conflict*; and Conley, *Memory from the Margins*.
22. See Gutman, *Memory Activism*.
23. See Steir-Livny, "Remembrance in the Living Room" [Zikaron b'Salon].
24. See Arad, "Israel and the Shoah"; Ofer, "The Strength of Remembrance"; and Steir-Livny, *Har Hazikaron Yizkor Bimkomi* [Let the Memorial Hill remember].
25. See Handelman, *Nationalism and the Israeli State*. For a discussion of paradigmatic ceremonies, see Hermoni and Lebel, "Politicizing Memory."
26. See Meyers, Zandberg, and Neiger, "Prime Time Commemoration."
27. See Shafir and Peled, *Being Israeli*.
28. See Prusher, "Building Communities of Kindness."
29. See "Zikaron Basalon" [Memory in the Living Room].
30. See "Zikaron B'salon: Iruay Hazikaron Hameyuchadim V'haintimim L'yom HaShoah" [Memory in the Living Room: Unique and Intimate Memory Events on Holocaust Memorial Day].
31. Shira, (founding member Zikaron Basalon) in discussion with the author, May 2021. All names listed for interviews are pseudonyms to protect the privacy of the participants.
32. Such as *nrg* website (retrieved 23 July 2022 from https://www.nrg.co.il); *ynet* website (retrieved 23 July 2022 from https://www.ynet.co.il); *Radio Kol Rishonim 106.2* website (retrieved 23 July 2022 from https://www.106-2fm.co.il).

33. "Zikaron Basalon" [Memory in the Living Room].
34. Kook, "Agents of Memory."
35. Nir, "Official or Privatized."
36. "Zikaron Basalon" [Memory in the living room].
37. Kook, "Agents of Memory."
38. Prusher, "Building Communities of Kindness."
39. See Shimony, "On 'Holocaust Envy' in Mizrahi Literature"; and Oppenheimer, "The Holocaust: A Mizrahi Perspective."
40. Mizrachi and Herzog, "Participatory Destigmatization Strategies."
41. Ben, (founding member Zikaron Basalon) in discussion with the author, December 2018.
42. Ruth, (founding member Zikaron Basalon) in discussion with the author, March 2019.
43. Ben, (founding member Zikaron Basalon) in discussion with the author, December 2018.
44. "Misaviv La'medoora" [Around the campfire].
45. "Ha'achim Shelanu" [Our brothers].
46. "Sipour al Ha'derech" [Story on the Road].
47. Shira, (founding member Zikaron Basalon) in discussion with the author, January 2019.
48. Shira, (founding member Zikaron Basalon) in discussion with the author, January 2019.
49. Neta, (founding member Zikaron Basalon) in discussion with the author, November 2018.
50. Yael, (founding member Zikaron Basalon) in discussion with the author, October 2018.
51. Prusher, "Building Communities of Kindness."
52. Shimony, "On 'Holocaust Envy' in Mizrahi Literature."
53. van Dijck, *The Culture of Connectivity*; Plantin et al., "Infrastructure Studies Meet Platform Studies."
54. Noa, (founding member Zikaron Basalon) in discussion with the author, February 2019.
55. Michal, (founding member Zikaron Basalon) in discussion with the author, December 2018.
56. Yael, (founding member Zikaron Basalon) in discussion with the author, October 2018.
57. Moshe, (founding member Zikaron Basalon) in discussion with the author, November 2018.
58. Ruth, (founding member Zikaron Basalon) in discussion with the author, March 2019.
59. "From there" refers to the Zionist distinction made between Here (Israel) and There (the Diaspora). See Arad, "Israel and the Shoah."
60. On the exclusion of marginal communities from Holocaust memory in Israel, see Steir-Livny, *Har Hazikaron Yizkor Bimkomi* [Let the Memorial Hill remember].
61. On the marginalization of these minority communities within Israel, see Shafir and Peled, *Being Israeli*.
62. Corning and Schuman, *Generations and Collective Memory*.
63. Young, "When a Day Remembers."
64. Connerton, *How Societies Remember*.
65. For an interesting complementary approach, see Tirosh and Schejter's discussion of Sen's capabilities approach in their chapter in this volume, as it, too, builds on the human capacity (and need) for sociability and identity as a basis for the distribution of rights.

Bibliography

Anderson, Benedict. *Imagined Communities: Reflections on the Origins and Spread of Nationalism*. London: Verso, 1991.

Arad, Gulie Ne'eman. "Israel and the Shoah: A Tale of Multifarious Taboos." *New German Critique* 90 (2003): 5–26.
Assmann, Jan. *Cultural Memory and Early Civilization: Writing, Remembrance, and Political Imagination*. Cambridge: Cambridge University Press, 2011.
Baines, Gary. "A Duty to Remember (and Forget?): A Transnational Perspective on Commemorating War." In *War and Memorials: The Age of Nationalism and the Great War*, edited by Frank Jacob and Kenneth Pearl, 23–44. Paderborn: Ferdinand Schöningh, 2019.
Bakiner, Onur. *Truth Commissions: Memory, Power, and Legitimacy*. Philadelphia: University of Pennsylvania Press, 2015.
Beiner, Guy. *Forgetful Remembrance: Social Forgetting and Vernacular Historiography of a Rebellion in Ulster*. Oxford: Oxford University Press, 2018.
Cameron, John David. "Communicating Cosmopolitanism and Motivating Global Citizenship." *Political Studies* 66, no. 3 (2018): 718–34.
Confino, Alon. "Telling about Germany: Narratives of Memory and Culture." *The Journal of Modern History* 76, no. 2 (2004): 389–416.
Conley, Bridget. *Memory from the Margins: Ethiopia's Red Terror Martyrs Memorial Museum*. London: Palgrave Macmillan, 2019.
Connerton, Paul. *How Societies Remember*. Cambridge: Cambridge University Press, 1989.
"Convention on the Prevention and Punishment of the Crime of Genocide." 1951. *United Nations*. Retrieved 7 December 2020 from https://www.ohchr.org/en/professionalinterest/pages/crimeofgenocide.aspx.
Corning, Amy, and Howard Schuman. *Generations and Collective Memory*. Chicago: University of Chicago Press, 2015.
Cunningham, Frank. *Theories of Democracy: A Critical Introduction*. London: Routledge, 2002.
David, Lea. "Against Standardization of Memory." *Human Rights Quarterly* 39, no. 2 (2017): 296–318.
———. *The Past Can't Heal Us: The Dangers of Mandating Memory in the Name of Human Rights*. London: Cambridge University Press, 2020.
Greenfeld, Liah. *Nationalism: Five Roads to Modernity*. Cambridge, MA: Harvard University Press, 1992.
Gutman, Yifat. *Memory Activism: Reimagining the Past for the Future in Israel-Palestine*. Nashville, TN: Vanderbilt University Press, 2017.
"Ha'achim Shelanu" [Our Brothers]. *Ha'achim Shelanu*. Retrieved 13 December 2020 from https://ourbrothers.co.il/.
Handelman, Don. *Nationalism and the Israeli State: Bureaucratic Logic in Public Events*. Oxford: Berg Publishers, 2004.
Hermoni, Gal, and Udi Lebel. "Politicizing Memory: An Ethnographical Study of a Remembrance Ceremony." *Cultural Studies* 26, no. 4 (2012): 469–91.
Huyssen, Andreas. "Present Pasts: Media, Politics, Amnesia." *Public Culture* 12, no. (2000): 21–38.
———. "International Human Rights and the Politics of Memory: Limits and Challenges." *Criticism* 53, no. 4 (2011): 607–24.
Jelin, Elizabeth. *State Repression and the Labors of Memory*, trans. Judy Rein and Marcial Godoy-Anativa. Minneapolis: University of Minnesota Press, 2003.
Kaiser, Wolfram, and Anette Homlong Storeide. "International Organizations and Holocaust Remembrance: From Europe to the World." *International Journal of Cultural Policy* 24, no. 6 (2018): 798–810.
Kook, Rebecca. "Agents of Memory in the Post-witness Era: 'Memory in the Living Room' and Changing Forms of Holocaust Remembrance in Israel." *Memory Studies*, 30 September 2020. https://doi.org/10.1177/1750698020959804.

Lee, Philip. "Towards a Right to Memory." *Media Development* 57, no. 2 (2010): 3–10.
Lessa, Francesca. *Memory and Transitional Justice in Argentina and Uruguay: Against Impunity.* London: Palgrave Macmillan, 2013.
Levy, Daniel, and Natan Sznaider. *The Holocaust and Memory in the Global Age.* Philadelphia, PA: Temple University Press, 2006.
Margalit, Avishai. *The Ethics of Memory.* Cambridge, MA: Harvard University Press, 2002.
Meyers, Oren, Eyal Zandberg, and Motti Neiger. "Prime Time Commemoration: An Analysis of Television Broadcasts on Israel's Memorial Day for the Holocaust and the Heroism." *Journal of Communication* 59, no. 3 (2009): 456–80.
"Misaviv La'medoora" [Around the campfire]. *Misaviv La'medoora.* Retrieved 13 December 2020 from https://www.misavivla.com/blank.
Mizrachi, Nissim, and Hanna Herzog. "Participatory Destigmatization Strategies among Palestinian Citizens, Ethiopian Jews, and Mizrahi Jews in Israel." *Ethnic and Racial Studies* 35, no. 3 (2012): 418–35.
Nir, Shai, "Official or Privatized: From Yad Vashem to Zikaron Basalon, What Is Happening to the Way We Remember the Holocaust?" [In Hebrew.] *Davar Hayom,* 23 July 2017. Retrieved 4 September 2021 from https://www.davar1.co.il/64403//.
Ofer, Dalia. "The Strength of Remembrance: Commemorating the Holocaust During the First Decade of Israel." *Jewish Social Studies* 6, no. 2 (2000): 24–55.
Oppenheimer, Yochai. "The Holocaust: A Mizrahi Perspective." *Hebrew Studies* 51(2010): 303–28.
Plantin, Jean-Christophe, Carl Lagoze, Paul N. Edwards, and Christian Sandvig. "Infrastructure Studies Meet Platform Studies in the Age of Google and Facebook." *New Media & Society* 20, no. 1 (2010): 293–310.
Prusher, Ilene. "Building Communities of Kindness." *TIME.com,* 12 September 2014. Retrieved 13 May 2019 from https://time.com/collection-post/3270757/adi-altschuler-next-generation-leaders/.
Reading, Anna. "Identity, Memory and Cosmopolitanism: The Otherness of the Past and a Right to Memory?" *European Journal of Cultural Studies* 14, no.4 (2011): 379–94.
Recuber, Timothy. "The Presumption of Commemoration: Disasters, Digital Memory Banks, and Online Collective Memory." *American Behavioral Scientist* 56, no. 4 (2012): 531–49.
Ricoeur, Paul. *Figuring the Sacred: Religion, Narrative, and Imagination.* Minneapolis: Augsburg Fortress, 1995.
Shafir, Gershon, and Yoav Peled. *Being Israeli: The Dynamics of Multiple Citizenship.* Cambridge: Cambridge University Press, 2002.
Shimony, Batya. "On 'Holocaust Envy' in Mizrahi Literature." *Dapim: Studies on the Holocaust* 25, no. 1 (2011): 239–71.
"Sipour al Ha'derech" [Story on the Road]. *Sipour.* Retrieved 13 December 2020 from https://www.sipur.org.il/index.php.
Smith, Anthony D. "The Ethnic Sources of Nationalism." *Survival: Global Politics and Strategy* 35, no. 1(1993): 48–62.
Sorek, Tamir. *Palestinian Commemoration in Israel: Calendars, Monuments, and Martyrs.* Stanford, CA: Stanford University Press, 2015.
Steir-Livny, Liat. *Har Hazikaron Yizkor Bimkomi: HaZikaron HaHadash Shel HaShoah B'Tarbut HaPopularit B'Israel* [Let the Memorial Hill remember: Holocaust representation in Israeli popular culture]. [In Hebrew.] Tel Aviv: Resling Publishing, 2014.
Steir-Livny, Liat. "Remembrance in the Living Room [Zikaron b'Salon]: Grassroots Gatherings as New Forms of Holocaust Commemoration in Israel." *Holocaust Studies* 26, no. 2 (2020): 241–58.

Tirosh, Noam. "iNakba, Mobile Media and Society's Memory," *Mobile Media & Communication* 6, no. 3 (2018): 350–66.

Tirosh, Noam, and Yifat Gutman. "On Media, Memory and Laws: The Israeli 'Law Commemorating the Exile of Jews from Arab Countries and Iran' (2014) as a Case Study." *International Journal of Media & Cultural Politics* 15, no. 1 (2019): 49–67.

van Dijck, José. *The Culture of Connectivity: A Critical History of Social Media.* New York: Oxford University Press, 2013.

Viejo-Rose, Dacia. "Memorial Functions: Intent, Impact and the Right to Remember." *Memory Studies* 4, no. 4 (2011): 465–80.

Wang, Zheng. *Memory Politics, Identity and Conflict: Historical Memory as a Variable.* London: Palgrave Macmillan, 2017.

Young, James E. "When a Day Remembers: A Performative History of Yom Ha-shoah." In *The Texture of Memory; Holocaust Memorials and Meaning*, edited by James E. Young, 263–83. New Haven, CT: Yale University Press, 1993.

"Zikaron Basalon" [Memory in the living room]. *Zikaron Basalon*. Retrieved 7 December 2020 from https://www.zikaronbasalon.com/about.

"Zikaron B'salon: Iruay Hazikaron Hameyuchadim V'haintimim L'yom HaShoah" [Memory in the living room: Unique and intimate memorial events on Holocaust Memorial Day]. *MAKO*, 30 April 2019. Retrieved 13 May 2019 from https://www.mako.co.il/culture-books-and-theatre/Article-3f6db5adefd6a61026.html.

Chapter 6

USING AND ABUSING MEMORY LAWS IN SEARCH OF "HISTORICAL TRUTH"

The Case of the 2018 Amendments to the Polish Institute of National Remembrance Act

Aleksandra Gliszczyńska-Grabias and Grażyna Baranowska

Struggling over "Historical Truth"

"Historical truth" is an extremely complex phenomenon that historians and scholars of memory studies struggle to grasp and define. "Truth" can be demanded by both those who seek recognition of their community's suffering and the crimes committed against them and by those who deny such suffering and crimes.[1]

For this chapter, we propose two quotes from Václav Havel, a legendary Czech oppositionist, to frame our understanding of historical truth: "When a truth is not given complete freedom, freedom is not complete" and "The truth is not simply what you think it is. It is also the circumstances in which it is said, and to whom, why, and how it is said."[2] Although these words do not directly refer to the issue of legal governance of history, they actually touch its very essence. Truth and freedom remain in a close, inseparable relationship with each other and this relationship applies to the research and public discourse in search of historical truth. At the same time, truth is subject to so many conditions, dependencies, and variables that the context in which it is expressed or defined sometimes becomes a factor that shapes its very content and essence. Thus, it is even more important to secure the freedom to search for historical truth in all of its intricacies.

The legal concept of the "right to truth" originated in the field of international humanitarian law and essentially refers to the right of relatives to know the truth about the fates of missing persons (as will be more closely assessed in a later section of this chapter). The concept only recently started to penetrate other areas of legal research. Thus, with subsequent states adopting so-called memory laws, many began to appeal to "the right to historical truth."[3] Memory laws stem from the actions of authorities who claim to execute this right by declaring a legally defined, singular historical narrative that excludes contrary or divergent narratives, often under the threat of legal sanctions.[4]

Every community and its story—sometimes kept for centuries and often distorted to build the community's identity in the least painful way—has a natural tendency to portray itself in a positive way.[5] Of course, this tendency is also typical of individuals, but in the communal and collective dimension, it can become a socially dangerous phenomenon, positioned close to nationalism, messianism, and xenophobia. Obviously, these are not the attitudes that characterize entire uniform societies. However, the executive power of authorities with nationalistic and authoritarian inclinations gives their official policies regarding the past and how it should be addressed the ability to influence societies and become dominant social perspectives. And if not "dominant," then at least imposed by so many various instruments of power that their opponents begin to experience a chilling effect and try to avoid a direct confrontation with defenders of the "official truth" about the past. Meanwhile, those who do confront these defenders, even in academic research, must brace for related risks. Such is the situation in Poland, where scholars and prominent Holocaust experts—Professors Jan Grabowski and Barbara Engelking—were sued for the contents of an academic publication they edited.[6] Grabowski and Engelking were brought to court by the descendants of a person they had described in their text as co-responsible for denunciations of Jews hiding during the Holocaust.[7] The lawsuit was based on the civil code provisions on protection of personal rights and thus not directly on any of the memory laws. Nevertheless, there is no doubt that it has a very clear link with the recent trend of legal governance of history in Poland having a very tenuous connection with the search for historical truth.

This chapter speaks to two of the four ways memory rights are framed internationally, as identified in Anna Reading's chapter on memory rights in international law in this volume as "national memory" and "victim memory." We show that while the "right to truth" is provided to victims under international law, and can be thus interpreted in the light of "victim memory," in the discussion of amendments to the Institute of National Remembrance Act (INRA), it has been invoked to protect the narratives of national identity.

This chapter further situates the "right to memory" within the context of "right to truth" and "memory laws." It starts with a definition of "memory laws" and the circumstances in which they have been used in Central and Eastern Europe. It shows that in certain forms, they are clearly in violation of international human rights standards. The next section focuses on Poland, in particular the 2018 INRA amendments, in the context of the debate on historical narrative. We show the danger this provision poses, as well as argue why it should not be labeled only as "Holocaust Bill." In the following section, we analyze the INRA amendments in light of the right to historical truth, which is a concept that has been advanced to argue for the adoption of this act. However, we show that the concept was misunderstood and should not have been invoked in this context.

Governing the Past with the Use of the Law: Challenges and International Human Rights Law Standards

Law, including international human rights law, does not function in a vacuum. One of its roles is to respond to constant social changes, challenges, and needs. This includes the shifting perception of the past, current concerns about the geopolitical situation, and changes associated with the process of transition from a totalitarian or authoritarian system to a democratic one, along with the implementation of transitional justice instruments. Such are also the roles of memory laws. For the purpose of this chapter, we use the definition of memory laws proposed by Aleksandra Gliszczyńska-Grabias and Uladzislau Belavusau, who understand them as "various forms of legal measures governing history, including punitive measures against the denial of historical atrocities and bans prohibiting the use of totalitarian symbols of the past."[8] Our broad notion of memory laws also covers legal acts recognizing and commemorating historical events and figures, including laws establishing state holidays, commemorations and dates of mourning, street (re-)naming and monument installations in honor of historical figures, status and access to historical archives, as well as regulations regarding museums and school curricula on historical subjects.[9] At the same time, it should be noted that the typology of memory laws varies. For example, Eric Heinze uses the concept of "laws affecting historical memory" and defines them as norms that give preference, or expressive importance, to narratives about the past while at the same time directly restricting specific rights and freedoms of individuals.[10]

The concept of memory laws emerged in the Western European context almost three decades ago as a specific phenomenon in criminal law, designed to counteract negationism, specifically Holocaust denial.[11] However, over time, this legislation expanded to include additional types of negation, such as the Turkish denial of the Armenian genocide and the Tutsi genocide in Rwanda. It has also transcended criminal legislation to acquire constitutional significance, framed as mnemonic constitutionalism. This is a phenomenon observed primarily in Central and Eastern Europe (hereafter CEE), which sought ways to consolidate its historical identity after the communist period and to highlight its historical suffering, which for decades had remained beyond a Western European focus.[12] Some states even use memory laws to advance their politics of mnemonical security, understood as securing the very identity of a state.[13] This is certainly the case with Ukraine, whose legal management of memory inextricably links it with Russia or, rather, with the defense against Russia's aggressive historical propaganda on "Great Patriotic War" and the exclusively heroic deeds of the Soviet Army that in February 2022 led to the brutal military aggression and war against Ukraine. At the same time, such mnemonical security orientation stands in contrast to the European ideals of a reflective and self-critical relationship with the past.

However, what remains extremely problematic is that these specific forms of imposing a legal "duty to remember," as defined by Lea David in this volume, very often violate international human rights protection standards. The matter was raised by the UN Human Rights Committee (hereafter the Committee), among others, which addressed this problem in its General Comment No. 34 on freedoms of opinion and expression, enshrined in Article 19 of the International Covenant on Civil and Political Rights. The General Comment states that: "Laws that penalize the expression of opinions about historical facts are incompatible with the obligations that the Covenant imposes on States parties in relation to the respect for freedom of opinion and expression. The Covenant does not permit general prohibition of expressions of an erroneous opinion or an incorrect interpretation of past events."[14] The Committee referred here mostly to the controversies of penalizing negationism and Holocaust denial, as such cases also appeared before the Committee and were considered to be some of the most challenging among those that relate to freedom of speech.[15] The EU law, as another example, also applies to these phenomena with the EU Council Framework Decision 2008/913/JHA of 28 November 2008 on combating certain forms and expressions of racism and xenophobia by means of criminal law also applies to these phenomena.[16] This legislation obliges EU member states to take the measures necessary to ensure that publicly condoning, denying, or grossly trivializing crimes of genocide, crimes against humanity, and war crimes (as defined in particular and listed in the Framework Decision on international treaties) is punishable if such acts are directed against a group of persons or a member of such a group defined by reference to race, color, religion, descent, or national or ethnic origin when the conduct is carried out in a manner likely to incite violence or hatred against such a group or a member of such a group.

The risks for freedom of expression and academic research brought by memory laws are analyzed in the jurisprudence of the European Court of Human Rights (ECtHR) in Strasbourg. There, we can observe a very interesting legal struggle to prevent the courtroom of the international tribunal from becoming a forum for judging history. As argued by the ECtHR: "The Court considers that it is an integral part of freedom of expression to seek historical truth and it is not the Court's role to arbitrate the underlying historical issues, which are part of a continuing debate between historians that shapes opinion as to the events which took place and their interpretation."[17] However, the ECtHR itself is not always faithful to such an assumption. The institution already embarked on "the search for historical truth" several times, such as when it analyzed the memory of communist crimes in Hungary in a case concerning the public display of the red star symbol, when comparing Holocaust and Armenian genocide denials, and when evaluating the status of the Katyń massacre as a war crime.[18]

Moreover, the ECtHR evidently makes an exception in its general unwillingness to enter into debates over history for one type of memory—the European meta-memory of the Holocaust.[19] Thus, in the case law of the ECtHR, the memory of the Holocaust is strictly protected. However, the ECtHR offers this protection in a specific way.[20] In the above-mentioned cases, the ECtHR addressed historical complexities by examining the risk of re-establishing an authoritarian regime or whether a criminal ideology is promoted. At the same time, in cases concerning restrictions on the freedom of expression for any neo-Nazi or neo-fascist movement, its analysis of facts is minimal. Moreover, the ECtHR does not distinguish subtly between certain behaviors, as if a priori considering any such activity to violate the European Convention on Human Rights, and the ECtHR is usually willing to find the complaints by those who promote pro-Nazi activities or contents manifestly inadmissible. Insulting the memory of Holocaust victims is treated by the ECtHR in a similar way. Even though the ECtHR considers freedom of expression to be one of the most fundamental and broadly interpreted freedoms, in cases of even the most well-intentioned references to the Holocaust—for instance, made by authors of animal rights campaigns or anti-abortion activists—it finds such comparisons to be inadmissible abuses of the Holocaust victims' memory. Likewise, the ECtHR considers comparing someone's contemporary activities to Nazi practices unacceptable, due to the specific odium involved in calling someone a "Nazi." Also, the ECtHR has never granted the protection of free speech to any Holocaust denier complaining about being punished at national level for denying the Holocaust.

Compliance with international human rights protection, in particular regarding excessive interference with freedom of expression, also appears with regard to national memory laws. However, there appears to be an additional political factor very often associated with the nationalist historical narrative of a given government. These dilemmas are very well illustrated by the example of the Polish INRA, whose connections with "right to truth," "right to historical truth," and the category of "memory laws" will be analyzed later in this chapter.

Searching for Historical Truth in Poland: Defective Codes of Memory in the Context of the 2018 Amendments to INRA

Defective Codes of Memory is the title of a book published by the Polish Ministry of Foreign Affairs in 2015.[21] The book is an academic publication with an extensive range of contributions from renowned scholars who try to answer the subtitle's question of "How the memory of international crimes is distorted in public discourse?" The work analyzes individual elements of memory distortion substantively and rigorously. It sharply focuses on the term "Polish concentration camps" or "Polish death camps," which appear mostly in foreign media, explaining why it is of crucial importance to avoid these kinds of misleading descriptions. However, concurrent with this publication, the Law and Justice Party (PiS) in Poland won parliamentary elections and announced the end of the "pedagogy of shame" both in international relations and in the internal national narrative about the past.[22] It soon became clear that "Polish historical truth" would be protected by criminal law rather than by scholarly arguments and diplomatic efforts.

Similar legislative initiatives had already appeared before. These were regarded as active opposition to the truth about Polish involvement in World War II crimes against minorities and forbade the dissemination of this truth abroad. As a result, in 2006 a new amendment to the Polish Penal Code appeared. Article 132a, stated that "Whoever publicly accuses the Polish Nation of participation in, organization of, or responsibility for Communist or Nazi crimes, is punishable by imprisonment for up to three years."[23] The law made not only Polish citizens criminally liable for defamation but every individual, regardless of the laws in force at the place where the alleged offense was committed. The authors of this legal change, which was often called *Lex Gross*,[24] argued that prosecuting the statements enumerated in Article 132a was necessary because: "in the international arena, we very often witness untruthful accusations against the Polish Nation and citizens for their alleged help or collaboration with criminal Nazi and communist regimes. The proposed change will equip the Institute of National Remembrance with new tools to improve and accelerate the prosecution of such crimes and defend the historical truth."[25] However, the Constitutional Tribunal—at that time still independently functioning in Poland—ruled on procedural grounds that this attempt to decree history with the aid of law was unconstitutional.[26]

The same idea returned a decade later, and on the eve of the 2018 International Holocaust Remembrance Day, the amendment to INRA was passed instantly, in violation of the rules of proper legislation and constitutional and international free speech protection standards.[27] The legal mechanisms of introducing this regulation into the Polish legal system have been already widely described.[28] Thus, only three most important aspects of the amendment should be highlighted here:

1. The January 2018 amendment to INRA stipulated that "Anyone who publicly and falsely attributes responsibility or co-responsibility to the Polish nation or the Polish State for the crimes committed by the German Third Reich . . . or for any other crimes that are crimes against peace, crimes against humanity, or war crimes, or who otherwise glaringly trivializes the responsibility of their actual perpetrators, shall be subject to a fine or the penalty of imprisonment of up to three years. The sentence shall be made public";

2. President Andrzej Duda signed the law, ignoring all protests and arguments proving the amendment was unconstitutional and contrary to international law standards. At the same time, President Duda filed a motion to the politically captured Constitutional Tribunal for an ex post constitutional review of the law. As a consequence of political interventions into the composition of the Tribunal, one could predict that the result of the Tribunal's control will be in full conformity with the political will and need;[29]

3. As a result of international pressure, in June 2018, another amendment to INRA was introduced, nullifying the criminal law sanctions. In its present form, the law says that the relevant provisions of the Civil Code, concerning the protection of personal rights, shall apply to the protection of the good name of the Republic of Poland and the Polish nation.[30]

The amendment to INRA has been labeled a Holocaust Bill, since in the opinion of most commentators its prime aim was to counteract the dissemination of views and academic research revealing the difficult truth about the behavior of large parts of Polish society toward persecuted Jews during the Holocaust. In response to such claims, the authors of the new law tried to legitimize the introduced penalization by binding it to the regulations on penalizing Holocaust denial. However, we must clarify the fundamental difference between these two models of legal governance of history: while the penalization of Holocaust denial remains closely linked to preventing and combating anti-Semitism, the amendment to the INRA case places the protection of the state's and nation's good name at the fore. The good name, understood as a protected "personal right," remains highly questionable and poses a threat of punishment for the very process of seeking historical truth and, sometimes, historical justice.[31] Further, laws against Holocaust denial normally penalize statements of demonstrable untruth while the INRA law penalized opinions and assessments difficult to verify or falsify.

The January 2018 INRA amendment sparked an enormous international reaction and outcry. In this "war over memory" whose participants were Polish government *versus* Israel and the United States, who very openly opposed this form of restricting the freedom of expression, the most interesting element was the Polish-Israeli governmental declaration signed by Prime Ministers Netanyahu and Morawiecki only a few hours after the June amendment to INRA.[32] There is no doubt that the declaration had a purely political meaning, which makes it difficult to see and acknowledge true historical truth-seeking in it. The declaration is a puzzling mixture of accurate statements and deeply disturbing ones. It says that both sides "have always agreed that the term 'Polish concentration/death camps' is blatantly erroneous," which is an obvious and rightful claim.[33] At the same time, the declaration states:

> We acknowledge and condemn every single case of cruelty against Jews perpetrated by Poles during World War II. We reject the actions aimed at blaming Poland or the Polish nation as a whole for the atrocities committed by the Nazis and their collaborators of different nations. Both governments vehemently condemn all forms of anti-Semitism. Both governments also express their rejection of anti-Polonism.[34]

Thus, the crimes committed by Poles against their Jewish compatriots during World War II are evidently downplayed in the document.[35] The declaration also equates anti-Semitism, whose history is the history of the "oldest hatred," as Robert Wistrich called it, with a hardly discernible anti-Polonism (a concept used often in the xenophobic propaganda and smacking of paranoia).[36] However, the most bizarre element of the declaration is a statement that the governments of both states "support free and open historical expression and research on all aspects of the Holocaust."[37] It seems extremely difficult to reconcile the Polish government's declaration of commitment to the freedom of speech and academic research in a situation when just a few months earlier it had intended to punish such research with imprisonment of up to three years. Yehuda Bauer, a world-class Holocaust scholar, denounced the declaration as not only factually erroneous but also a betrayal of the genocide victims' memory, motivated by mundane present-day political considerations.[38] Abrupt reactions also appeared in the nationalist and right-wing public discourses in Poland. The reactions included accusations appearing in social media that the Polish government officially accepted "Jewish hegemony," understood as imposing decisions on the Polish sovereign state by "the Jews." However, all of these expressions of unease were silenced over time.

The INRA's amendment has remained practically a dead legal regulation that serves to produce a chilling effect, warning Poles against engaging in difficult debates about the past. This only confirms that the adoption of this memory law was strictly political and had nothing to do with the search for historical truth.

The example of the way INRA was amended should serve as a warning and illustration for what can happen when nationalistic political forces decide to treat the law instrumentally, misuse it for political purposes, create a dangerous legal precedent, and trigger a chilling effect. While the chilling effect will probably not affect those who are privileged enough to present their scientific research and conclusions in international academic forums, it will influence those who teach the hard truth about the history of difficult Polish-Jewish relations in elementary schools or who would like to address the issue in the local press.

Amendments to INRA in Light of the Right to Historical Truth

The authors of the legislative initiatives that amended INRA in 2018 justified the need for the amendments through appeals to "the right to historical truth," which they defined as counteracting the falsification of history and the public propagation of lies concerning the past.[39] The justifications included lengthy explanations of Ukrainian memory politics and memory laws, as well as EU Council Framework Decisions, relevant judgments of the ECtHR, legal discussions concerning the states' practice with regard to regulating memory politics—including by criminal law. However, in effect, the concept of the right to historical truth remains irrelevant for the INRA amendments and was misunderstood by those referring to it in the context of the Polish law.[40]

The "right to historical truth" is closely linked to the "right to truth." However, the two differ significantly, and only the former has a strong legal basis.[41] The "right to truth" relates to the obligation of a state to provide information about the circumstances surrounding serious violations of human rights. As mentioned above, it originated in the rights of families of missing persons to know the fates of their relatives. While it has gradually expanded to include other human rights violations,[42] only families of forcibly disappeared persons are provided the "right to truth" in a universal treaty.[43] In contrast, the "right to historical truth" is not limited to victims of human rights violations, but is also due to society, people or nations. However, as with the "right to truth," it concerns the obligation of a state to provide certain information about historical facts. No international treaty contains the "right to historical truth," but it has been addressed in UN documents and case law. What follows is a brief description of how the "right to historical truth" is to be understood and how to situate INRA amendments against this background.

In 2007, the UN Office of the High Commission of Human Rights published a "set of principles to combat impunity" (hereafter: set of principles), which inter alia dealt with the right to truth. It distinguished between "the victims' right to know the truth" (Principle 4) and the collective peoples' "right to know the truth about past events" (Principle 2 and 3).[44] The first, individual dimension of the right to truth is outside the scope of the INRA amendments and, consequently, of this chapter. The "historical truth" invoked in the INRA amendments touches upon the collective dimension of the right to truth. The set of principles approaches this dimension from two perspectives: as a right (of victims) (Principle 2) and as a duty (of states) (Principle 3).

It begins by stating: "Every people has the inalienable right to know the truth" about past heinous crimes, their circumstances, and their reasons (Principle 2). Consequently, the right relates not to all historical events, but only to those that can be described as "heinous crimes." While the set of principles does not explicitly specify which people are to benefit from this right, it appears to concern all those that were somehow connected to the crimes: societies where the victims and perpetrators of the crimes came from, people who lived on the territories where the crimes occurred, as well as those who were involved or affected in any other way. This clearly concerns the substance of the INRA amendments, as they concerned crimes committed on the territory of Poland, in which citizens of Poland were both victims and perpetrators. However, the right as stipulated in Principle 2 relates to knowing the truth about past events and not criminalizing statements about the past. The next principle tackles the duty to preserve memory (Principle 3) and relates to a "people's knowledge of the history of its oppression." In this context the state is obliged to take appropriate measures to "preserve archives and other evidence concerning violations of human rights and humanitarian law," as well as to "facilitate knowledge of those violations." The aim of such actions is to preserve the collective memory from extinction and to guard "against the development of revisionist and negationist arguments."[45] Thus, the set of principles addresses the falsification of history and propagation of lies concerning history, which were mentioned as the justifications for the INRA amendments. However, according to the UN document, states should address such endeavors with measures to preserve memory. While criminal sanctions for certain statements about the past are not violating the principles, it is clear that they are not included in what the set of principles understands as the right to truth in its collective dimension.

Individual and collective dimensions of the right to truth have also been recognized by international courts.[46] The Inter-American human rights system was crucial in bringing the concept of the "right to truth" to reality, inferring it from the right of access to justice.[47] The ECtHR, which sets European standards that Polish authorities have to comply with, has been less vocal about the right to truth than its US counterpart. The ECtHR tackled it for the first time in a 2011 judgment concerning the failure of Romania to investigate the circumstances of the massacres of anti-government protestors in 1989, stating that the victims, their families, and their dependents have the right "to know the truth."[48] Subsequently, a number of judgments concerning extraordinary rendition cases in the ECtHR in 2012 and 2014 mentioned that the "general public . . . had the right to know what had happened,"[49] thereby recognizing the collective dimension of the right to truth. However, none of those cases concerned historical debate. In cases dealing with discussions about the past, the ECtHR did not invoke the "right to truth," but instead recognized that seeking "historical truth" is an "integral part of freedom of expression."[50] When dealing with cases concerning the criminalization of denying crimes, such as the Holocaust, the ECtHR did not invoke the right to truth or historical truth, but deliberated on the right to freedom of expression. Thus, for the ECtHR, the right to truth cannot be invoked to criminalize certain statements about the past, as has been introduced by the 2018 INRA amendments.[51]

The right to truth and the right to historical truth as understood in international law are not exactly the same as the "right to memory." At the heart of the right to truth lies the right of victims of human rights abuses to learn what happened; it does not require them, or anyone else, the right to memorialize or commemorate. However, there is clearly an important overlap, as revealing the truth to individuals or the society as a whole (collective dimension of the right to truth) will lead a narrative of the past to be present in the public discourse. Furthermore, the "right to truth" has been raised to justify the need for memorialization. This, however, should always be seen through the lens of the wishes of the victims. The division between the "right to historical truth" and "right to memory" appears to be less clear-cut, as both appeal to narrative(s) about the past.

From the right to historical truth as understood in international human rights law derives the right of society to know the factual truth about past crimes. It does not relate to prohibiting denial of certain crimes by criminal law and neither does the "right to memory," as explored in this volume. This fact is of crucial importance as the current Polish authorities are not the only ones using criminal law to prohibit statements that contradict what is considered by a given government to be the rightful "historical truth." Other states have adopted similar laws. The INRA amendments in particular have been compared with laws prohibiting the denigration of the Turkish nation and a provision of the Russian criminal code that criminalizes dissemination of knowingly false information on the activities of the Soviet Army during World War II.[52]

In Turkey, there is not one law relating to a particular historical event, instead there are a number of different laws that have been used for many decades to prosecute persons who made statements about the past, which were contravening the official memory politics of the state authorities, including the Armenian genocide and more recent human rights violations.[53] The above-mentioned Russian law, for another example, criminalizes the dissemination of knowingly false information on the activities of the Soviet Army during World War II, in this way trying to impose, as claimed by Nikolay Koposov, an interpretation of the war focused on the Soviet Union's decisive role in the victory over fascism. This perspective on World War II is one of the main factors leading Eastern Europe to become an important center for legislative activity concerning the past, including Polish initiatives.[54]

Conclusion

While the concept of historical truth, as well as the right to historical truth, is not clearly defined, in recent years it has been used to substantiate the necessity to introduce criminal law restrictions to the freedom of expression, such as the 2018 INRA amendments in Poland. As we have tried to argue, and as interpreted by various UN bodies and in international case law, the right to historical truth should be understood as a right to information about historical events and not to restrict certain information or opinions.[55] The "right to memory" has not been invoked in this context, but it also does not seek to limit information, research, or speech.

According to Václav Havel, "the circumstances in which [truth is] said, and to whom, why, and how it is said" are inherent elements of truth. This is even more relevant for historical truth, as it appears to be impossible to agree on a singular "truth" through historical discourse.[56] At the same time, an official version of historical truth promoted by state authorities can have a significant effect on how certain events are remembered, as well as whether they should or should not be remembered. The exclusion of selected facts from the social memory, for example, crimes committed by members of one's own ethnicity against another ethnic group, can be amplified by restrictions on freedom of speech. The INRA amendments most likely have a chilling effect on statements concerning a particular part of Polish history, the involvement of Poles in the crimes committed against the Jews during the Holocaust.

Lastly, the 2018 INRA amendments were not adopted in order to protect victims, but to protect the Polish nation's "good name." As such, they are, as framed by Eric Heinze: "self-exculpatory" memory laws: regulations that are adopted to punish or discipline those who accuse a particular state of having committed human rights abuses.[57] The above-mentioned memory laws in

Turkey and Russia also fit this category. Holocaust denial bans, on the other hand, can be considered "self-inculpatory" laws that apply when speakers are punished for denying the genocide officially acknowledged by a given state (and most often, also international law). While these bans also limit historical discussions, they are being introduced with the aim to instill a critical attitude toward past state conduct and counteract hatred still targeting the members of a group subjected to genocide or other gross crimes in the past. This was clearly not the case with the 2018 INRA amendments. If anything, the amendments were introduced to promote a certain version of Polish heroic and noble history, and silence its critics.

The phenomenon of the "proliferation of the human rights memorialization agenda," to use Lea David's phrase from this volume, includes all legal concepts invoked in this chapter. Memory laws, the right to truth, and the right to historical truth emerged within the human rights environment and have since been invoked as legal tools for securing the particular aspects of the right to memory. At the same time, the process of abusing them with the intention to distort social perception of the past, former atrocities, and the question of guilt and responsibility has been observed in many legislations, including those of authoritarian and populist tendencies. For such governments, the right to truth is reserved almost exclusively for *their* truth, defined by the imperative of heroism and victimhood. Such attempts are inconsistent with one of the core conclusions arising from the analysis of relevant human rights law standards, which has been expressed by the ECtHR in its case law discussions about the past. The ECtHR does not invoke the "right to truth" but instead recognizes that seeking "historical truth" is an integral part of freedom of expression. This historical truth-seeking process should not be disturbed by law or court rulings; unfortunately, this has started to become common practice in many parts of CEE.

Aleksandra Gliszczyńska-Grabias is Assistant Professor at the Institute of Law Studies,Polish Academy of Sciences. Expert in anti-discrimination law, freedom of speech and memory laws, she also the co-editor and co-author of *Constitutionalism under Stress* (Oxford University Press, 2020) and *Law and Memory: Towards Legal Governance of History* (Columbia University Press, 2017). She was a Bohdan Winiarski Fellow (University of Cambridge), Yale University Initiative for the Study of Antisemitism Fellow, and Braudel Fellow (European University Institute). Aleksandra is the Principal Investigator for the international research consortiums "Memory Laws in European and Comparative Perspective" (2016–19) and "The Challenge of Populist Memory Politics for Europe: Towards Effective Responses to Militant Legislation on the Past" (2021–24).

Grażyna Baranowska is pursuing a Marie Skłodowska-Curie Action grant on missing migrants at the Hertie School in Berlin. She is an Assistant Professor at the Institute of Law Studies, Polish Academy of Sciences, where she works with the international research consortium "The Challenge of Populist Memory Politics for Europe: Towards Effective Responses to Militant Legislation on the Past" (2021–24). Since August 2022, she has been a member of the UN Working Group on Enforced and Involuntary Disappearances. Her book titled *Right of Families of Disappeared Persons* was published by Intersentia in 2021.

Notes

The study was funded by the Volkswagen Foundation MEMOCRACY project.

1. Recent years have brought an enormous rise in memory studies academic literature. Some key works include Baer and Sznaider, *Memory and Forgetting*; Chaionglou et al., *Injustice, Memory and Faith*; Sierp, *History, Memory and Transeuropean Identity*; Wawrzyniak and Pakier, *Memory and Change in Europe*; and Malcontent, *Facing the Past*.
2. Havel, *Disturbing the Peace*.
3. Some of the most significant recent academic works on memory laws include: Fronza, *Memory and Punishment*; Koposov, *Memory Laws, Memory Wars*; Belavusau and Gliszczyńska-Grabias, *Law and Memory*; and Löytömäki, *Law and Politics of Memory*.
4. See examples from Turkey and Ukraine in the last section of the chapter.
5. For interesting remarks concerning the role of narrative in the construction of social theory and perception of the past, see Patterson and Monroe, "Narrative in Political Science."
6. "Warsaw Court Launches 'Night without an End' Lawsuit."
7. Glanville, "'A Gift for Holocaust Deniers.'"
8. Belavusau and Gliszczyńska-Grabias, "Mnemonic Constitutionalism," 3.
9. Belavusau and Gliszczyńska-Grabias, "Mnemonic Constitutionalism," 3.
10. Heinze, "Theorizing Law and Historical Memory," 13.
11. Czech law can serve as an example here. The Law against Support and Dissemination of Movements Oppressing Human Rights and Freedoms (2001), article 405, stipulates that: "Anyone who publicly denies, disputes, approves or attempts to justify a Nazi, Communist or other genocide or Nazi, Communist or other crimes against humanity or war crimes or crimes against peace will be punished by imprisonment for six months to three years," quoted in Naamat, Osin, and Porat, *Legislating for Equality*, 118.
12. For more on particular aspects of governing the past with the use of law in CEE, see Fedor et al., *War and Memory*; Khapaeva, "Triumphant Memory of the Perpetrators"; and Mälksoo, "Kononov v. Latvia as an Ontological Security Struggle."
13. The term has been coined and promoted in scholarly circles mostly by Mälksoo. See Mälksoo, "'Memory Must Be Defended.'"
14. "General Comment No. 34," CCPR/C/GC/34, para 49.
15. See Faurisson, "Communication No. 550/93," *Faurisson v. France*.
16. "Council Framework Decision 2008/913/JHA," OJ L 328, 6.12.2008, 55–58.

17. ECtHR *Chauvy and Others v. France* (2004).
18. In 2012, the ECtHR handed down a judgment on the complaint of the families of the victims of the Katyń massacre of Polish Army officers by the Soviets, against the Russian authorities. The ECtHR ruled that Russia violated Art. 3 of the European Convention on Human Rights, by "inhuman and degrading treatment" toward some relatives of the victims by concealing documents from the investigation, failing to indicate the place of burial of the murdered officers, and denying the historical truth about the Katyń massacre. The judges also found that Russia violated Art. 38 of the Convention, refusing to present to the Court a document on the conclusion of the Russian investigation into the Katyń massacre (closed in 2004 due to the "death of the perpetrators"). However, with regard to Art. 2 of the Convention (right to life), which was of crucial importance for the Poles, the judges decided that the assessment of the reliability of the Russian investigation exceeded the jurisdiction of the ECtHR due to the fact that the main part of the investigation initiated in 1990 took place before the adoption of the Convention by Russia in 1998. See the judgment in ECtHR *Janowiec and Others v. Russia* (2013).
19. Gliszczyńska-Grabias, Aleksandra. "'Never Again' as a Cornerstone of the Strasbourg System."
20. For an analysis of the specific attitude of the ECtHR toward different regimes, see Gliszczyńska-Grabias, "Jurisprudence of the European Court."
21. Nowak-Far and Zamecki, *Defective Codes of Memory*.
22. For more on the phenomenon of the "pedagogy of shame" repeatedly referred to by members of PiS and the government, see Majmurek, "Pedagogika wstydu."
23. *1592* (2006) *Polish Journal of Laws*. For a comprehensive analysis of the provision, see Kamiński, "Kontrowersje prawne."
24. In 2000, Jan Tomasz Gross published a groundbreaking book in which he described a pogrom carried out by Poles in the small town of Jedwabne, against more than three hundred of their Jewish neighbors. The book caused a wave of hateful, negationist reactions, denying historical findings. The law introduced in 2006 was considered to be another manifestation of rejecting the claims by Gross. See Gross, *Neighbors*.
25. Print no. 334.
26. Judgment of the Constitutional Tribunal of Poland, 19 September 2008.
27. Print no. 806: The Government Bill to Amend the Act on the Institute of National Remembrance (29 August 2016). Retrieved 15 April 2022 from https://www.sejm.gov.pl/sejm8.nsf/PrzebiegProc.xsp?nr=806.
28. See Gliszczyńska-Grabias, "Deployments of Memory."
29. Judgment of the Constitutional Tribunal of Poland, 17 January 2019. The Tribunal decided that the wording "Ukrainian nationalists" was in conflict with one of the principles deriving from Article 2 of the Constitution, namely, the principle of specificity of legal provisions, and Article 42.1, concerning the principles of restricting rights and freedoms. Simultaneously, it discontinued proceedings initiated by President Duda in the remaining scope, that is, regarding compliance with Article 55a of INRA, as it had been removed by the June 2018 amendment to INRA.
30. "Ustawa o zmianie ustawy o Instytucie Pamięci Narodowej" [The law amending the Act on the Institute of National Remembrance].
31. See Gliszczyńska-Grabias and Jabłoński, "Is One Offended Pole Enough."
32. The official text of the Declaration of 27 June 2018 is available at https://www.gov.pl/web/premier/joint-declaration-of-prime-ministers-of-the-state-of-israel-and-the-republic-of-poland
33. 27 June 2018 Declaration.

34. 27 June 2018 Declaration.
35. In response to the Declaration, Yad Vashem stressed: "The statement contains highly problematic wording that contradicts existing and accepted historical knowledge in this field." "Yad Vashem historians respond."
36. Wistrich, *Antisemitism*.
37. Wistrich, *Antisemitism*.
38. As quoted in Arhen, "Israeli-Polish Holocaust Law Agreement?"
39. The 2018 INRA amendments originated in two legislative initiatives. First, a parliamentary project was submitted to the Sejm in July 2016 and concerned "crimes committed by Ukrainian nationalists and Ukrainian formations collaborating with the Third Reich." Second, a governmental project submitted to the Sejm in August 2016 regarding the "effective protection of the good name of Poland" aimed at eliminating the use of the term "Polish concentration camps" as well as the care for war graves and cemeteries. July 2016 Project: 'Print 771,' https://www.sejm.gov.pl/Sejm8.nsf/druk.xsp?nr=771; August 2016 project 'Print 806', https://www.sejm.gov.pl/Sejm8.nsf/druk.xsp?nr=806.
40. The "right to historical truth" was included in the justification to the INRA amendments (see above), as well as in comments of leading politicians, for example see prime ministers' statements ("Amendment to the Act," 27 June 2018), and by the Institute for National Remembrance.
41. Despite its increasing recognition, the concept of the "right to truth" raises questions as to its scope and implementation as well as its existence as a free-standing right, see inter alia, Méndez and Bariffi, "Right to Truth." See also Baranowska and Gliszczyńska-Grabias, "'Right to Truth' and Memory Laws."
42. Naqvi, "Right to Truth in International Law."
43. Article 24, paragraph 2 of "The International Convention for the Protection of All Persons from Enforced Disappearance."
44. Orentlicher, "Updated Set of Principles."
45. Orentlicher, "Updated Set of Principles."
46. *Inter-American Court of Human Rights, Bámaca-Velásquez v. Guatemala*, Judgment of February 22, 2002 (Reparations and Costs), para. 197. See also comments on the collective dimension of the right to truth in the separate opinion of Judge Cançado Trindade, separate concurring opinion of Judge Salgado Pesantes, and separate concurring opinion of Judge García Ramírez.
47. Ferrer Mac-Gregor, "Right to Truth as an Autonomous Right"; and Naftali, "'Right to Truth' in International Law."
48. ECtHR *Association '21 December 1989' v. Romania* (2011).
49. ECtHR *El-Masri v. Macedonia* (2021); ECtHR *Al-Nashiri v. Poland* (2014); and ECtHR *Abu Zubaydah v. Poland* (2015).
50. See, for example, ECtHR *Monnat v. Switzerland* (2006); ECtHR *Chauvy and Others v. France* (2004); and ECtHR *Fatullayev v. Azerbaijan* (2010).
51. The INRA amendments raise serious doubts as to their comprehensiveness with ECtHR standards. See Gliszczyńska-Grabias, Baranowska, and Wójcik, "Law-Secured Narratives of the Past."
52. See, for example, Belavusau and Wójcik, "Polish Memory Law."
53. Baranowska, "Penalizing Statements about the Past in Turkey."
54. Koposov, *Memory Laws, Memory Wars*.
55. *El-Masri v. Macedonia* (2021).
56. Maier "Doing History, Doing Justice."
57. Heinze, "Should Governments Butt Out of History?"

Bibliography

Arhen, Raphael. "Does the Israeli-Polish Holocaust Law Agreement Defend Truth or Betray History?" *The Times of Israel*, 4 July 2018. Retrieved 27 July 2022 from https://www.timesofisrael.com/does-the-israeli-polish-holocaust-law-agreement-defend-truth-or-betray-history/.

Baer, Alejandro, and Natan Sznaider. *Memory and Forgetting in the Post-Holocaust Era: The Ethics of Never Again*. London: Routledge, 2017.

Baranowska, Grażyna. "Penalizing Statements about the Past in Turkey." In *Responsibility for Negation of International Crimes*, ed. Patrycja Grzebyk, 249–58. Warsaw: Institute of Justice, 2020.

Baranowska, Grażyna, and Aleksandra Gliszczyńska-Grabias. "'Right to Truth' and Memory Laws: General Rules and Practical Implications." *Polish Yearbook of Political Science* 47, no. 1 (2018): 97–109.

Belavusau, Uladzislau, and Aleksandra Gliszczyńska-Grabias. *Law and Memory: Towards Legal Governance of History*. Cambridge: Cambridge University Press, 2017.

———. "Mnemonic Constitutionalism in Central and Eastern Europe." *European Papers* 5, no. 3 (2020): 1231–46.

Belavusau, Uladzislau, and Anna Wójcik. "Polish Memory Law: When History Becomes a Source of Mistrust." *New Eastern Europe*. Retrieved 24 December 2020 from http://neweasterneurope.eu/2018/02/19/polish-memory-law-history-becomes-source-mistrust/.

Chaionglou, Kalliopi, Barry Collins, Michael Phillips, and John Strawson. *Injustice, Memory and Faith in Human Rights*. London: Routledge, 2018.

Fedor, Julie, Markku Kangaspuro, Jussi Lassila, and Tatiana Zhurzhenko, eds. *War and Memory in Russia, Ukraine and Belarus*. London: Palgrave Macmillan, 2017.

Ferrer Mac-Gregor, Eduardo. "The Right to Truth as an Autonomous Right under the Inter-American Human Rights System." *Mexican Law Review* 9, no. 1 (2016): 121–39.

Fronza, Emanuela. *Memory and Punishment: Historical Denialism, Free Speech and the Limits of Criminal Law*. The Hague: TMC Asser Press / Berlin: Springer, 2018.

Glanville, Jo. "'A Gift for Holocaust Deniers': How Polish Libel Ruling Will Hit Historians." *The Guardian*, 29 October 2019. Retrieved 5 September 2022 from https://www.thefirstnews.com/article/warsaw-court-launches-night-without-an-end-lawsuit-8381.

Gliszczyńska-Grabias, Aleksandra. "'Never Again' as a Cornerstone of the Strasbourg System: The Reminiscence of the Holocaust in the Jurisprudence of the European Court of Human Rights." In *The European Court of Human Rights: Current Challenges in Historical and Comparative Perspective*, edited by Helmut Ast and Esra Demir, 200–20. Cheltenham: Edward Elgar, 2021.

———. "Deployments of Memory with the Tools of Law—the Case of Poland." *Review of Central and East European Law* 44 (2019): 464–92.

———. "The Jurisprudence of the European Court of Human Rights in the Area of Europe's Totalitarian Past—Selected Examples." In *Responsibility for Negation of International Crimes*, edited by Patrycja Grzebyk, 85–92. Warsaw: Institute of Justice, 2020.

Gliszczyńska-Grabias, Aleksandra, Grażyna Baranowska, and Anna Wójcik, "Law-Secured Narratives of the Past in Poland in Light of International Human Rights Law Standards." *Polish Yearbook of International Law* (2018): 67–72.

Gliszczyńska-Grabias, Aleksandra, and Michał Jabłoński, "Is One Offended Pole Enough to Take Critics of Official Historical Narratives to Court?" *Verfassungsblog*, 12 October 2019. Retrieved 24 December 2020 from https://verfassungsblog.de/is-one-offended-pole-enough-to-take-critics-of-official-historical-narratives-to-court/.

Gross, Jan Tomasz. *Neighbors: The Destruction of the Jewish Community in Jedwabne, Poland.* Princeton, NJ: Princeton University Press, 2001.

Havel, Václav. *Disturbing the Peace: A Conversation with Karel Huizdala.* New York: Vintage, 1991.

Heinze, Eric. "Theorizing Law and Historical Memory: Denialism and the Pre-Conditions for Human Rights." *Journal of Comparative Law* 13, no. 1 (2018): 43–60.

———. "Should Governments Butt Out of History?" *Free Speech Debate*, 12 March 2019. Retrieved 24 December 2020 from https://freespeechdebate.com/discuss/should-governments-butt-out-of-history/.

Kamiński, Ireneusz C. "Kontrowersje prawne wokół przestępstwa polegającego na pomawianiu narodu o popełnienie zbrodni" [Legal controversy surrounding the crime of accusing the nation of committing a crime]. *Problemy Współczesnego Prawa Międzynarodowego, Europejskiego i Porównawczego* [Problems of contemporary international, European and comparative law] 8 (2010): 5–34.

Khapaeva, Dina. "Triumphant Memory of the Perpetrators: Putin's Politics of Re-Stalinization." *Communist and Post-Communist Studies* 49, no. 1 (2016): 61–73.

Koposov, Nikolay. *Memory Laws, Memory Wars: The Politics of the Past in Europe and Russia.* Cambridge: Cambridge University Press, 2017.

Löytömäki, Stiina. *Law and Politics of Memory: Confronting the Past.* London: Routledge, 2014.

Maier, Charles S. "Doing History, Doing Justice: The Narrative of the Historian and of the Truth Commission." In *Truth v. Justice: The Morality of Truth Commissions*, edited by Robert I. Rotberg and Dennis F. Thompson, 261–78. Princeton, NJ: Princeton University Press, 2000.

Malcontent, Peter. *Facing the Past.* Cambridge: Intersentia, 2016.

Mälksoo, Maria. "Kononov v. Latvia as an Ontological Security Struggle over Remembering the Second World War." In *Law and Memory: Towards Legal Governance of History*, edited by Uladzislau Belavusau and Aleksandra Gliszczyńska-Grabias, 91–108. Cambridge: Cambridge University Press, 2017.

———. "'Memory Must Be Defended': Beyond the Politics of Mnemonical Security." *Security Dialogue* 6, no. 3 (2015): 221–37.

Majmurek, Jakub. "Pedagogika wstydu, której nigdy nie było" [A pedagogy of shame that never existed]. *OKOpress*, 6 August 2016. Retrieved 24 December 2020 from https://oko.press/pedagogika-wstydu-ktorej-nigdy-bylo/.

Méndez, Juan E., and Francisco J. Bariffi. "Right to Truth." In *Max Planck Encyclopedia of Public International Law*. Heidelberg: Oxford University Press, 2012.

Naamat, Talia, Nina Osin, and Dina Porat, eds. *Legislating for Equality: A Multinational Collection of Non-Discrimination Norms. Volume I: Europe.* Leiden: Martinus Nijhoff Publishers, 2011.

Naftali, Patricia. "The 'Right to Truth' in International Law: The 'Last Utopia'?" In *Law and Memory*, edited by Uladzislau Belavusau and Aleksandra Gliszczyńska-Grabias, 70–88. Cambridge: Cambridge University Press, 2017.

Naqvi, Yusra. "The Right to Truth in International Law: Fact or Fiction?" *International Review of the Red Cross* 862 (2006): 245–73.

Nowak-Far, Artur, and Łukasz Zamecki, eds. *Defective Codes of Memory: How the Memory of International Crimes Is Distorted in Public Discourse.* Warsaw: Ministry of Foreign Affairs of the Republic of Poland, 2015.

Patterson, Molly, and Kristen Renwick Monroe. "Narrative in Political Science." *Annual Review of Political Science* 1 (1998): 315–31.

Sierp, Aline. *History, Memory and Transeuropean Identity: Unifying Divisions.* London: Routledge, 2014.

"Warsaw Court Launches 'Night without an End' Lawsuit." *The First News*, 29 October 2019. Retrieved 24 December 2020 from https://www.thefirstnews.com/article/warsaw-court-launches-night-without-an-end-lawsuit-8381.

Wawrzyniak, Joanna, and Małgorzata Pakier, eds. *Memory and Change in Europe: Eastern Perspectives*. Oxford: Berghahn Books, 2016.

Wistrich, Robert S. *Antisemitism: The Longest Hatred*. New York: Pantheon Books, 1994.

Declarations

"Yad Vashem Historians Respond to the Joint Statement of the Governments of Poland and Israel Concerning the Revision of the 26 January 2018, Amendment to Poland's Act on the Institute of National Remembrance." *Yad Vashem*, 5 July 2018. Retrieved 27 July 2022 from https://www.yadvashem.org/press-release/05-july-2018-07-34.html.

"Joint declaration of prime ministers of the State of Israel and the Republic of Poland." 27 June 2018. Retrieved 4 September 2022 from https://www.gov.pl/web/premier/joint-declaration-of-prime-ministers-of-the-state-of-israel-and-the-republic-of-poland.

Laws, Judgments, and Official Documents

1592 (2006) *Polish Journal of Laws* 218 p.10809. Retrieved 15 April 2022 from https://isap.sejm.gov.pl/isap.nsf/download.xsp/WDU20062181592/O/D20061592.pdf.

Al-Nashiri v. Poland (24 July 2014). Retrieved 15 April 2022 from https://hudoc.echr.coe.int/eng#{%22fulltext%22:[%22AlNashiri%22],%22documentcollectionid2%22:[%22GRANDCHAMBER%22,%22CHAMBER%22],%22itemid%22:[%22001-146044%22]}.

Association '21 December 1989' v. Romania (24 May 2011). Retrieved 15 April 2022 from https://hudoc.echr.coe.int/eng#{%22fulltext%22:[%2233810/07%22],%22documentcollectionid2%22:[%22GRANDCHAMBER%22,%22CHAMBER%22],%22itemid%22:[%22001-104864%22]}.

Chauvy and Others v. France (29 September 2004). *HUDOC: European Court of Human Rights*. Retrieved 15 April 2022 from https://hudoc.echr.coe.int/fre#{%22itemid%22:[%22001-61861%22]}.

"Council Framework Decision 2008/913/JHA: On Combating Certain Forms and Expressions of Racism and Xenophobia by Means of Criminal Law." *EUR-Lex*. 28 November 2008. Retrieved 15 April 2022 from https://eur-lex.europa.eu/legal-content/EN/TXT/?uri=celex%3A32008F0913.

El-Masri v. The Former Yugoslav Republic of Macedonia (13 December 2021). Retrieved 15 April 2022 from https://hudoc.echr.coe.int/eng#{%22fulltext%22:[%22el%20masri%22],%22documentcollectionid2%22:[%22GRANDCHAMBER%22,%22CHAMBER%22],%22itemid%22:[%22001-115621%22]}.

Fatullayev v. Azerbaijan (22 April 2010). Retrieved 15 April 2022 from https://hudoc.echr.coe.int/eng#{%22fulltext%22:[%22Fatullayev%20v%20Azerbaijan%22],%22documentcollectionid2%22:[%22GRANDCHAMBER%22,%22CHAMBER%22],%22itemid%22:[%22001-98401%22]}.

Faurisson, Robert. "Communication No. 550/93." *Jurisprudence, Office of the High Commissioner on Human Rights*. 8 November 1996. Retrieved 15 April 2022 from https://juris.ohchr.org/Search/Details/654.

"General Comment No. 34." *International Covenant on Civil and Political Rights.* (12 September 2011). Retrieved 15 April 2022 from https://www2.ohchr.org/english/bodies/hrc/docs/gc34.pdf.

Husayn (Abu Zubaydah) v. Poland (16 February 2015). Retrieved 15 April 2022 from https://hudoc.echr.coe.int/eng#{%22fulltext%22:[%22Abu%20Zubaydah%22],%22documentcollectionid2%22:[%22GRANDCHAMBER%22,%22CHAMBER%22],%22itemid%22:[%22001-146047%22]}.

Inter-American Court of Human Rights, Bámaca-Velásquez v. Guatemala (22 February 2002). Retrieved 15 April 2022 from https://www.corteidh.or.cr/docs/casos/articulos/Seriec_91_ing.pdf.

"The International Convention for the Protection of All Persons from Enforced Disappearance." *United Nations Treaty Collection.* 20 December 2006. Retrieved 15 April 2022 from https://treaties.un.org/pages/ViewDetails.aspx?src=TREATY&mtdsg_no=IV-16&chapter=4.

Janowiec and Others v. Russia (21 October 2013). *HUDOC: European Court of Human Rights.* Retrieved 15 April 2022 from https://hudoc.echr.coe.int/eng#{%22fulltext%22:[%22janowiec%22],%22documentcollectionid2%22:[%22GRANDCHAMBER%22,%22CHAMBER%22],%22itemid%22:[%22001-127684%22]}.

Judgment of the Constitutional Tribunal of Poland (19 September 2008). Retrieved 15 April 2022 from https://isap.sejm.gov.pl/isap.nsf/download.xsp/WDU20081731080/T/D20081080TK.pdf.

Judgment of the Constitutional Tribunal of Poland (17 January 2019). Retrieved 15 April 2022 from https://ipo.trybunal.gov.pl/ipo/view/sprawa.xhtml?&pokaz=dokumenty&sygnatura=K%20 1/18.

Monnat v. Switzerland (21 December 2006). Retrieved 15 April 2022 from https://hudoc.echr.coe.int/eng#{%22fulltext%22:[%22Monnat%20v.%20Switzerland%22],%22documentcollectionid2%22:[%22GRANDCHAMBER%22,%22CHAMBER%22],%22itemid%22:[%22001-76947%22]}.

Orentlicher, Diane. "Updated Set of Principles for the Protection and Promotion of Human Rights through Action to Combat Impunity." *Official Document System UN,* 8 February 2005. Retrieved 15 April 2022 from https://documents-dds-ny.un.org/doc/UNDOC/GEN/G05/109/00/PDF/G0510900.pdf?OpenElement.

Print no. 334: Parliamentary Draft Act Amending the Act on the Institute of National Remembrance (2016). Retrieved 15 April 2022 from https://www.sejm.gov.pl/Sejm8.nsf/druk.xsp?nr=334.

Print no. 771: Parliamentary Draft Act Amending the Act on the Institute of National Remembrance (6 July 2016). Retrieved 15 April 2022 from https://www.sejm.gov.pl/sejm8.nsf/druk.xsp?nr=771.

Print no. 806: The Government Bill to Amend the Act on the Institute of National Remembrance (29 August 2016). Retrieved 15 April 2022 from https://www.sejm.gov.pl/sejm8.nsf/PrzebiegProc.xsp?nr=806.

Ustawa o zmianie ustawy o Instytucie Pamięci Narodowej [The law amending the Act on the Institute of National Remembrance] (2018) *Polish Journal of Laws* 369. Retrieved 15 April 2022 from https://isap.sejm.gov.pl/isap.nsf/download.xsp/WDU20180000369/T/D20180369L.pdf.

Chapter 7

THE RIGHT TO PRODUCE MEMORY

Social Memory Technology as Cultural Work

Karen Worcman and Joanne Garde-Hansen

Introduction

Founded in São Paulo, Brazil, in 1991, the Museu da Pessoa (Museum of the person) is a state independent institution; a virtual and collaborative museum of life stories that aims to record, preserve, and transform memories into a source of digital information and online connection between people around the world. The Museu da Pessoa emerged from a cultural shift toward a politics of identity (recognizing that every person is a citizen with rights to their own story and culture) that is transcultural in approach (recognizing that every person has distinctive and different cultural heritages that transfer beyond Brazil). On the one hand, a right to memory encounters currency, value, and valuation explicitly.[1] Indeed, empowering local communities and unlocking new levels of memory via digital technologies, the goal of the Museu da Pessoa, was and is sponsored by public agencies, subsidies, tax exemptions and corporate financing. On the other hand, while such value creation is within the wheelhouse of neoliberal entrepreneurialism, the museum has been concerned with how the cultural value of an individual life story can speak back to official histories and expand what a rights-based development of cultural belonging might look like. The right of the individual to tell their story in a society, not simply as part of a collective or community or nation, but as a cultural right that is expansive, connective, and increasingly digital and multitudinous,[2] will be explored in this chapter.

In Brazil, the emergence of the memories of the people has been part of a wider Latin American discussion about creating memories to promote social change. A study coordinated by Elizabeth Jelin used three definitions of memory to gather and examine memories of repression in the Southern Cone: memory understood as a subjective process, based upon experiences and symbolic and material milestones; memory as a focus of conflicts and struggles between different players and memory producers (including the state); and memory as a historical production, a result of the context, culture, and political and ideological spaces in which it is found.[3] The disputes and conflicts concerning memory are present in Brazil in the memories of socially excluded individuals and groups (above all, the history of indigenous and Afro-descendant groups that are not officially included on the educational curriculum) in the historical narratives that result from the colonial pasts and, more recently, from the issues that involve memories of the dictatorship.[4]

The democratization of Brazil in the 1980s allowed the development of public policies that, in the field of memory, meant that many of these issues could be faced. Under the Lula government, public policies concerning culture were created to address, as pointed out by Eliane Costa, these challenges and "to overcome what Paulo Freire called a 'culture of silence.'"[5] This political and cultural debate in Brazil and in Latin America as a whole gave birth to many initiatives among artists, museologists and culture activists in the 1970s and 1980s that have created different methods and strategies to develop grassroots community content creation together with political mobilization. In Brazil, Freire's pedagogy of the oppressed, Augusto Boal's theater of the oppressed, and the street theater of Amir Haddad, among others, were all looking for popular participation and social change through Art. On the museum's side, since the Manifesto of Santiago in 1972,[6] there has been a strong concern for discussing the role of museums for reversing colonial heritage and narratives and for creating new possibilities for debating social exclusion. The Santiago Round Table was the first public expression of what would become a New Museology. Paulo Freire, at the time exiled by the military dictatorship in Brazil, was invited by Hugh de Varine, then director of the International Council of Museums (ICOM), to chair the event, but his participation was vetoed by the Brazilian government. However, the resolutions adopted by the Santiago Round Table, including expanding museums' commitment to the socio-political cultural reality of Latin American countries, and stressing the need to integrate urban and rural communities as the museums' priority publics, were heavily influenced by his thinking.

The Museu da Pessoa has pragmatically, skillfully, and creatively used the cultural work of producing individual memories as a way of addressing the problem of rights in Brazil. Given the global profile of human rights so well expressed in this book, why do "cultural rights" (to memory) remain ambiguous? How has the Museu da Pessoa used its methodology of social memory technology as a form of cultural intervention to communicate knowledge of rights as memory? If "cultural rights" are inseparable from human rights, as Article 5 of the 2001 UNESCO Declaration on Cultural Diversity declares, then how is remembering one's own story a demonstration of human rights, a right to be recognized as a historian of one's life?[7]

In this chapter, we adopt Jonathan Vickery's perspective that it is "with the United Nations and its global political discourse of rights, that a transformation in the conception of basic 'human life,' and even of culture, is still being developed, and developed according to an ever-proliferating interpretation and application of rights-based ethical thought."[8] Thus, a right to memory, as a cultural right, is open and iterative. To recognize that cultural memory is more than collective or social memory means collecting, building, and sharing memories to produce a set of obligations that prioritize "individual beneficiaries" and make visible the "individuals who bear the cost" of developing rights in Brazil.[9] All of which "awards attention to social exclusion, disparities and injustice" and "offers a way of interconnecting social, economic and cultural factors in a civil and political context—not just the practical aims of development."[10] The Museu da Pessoa's rights-based approach to memory has challenged power structures around who gets to tell their story and has devolved responsibility for cultural expression to individuals who are both responsible for and personal beneficiaries of culture.

Cultural rights to memory performed in, by, and with the Museu da Pessoa as a remembering by, with, and through the "more or less" digital,[11] become ongoing cultural work co-produced by participants and the museum. Its ongoing-ness, as Maria Puig de la Bellacasa suggests, is a "thinking-with [a remembering with] that creates new patterns out of previous multiplicities, intervening by adding layers of meaning rather than questioning or conforming to ready-made categories."[12] The Museu da Pessoa has been creating an archive of memories of many different kinds of people, places, objects, and experiences, which are connective and suffused with intimacy, openness, and fluidity, ready to be re-made and re-ordered. It has taken its concept-theory-method of building, organizing, and sharing memory and socialized it beyond the walls of the museum, long before digital and social media expanded this hyperconnectivity of memories into more recent demands for a right to be forgotten. The Museu da Pessoa stands as an early and important example of a cultural organization designed and funded to protect and legitimate individuals' rights to tell their story, to share their memories and preserve their histories. The right to tell stories means, in this case, the understanding that everyone is a potential protagonist of their own history and that everyone is an important social and cultural player when it comes to the definition of who has the right (and historians often claim that they are the official writers) to contribute to the social construction of historical narratives.

Therefore, the trajectory of the Museu da Pessoa is an interesting example for this book as it illustrates that economic sustainability, rights development, and cultural and political aims in Brazil are interconnected and can influence the final results of cultural and social initiatives. While the Museu da Pessoa produces memories it also continues to think and remember with those memories, creating space for future cultural and media work. Out of memory work, we bring more culture; out of this memory culture, we expand cultural values. In this chapter, we select key examples from the Museu da Pessoa and map the connections of memory work to cultural work and research. Our examples relate the ongoing nature of sustainable cultural memories that are both commemorative and pedagogic to Paulo Freire's sense of the pedagogy of the oppressed. They also show that ordinary Brazilian citizens enact their rights to memory as a form of civic participation in memory culture. As Vickery argues, the question of rights is somewhat more urgent and complex in the Global South, and is becoming more so in the Global North, for "a global cultural view might understand rights as a legal term that appeals to a sphere of language, litigation and authority so often alien to the cultural realms of many countries in the Global South. In fact, to define cultural life at all in legal terms raises a range of questions on the autonomy of culture."[13]

The right to memory is understood as the right to produce memory and this is important to both the Global South and the Global North. In the Global South, it is a means of including new visions, experiences, and histories in the official historical (and decolonized) narrative. It means changing who is in and who is out, and including, for example, First Nations' perspectives on the European arrival on the continent. In the Global North, the right to memory can mean a revision of the historical narratives that are part of monuments, curriculums, and official celebrations. In Portugal, for example, a clear revision is needed of the role the country played in the colonization of Brazil, Africa, and so on.[14]

Social Memory Technology

In 2016, we published the book *Social Memory Technology: Theory, Practice, Action* in order to forward the theory-in-practice methodology of the Museu da Pessoa in Brazil, which had transferred itself to research and heritage projects in many parts of the world, including the United Kingdom.[15] We promoted the notion that the concept and method of social memory technology should be thought together. As a theory-concept-method, social memory has cultural value, bestows a right to one's story as a cultural expression determined and shared by the person, and is an embodied transaction of digital and cultural work between those who remember and the memory worker. It is far more than a "remembering me" style of memorialization or an inclusive heritage process.[16]

Social memory technology addresses Marianne Hirsch's call for a "shift in attention and methodology" in memory studies to "outside official structures of commemoration."[17] Bodies, places, sites, and memories become together. Like Rebecca Kook's analysis of the domestication and democratization of memory in Israel in this volume, we see a right to memory as informed by digitalization and personalization. The Museu da Pessoa's turn to the digital in the context of a national history of trauma or violence seeks out "experiential, interactive and affective strategies" to "inspire empathy," even if they too have a political intent (democracy, peace, creating a better future, justice, and reparations, etc.).[18] As Kook does, we explore the idea (from a Brazilian perspective) that to have the right to memory is more than to have the right to have the content of a specific memory or a group recognized by the rest of society (the identity politics of recognition). It is the right to produce, own, manage, and practice that memory (the politics of administration), to have access to it (the archive), to have ownership of one's own archive and the power to decide what to share and where to share it (privacy and the public sphere), and the right to re-use one's archive of memories for future resilience (sustainable humanity in a changing natural world). The right to memory is the right to culturally, personally, and socially produce memory and to have the power to establish it productively, technically, and archivally (which means in all the different ways it could be used as a tool to leverage other rights).

The paradigm of a social memory technology has underlying principles. These are:

Principle 1: The idea that any individual can and should be considered a key actor in a global and a local (mediated) heritage through the narration of his or her life story. Principle 2: The right of every group to produce their own memory. Principle 3: The practice and outcomes of communities and individuals producing their memories, life stories, and heritage, should be open, transparent, and inclusive. Principle 4: The potential for change—social, cultural, and theoretical—should be a key outcome of (re)constructing and (re)performing the past in the present as personal memory. These four principles have developed out of and in response to the various academic research findings and applied social practices that have privileged the use of memory and life histories as a tool for social change.[19]

"Social technology" is a concept and practice developed in India and appropriated by Latin American thinkers in the 1960s who defended the idea that neither science nor technology is neutral.[20] It is defined as "the whole process, method or tool of solving any kind of social problem and which meets the requisites of simplicity, low cost, ease of reapplication and proven social impact."[21] It was taken as a social alternative for development as by Amilcar Herrera in *Ciencia y tecnologia en el Desarrollo de la sociedad* (Science and technology in society's developments).[22] Social memory technology shares the basic premise of social technology, which is that through communal participation and use of knowledge, low-cost technologies can be created that will have greater social impact and enormous potential for reapplication. It starts with the understanding that the right to memory is the right to create, preserve, disseminate, and legitimize memories and is fundamentally concerned with the cultural rights of groups to be recognized inside a nation for their connections (past, present, and future) to persons outside their nation. The Museu da Pessoa's systematization of practices focused on enabling any individual, group, museum, community, or institution to construct, preserve, socialize, and legitimate their stories is based on social memory technology.

Brazilianization of Memory Rights and the Cost of Memory Work

Rather than searching for revisionist histories,[23] the Museu da Pessoa sought to rethink and recreate the whole process of producing memories. Thus, while Jean L. Cohen describes, in *Rethinking Human Rights*, the three waves of rights development from the 1940s to the end of the Cold War,[24] we find the Museu da Pessoa engaging in a new kind of cultural rights for development of minority groups within Brazil from the 1990s. This accords with other claims to cultural rights in Latin America, Australia, Canada, and New Zealand that have emerged in recent years. On the one hand, the museum amplifies a person's memories but not necessarily as an individual claim to be recognized. On the other hand, the museum amplifies the cultural group but not necessarily through a traditional notion of national identity.

To achieve this, the Museu da Pessoa encouraged the rise of participative memory experiences as a way of de-colonizing the methods for collecting stories and histories. Like Sarah Pink's suggestion that researchers "share with others the senses of place they felt as they sought to occupy similar places to those of their research participants, and to acknowledge the processes through which their sensory knowledge has become academic knowledge," the museum co-produced memory with participants.[25] It is a starting point for all memory work in the Museu da Pessoa that every life story (along with every social group) should be allowed to select, produce, and analyze its own history based on its own cultural values, cognizant of the cultural work that it involves, all of which has a cost. In fact, one of the biggest challenges for the museum was guaranteeing, through the development of an entrepreneurial model, the financial support to maintain a non-state-funded museum. This challenge brought culture and economics together in a way rarely addressed in Europe,[26] but which is only beginning to be acknowledged in a post-financial crisis context (after 2008). What is the value of culture, the politics of cultural work, the political economy of remembering, the sustainability of intangible heritage and the cost of recognizing the rights to memory of cultural groups? Many other questions have become crucial to the ongoing maintenance and management of an increasingly visible memory industry.

The participation of private companies funding memory projects such as the ones developed by the Museu da Pessoa for Petrobras (one of the biggest oil companies in the world) and for the Votorantim Group (a centennial, entirely Brazilian family-owned company and the biggest conglomerate in Brazil[27]) has become a cornerstone for financial sustainability and the creation of archives at the Museu da Pessoa.[28] This raises a series of questions about the development of these types of projects, above all in relation to the control of the narratives of memory produced with the workers or communities involved when there exists the risk of those interviewed remaining silent on internal problems, or the tendency to "sanitize" the story and highlight the benefits the company has made in everyone's lives. Despite all the tensions, it would be rather unfair to attribute the ethical responsibility of "trying" to control memory to the companies.[29] Memory is always an area of dispute, with this dispute taking place in various contexts, including families, schools, the state, museums, myths, etc., and the place of work is no different. As Jelin noted "it is necessary to recognize that memories are objects of dispute, conflict and struggle, and it is necessary to pay attention to the active role as producer of meaning of the participants in these struggles, characterized by their power relations."[30]

In Brazil, there was always a strong relationship between culture, politics, and the economy that defined the role of corporations, unions, civil society organizations, and the government. During the dictatorship (1964–1985) the biggest infrastructural companies benefited from the military government and had very few contacts with society. After democratization, there were some changes among the three sectors of the society, and there was a new collaboration to respond to social challenges of the country, like poverty, education, and the social environment.[31] For instance, the challenges for education in Brazil are numerous, and it is one of the main reasons for the continued social inequality, racism, and violence. The main idea behind Social Memory Technology (and behind all social technologies) is to achieve scale that can guarantee high impact and low cost. The main strategy used to achieve more impact and scale on the technology of social memory was to identify key places, such as institutions, communities, and social organizations, which could use it to face their social challenges. Public education became, therefore, one of our main goals, because social memory technology can help teachers and students to interview and register the history of their own communities. This process was guided by the idea that the right of memory should be incorporated in every school and changing the notion that history is a "faraway reality" and an unchangeable narrative. These kinds of projects were meant to develop new advocates in memory work and involve public school students (many from very poor and rural communities) to be the authors and protagonists of their own histories. This work engaged their families and their communities. Through researching, recording, drawing, retelling, and systematizing their stories, the students had the opportunity to become memory agents for their towns and teachers became aware of how this was empowering and valuable knowledge.[32]

During the early 2000s, the public policy for culture and memory work in Brazil changed completely. Gilberto Gil, renowned singer/songwriter and the then Minister of Culture (2003–2008) of the Lula Government,[33] identified several "quiescent points" in the "cultural body of the country" performed by both civil society and the government.[34] In his inauguration speech, when he affirmed that "The Ministry should be like a light that reveals, in the past and in the present, the things and the signs that made and make Brazil what it is," Gilberto Gil was already presenting the axis around which his mandate would revolve.[35] The concept stems from the presupposition that the favelas and excluded groups do not need to receive culture, but rather have their cultural expressions strengthened and recognized by society. These concepts bear a strong correlation with the ideas of Paulo Freire, who had called attention to the extent to which mass-oriented policies had resulted in cultures of silence that suffocated the lower classes. This initiative represented an enormous turnaround in the logic of what culture is and who is understood as a cultural producer in Brazil. One could argue that this turnaround is still slowly evolving in the UK and Europe, with less controversial investment in high art and high culture projects and growing attention to smaller and more local initiatives.

In 2005, the Points of Culture Program opened bidding rounds to all interested organizations and institutions in the country: indigenous communities, slave-descendant communities, musical groups, social movements, and universities. Cultural manifestations found in communities, quilombos, indigenous communities, cultural collectives, favelas, universities and different institutions were mapped through public call notices in which they participated and became a "Point of Culture."[36] The *Teias de Cultura* (Networks of culture) were born, which aimed to form a network between the Points of Culture that had, in digital studios, the possibility of developing productions and connections between each other.

It was in this context in 2005 that the Museu da Pessoa started a new strategy that was mainly focused on the articulation of grassroots organizations so they could produce and connect their own stories.[37] This strategy was based on the idea of using social memory technology as a way of stimulating new memory producers. This movement would also serve as a strong mobilizing axis for different social groups, and the initiative resulted in a national network of life stories called "Brazilian memory network,"[38] which involved around four hundred organizations throughout the country articulating their actions around memory. With the intention of allying memory with community development, the network was made up of all sorts of different kinds of organizations: universities, cultural foundations, grassroots organizations, and informal activist groups. Their aim was to use social memory technology to produce and share their own memories and, in this way, to strengthen the local actions of each organization involved.

Based on the same principles, Museu da Pessoa, together with thirteen youth organizations, created an initiative called the "One Million Life Stories of Youth" movement, involving young people from all over the country who would share their stories and use their content to fight for different public policies. The digital storytelling method created by Joe Lambert at Storycenter was adapted to support the creation of a large-scale youth voice initiative.[39] During this same period, there was also the campaign for the "International Day for Sharing Life Stories" promoted by the international Museu da Pessoa network, together with the Center for Digital Storytelling in California, in the United States, and other global partners.

The practical aspect of social memory technology is, then, a result of all this fieldwork that, after almost thirty years and more than three hundred different projects, has produced a life story archive with eighteen thousand stories and seventy-two thousand digitized personal images that tells, in some sense, the history of Brazil in the twentieth and twenty-first centuries. The multiple experiences with communities and public schools in more than 230 cities in Brazil and around 1,600 organizations (schools, organizations, and communities) had created opportunities to adapt the method in a way that it could work in places that have no Internet or no literacy at all. The main conceptual basis of all this work was that advocacy and collaboration are the elements that converge when thinking about a right to memory that connects with both Noam Tirosh and Amit Schejter's chapter in this book on personal control over producing and sharing life narratives, remembering and forgetting, and with Freire's affirmation that "The more men assume an active role in the investigation of their subject matter, the deeper their awareness will be in relation to their reality and, in exposing its most important subject matter, they will take possession of it."[40]

Digital Memory: Working Toward a Memory of the Multitude

Although social memory technology can be used without any ICT (Information Communication Technology) it is important to note that digital possibilities are, indeed, a strong element. Just as Tirosh and Schejter argued about the particular capabilities of digital memory technologies in terms of a rights-based theory focused on well-being, the museum's emphasis upon the person has always been central to the use of media and the digital. The Museu da Pessoa was defined as a virtual museum from the beginning. First it was just an idea and then, CDRoms, databases, and video booths became the different strategies used to promote authorships and collaboration. In 1996, the Museu da Pessoa launched its first website. In the beginning, there was a tendency among the traditional museums and cultural memory workers to reproduce the same logic of the broadcasters of traditional content (a collective memory approach that sought to establish an imagined community of Brazil, Brazilian culture as a homogeneous, and modernity as defined by the national majority). As Andreas Huyssen has argued in his essay "Natural Rights, Cultural Rights, and the Politics of Memory," cultures "affected by modernity" are split, perhaps vertically (high vs. low) or "in terms of privileging different media (print vs. music). Such stratifications will always be a site for struggle over meanings."[41] The museum's early adoption of the Internet was to take that struggle when the multitude was gathering away from the established media. That is, uploading the interviews and images that already existed seemed the "work to do" (confirming the established memories that already existed) and creating a new space for memory.

However, in 1997, it soon became clear that the Internet meant that the playing field had changed (multi-vocality was possible and necessary), since it could provide the visitor to the site with the possibility of recording his or her own story (and permitted the cultural work to diversify and become participatory). This was the beginning of "Tell Your Story," which encouraged new Internet users, an emerging multitude of connecting individuals who were creating archives (what Hoskins would later term "human-archival entanglements of communication through digital devices and networks"[42]), to take part in and create new content for the site.

This inevitably meant cultural work shifted from the producer to the audience. The stories were sent in by e-mail and uploaded directly in HTML format (after this became a database specially designed for cataloging life stories, narratives and personal images and videos). In 2003, the Museu da Pessoa launched the fourth version of its digital platform. Tools such as *Conte Sua História* (Tell your story) allowed the user to include their own stories, while the *Meu Museu* (My museum) tool allowed the user to collect their favorite stories together. The searches expanded the possibility of consulting the archive, numerous references encouraged the use of memory in education, and tools encouraged a more educational use of the content, such as sending a "postcard" with digitalized photographs from the archive.[43] In a study conducted by the Museu da Pessoa in 2009, Internet users were asked what had led them to use the space provided by the museum to tell their stories. Among the various replies that could help reach an understanding as to the most important reasons, there is one that summarizes and best illustrates the majority opinion: "I think that everyone imagines that they are alone when they think about talking about their personal issues, when, in fact, there is an institution like this one where there are people like you, who are in the minority, who are interesting, and are interested in the stories we have to tell."[44]

While the Web 2.0 and social media unevenly changed the whole world, it was based on capitalist principles of monetization and did not change necessarily the concepts underlying memory value in the world. On the contrary, it reinforced the programs of big companies such as Facebook (now called Meta), that create an illusion of authorship and disguise the fact that every person is a new product for consumption, whose "likes" became the business model (a "like economy," according to Carolin Gerlitz and Ann Helmond[45]) and whose tastes, sentiments and memories are to be captured, curated, and aggregated. This created a new perspective for discussing the relation between local and global and the right to memory.

To face this trend, the museum launched, in 2015, *Monte sua Coleção* (Build your collection), a new online tool designed to allow anyone to become a curator of the museum. *Monte sua Colecção* enabled individuals to build their own collections based, or not, on the museum's archives—to describe them, tag them, and publish them on the museum's website to share them through social networks.[46] By providing the community with possibilities to become curators of a museum's collections, such methods provided greater opportunities for the collective—and collaborative—construction of new memories, along with new spaces that challenge society's established perceptions and structures. *Monte sua Colecção* was first promoted by the museum team by publishing a series of thematic collections such as the fiftieth anniversary of the 1964 coup d'état,[47] an important moment in Brazilian history that would lead the country into a military dictatorship lasting twenty years. In the months that followed, the tool was taken up by Internet users who began assembling and disseminating their new collections. To date, more than two hundred new collections have been created and shared by the community, and around 4,500 personal stories have been uploaded by users and included in their collections.

In 2018, the Museu da Pessoa obtained the support of Brazil's National Bank of Development (BNDES), allowing it to digitize its entire archive, thereby providing the public with full access to it through a new platform that is able to meet every type of accessibility requirement. This period has been radically transforming the focus of the Museu da Pessoa, which has created online cultural programming and started experimenting with new digital models of online training.

The COVID-19 pandemic of 2020 onward and the periods of social lockdowns have provided the world with countless challenges, and these have affected cultural institutions, particularly museums.[48] During the pandemic, the Museu da Pessoa saw itself as an online museum that could keep its "doors" open to the public twenty-four hours a day. The staff dedicated themselves to adapting the initiatives of the museum's different areas of activity with the aim of increasing its social and digital relevance. This shift resulted in a wide and diverse program, which involved at least thirty professionals from different areas (including artists, video makers, web designers, and others). Alongside the initiatives mentioned above, the museum's archive was distributed over 2020–21 in the form of online exhibitions on social media networks such as Instagram, Facebook, Whatsapp, and LinkedIn, and was later included in the "Google Arts and Culture" platform and the Museu da Pessoa website, all of which open new horizons for exploring new channels of authorship and collaboration for sustainable memory work.

Conclusion: Sustainable Memory Work

We have argued that expanding the concept of the right to memory toward a collaborative action of intervening, in a practical manner, in the field of social and cultural activities is a powerful move toward social change. Change is only possible if individuals and groups assume the responsibility for creating, organizing, and socializing their own memories. This should be recognized as a right.

Social invisibility is born from the very sense of feeling invisible, both personally and socially. In this sense, cultural and digital memory work should be revealed as valuable work that produces a sense of recognition in one's own narrative as a part of humanity's heritage and as a politically transformative act. It is not enough to open new spaces for the inclusion of excluded memories. This concept draws upon the teachings of Freire to look upon history as a constructed reality rather than a given one. For this it is necessary that the communities themselves create, produce, and share their own stories alongside a process of social affirmation. It is also necessary that these individuals and communities (and schools) have the will to publicize and integrate their own local history in a more global culture. In UNESCO's 1995 Declaration of Principles on Tolerance, it is stressed that: "Tolerance is respect, acceptance and appreciation of the rich diversity of our world's cultures, our forms of expression and ways of being human"; and it is necessary that "attitudes of openness, mutual listening and solidarity should take place in schools and universities and through non-formal education, at home and in the workplace."[49]

These accounts reinforce the conclusions drawn from the impact evaluation studies undertaken by the Museu da Pessoa with users of its platform and participants on its training courses to understand the impact of voicing. The evaluation specifically asked "Does the contact with life histories contribute to a fight against intolerance?" The study showed that 98.9 percent of people felt that their empathy with those of different races, genres, social classes, ages, and cultures had increased; 98 percent recognized their own social importance and felt motivated to make social interventions against intolerance; 97.7 percent felt that the quality of their listening had improved; 100 percent felt that their understanding of social issues that lead to intolerance, such as discrimination and inequality, had increased; and 90.8 percent had intensified their ties with those they share their lives with, such as family, friends and workmates.

The power of voice should become the power of production because the right to memory is the right to be a part of history.

Karen Worcman is the founder and director of the Instituto Museu da Pessoa (Museum of the Person, founded in 1991). An historian and linguist, she is also a researcher and PhD candidate in the Diversitas group within the Humanidades, Direitos e Outras Legitimidades program of the University of São Paulo. She is the author (with Joanne Garde-Hansen) of *Social Memory Tecnhology: Theory, Practice, Action* (Routledge, 2016) and has co-edited several books, including *Historia Falada: memória, rede e mudança social* (2006), *Tecnologia Social de Memória* (2009), *Transformações Amazônicas* (2010), *Todo Mundo tem uma História para contar* (2012), *Quase Canções* (2017).

Joanne Garde-Hansen is Reader in Culture, Media and Communication, and directs the Centre for Cultural & Media Policy Studies at the University of Warwick. Her research and teaching focus upon media, memory, archives and heritage. This is manifest in two strands of research. The first, relates to the co-founding of the Centre for Television History, Heritage and Memory. The second, is in her collaboration with geographers, water scientists and the Centre for Floods, Communities and Resilience on the relationship between culture and water, rivers, flooding and drought. She has published on media and memory, television, archives, and water memories.

Notes

 1. See Garde-Hansen and Schwartz's, "Iconomy of Memory," in which they explore remembering as digital, civic and corporate currency in Brazil.
 2. Andrew Hoskins has argued that the digital has replaced the "collective" in memory studies with "the multitude" as "the defining digital organizational form of memory beyond but also incorporating the self." Hoskins, "Memory of the Multitude."
 3. See Jelin, *Los trabajos* [The works], 2.
 4. The Comissão Nacional da Verdade (CNV / National Commission of Truth) was created by Law 12.528/2011 on 16 May 2012. The purpose of the CNV is to ascertain serious violations of Human Rights that took place between 18 September 1946, and 5 October 1988. The CNV ended its activities in 2014. See *Comissão Nacional da Verdade* website. Retrieved 28 July 2022 from http://cnv.memoriasreveladas.gov.br/institucional-acesso-in formacao/a-cnv.html.
 5. Costa, *Jangada Digital*, 75.
 6. The regional UNESCO meeting in Santiago, Chile, in 1972 gave birth to the manifesto that started a new movement on social museology. See the manuscript: *Round Table on the Development and the Role of Museums in the Contemporary World*. Santiago de Chile, Chile, 20–31 May 1972. Retrieved 28 July 2022 from https://www.ces.uc.pt/projectos/somus/docs/Santiago%20declaration%201972.pdf.
 7. Donders defines "cultural rights" as "human rights that directly promote and protect cultural interests of individuals and communities and that are meant to advance their capacity to preserve, develop, and change their cultural identity," which can lead to change in the broader culture. Donders, "Cultural Human Rights," 117.
 8. Vickery, "Cultural Rights," 133.
 9. Vickery, "Cultural Rights," 134.
10. Vickery, "Cultural Rights," 134.
11. Samuel Merrill, Shanti Sumartojo, Angharad Closs Stephens, and Martin Coward have argued that "the more or less digital" elements of "commemorative public atmospheres" combine or create assemblages. Merrill et al., "Togetherness after Terror."
12. Puig de la Bellacasa, "'Nothing Comes without Its World,'" 200.
13. Vickery, "Cultural Rights," 134.
14. This could also be true of Belgium, whose role in the history of The Congo needs to be rewritten, and for other countries as well. This was pointed out by Ruth Philips in *Museum Pieces* on the politics of Canadian museums.
15. Worcman and Garde-Hansen, *Social Memory Technology*.
16. See Holloway et al., *Remember Me*; Smith and Waterton, "Constrained by Commonsense."
17. Altınay and Pető, "Gender, Memory and Connective Genocide Scholarship," 396.
18. Sodaro, *Exhibiting Atrocity*, 5.
19. The connection between life stories, memory, and social change has been pointed out by oral historians, such as Paul Thompson and Hugo Slim (in *Listening for a Change*). It has also been part of the debates around storytelling and peace building. See the report *The Evaluation of Storytelling as a Peace-building Methodology*; Mello and Peña, "Tecnologia Social" [Social technology]; and Worcman and Pereira, "História Falada" [Spoken history] for more on memory as a social technology. Memory for social change is also a crucial question when it comes to social museology and decolonization in the peripherical world. For this see Mbembe, *Crítica da Razão Negra* [Critique of Black reason]. Elizabeth Jelin points out the political elements of social change and memory in her *Los trabajos de La memória* [The works of memory].
20. Dagnino, Brandão, and Novaes, "Sobre o marco analítico" [About the analytical framework].

21. Mello and Peña, "Tecnologia social" [Social technology], 84.
22. Herrera, *Ciencia y tecnología*.
23. For more on revisionist history projects popularized in the 1980s, see Huyssen, *Present Pasts*.
24. Cohen, "Rethinking Human Rights."
25. Pink, *Doing Sensory Ethnography*, 2.
26. It was, in fact, the São Paulo football club that was one of the first big institutions to take a risk on the potential value of memory work in 1994.
27. For more on these cases, see Worcman and Garde-Hansen, *Social Memory Technology*, 86–101. Corporate memory work has guaranteed sustainability for the Museu da Pessoa over the last thirty years. It has developed almost a hundred different memory projects for corporations, unions, foundations, civil societies organizations, and families.
28. See more about the projects developed by the Museu da Pessoa in Thompson, *Voice of the Past*.
29. There has been a series of criticisms raised by the Oral History academic community in Brazil. One of the criticisms has been that the Museu da Pessoa was "selling" history. These criticisms have been overcome, but that is not to say that the debate over the control of historical narratives has gone away. This debate is not restricted to the development of memory projects for companies. This is an important debate that involves the academic world, museums, companies, and, above all, nation-states.
30. Jelin, *Los Trabajos* [The works], 2.
31. The government of Fernando Henrique Cardoso (1994–2003) created the Comunidade Solidária committee that gathered civil society, corporations, and the government together to face social challenges. It is important to say that this movement has had a resurgence since the Bolsonaro government took office in 2018.
32. Freire, *A Pedagogia do Oprimido*.
33. Lula—Luis Inácio Lula da Silva—was the first working-class President of Brazil. He was a union leader who emerged during the dictatorship when he led the first big strike in 1980. Lula created the PT Workers Party and won the presidential election in 2003. He was re-elected in 2006 and, in 2010, made his successor Dilma Roussef the first female President of Brazil, although she was impeached in 2016, the victim of a political coup d'état.
34. It is important to stress that a reversal of this repositioning of the state started in 2016, when Dilma Rousseff, the president at the time, was deposed. Since then, new disputes have come about involving historical narratives and, with the Bolsonaro government, in 2018, this revision assumed state proportions with, for example, the renaming of the 1964 Coup as the 1964 Revolution.
35. Costa, *Jangada Digital*, 70
36. Turino, *Ponto de Cultura*.
37. Up to that point the Museu da Pessoa had been more focused on its own work, which was to register, preserve, and disseminate life histories. This was performed by means of the different projects created at that time.
38. Worcman, Rogério, and Faleiros, *Brasil Memória em Rede* [Brazil memory net].
39. The digital storytelling movement was started by Joe Lambert, founder of Storycenter (retrieved 27 July 2022 from https://www.storycenter.org/) and Dana Atchley in California (see Lambert, *Digital Storytelling*). New initiatives of note in the same area include Cowbird (retrieved 27 July 2022 from http://cowbird.com/role/a-library-of-human-experience/stories/) and the well-known Storycorps (retrieved 27 July 2022 from https://storycorps.org/); Lambert, *Digital Storytelling*, 133.
40. Freire, *Pedagogia do Oprimido*, 94–97.
41. Huyssen, "Natural Rights."
42. Hoskins, "Memory of the Multitude," 86.

43. For more details, see Henriques, *Memória, museologia e virtualidade* [Memory, museology and virtuality], 108.
44. Answer to a question in a study performed by the Museu da Pessoa with Internet users in 2009.
45. Gerlitz and Helmond, "The Like Economy."
46. Worcman, "We're All Curators,"
47. See the collection at "Golpe at 64." *Museu da Pessoa*, 12 May 2014. Retrieved 27 July 2022 from https://acervo.museudapessoa.org/pt/conteudo/colecao/golpe-de-64-97503.
48. Ebbrecht-Hartmann, "Commemorating from a Distance."
49. At the 28th meeting of its General Conference held in Paris on 16 November 1995.

Bibliography

Altınay A. G., A. Pető. "Gender, Memory and Connective Genocide Scholarship: A Conversation with Marianne Hirsch." *European Journal of Women's Studies* 22, no. 4 (2015): 386–96.

Cohen, Jean L. "Rethinking Human Rights, Democracy, and Sovereignty in the Age of Globalization." *Political Theory* 36, no. 4 (2008): 578–606.

Costa, Eliane. *Jangada Digital: Gilberto Gil e as Políticas Públicas Para a Cultura Das Redes* [Digital Jangada: Gilberto Gil and public policies for the culture of networks]. Rio de Janeiro: Azougue, 2011.

Dagnino, Renato, Flávio Cruvinel Brandão, and Henrique Tahan Novaes. "Sobre o marco analítico- conceitual da tecnologia social" [About the analytical-conceptual framework of social technology]. In *Tecnologia Social: uma estratégia para o desenvolvimento*, edited by Daniel Seidl and Sandra Santos Cabral, 15–65. Rio de Janeiro: Fundação Banco do Brasil, 2004.

Donders, Yvonne. "Cultural Human Rights and the UNESCO Convention: More than Meets the Eye?" In *Globalization, Culture, and Development: The UNESCO Convention on Cultural Diversity*, edited by Christiaan De Beukelaer, Miika Pykkonen, and J. P. Singh, 117–31. Basingstoke: Palgrave, 2015.

Ebbrecht-Hartmann, Tobias. "Commemorating from a Distance: The Digital Transformation of Holocaust Memory in Times of COVID-19." *Media, Culture & Society* 43, no. 6 (2020):1095–112.

Freire, Paulo. *A Pedagogia do Oprimido* [Pedagogy of the oppressed]. Rio de Janeiro: Editora Paz e Terra, 2002.

Garde-Hansen, Joanne, and Gilson Schwartz. "Iconomy of Memory: On Remembering as Digital, Civic and Corporate Currency." In *Digital Memory Studies: Media Pasts in Transition*, edited by Andrew Hoskins, 217–33. New York: Routledge, 2017.

Gerlitz, Carolin, and Ann Helmond. "The Like Economy: Social Buttons and the Data Intensive Web." *New Media and Society* 15, no. 8 (2013): 1348–65.

Henriques, Rosali Maria Nunes. *Memória, museologia e virtualidade: um estudo sobre o Museu da Pessoa* [Memory, museology and virtuality: a study of Museu da Pessoa]. Portugal: Universidade Lusófona de Humanidades e Tecnologias Departamento de Arquitectura, Urbanismo e Geografia, 2004.

Herrera, Amilcar. *Ciencia y tecnología en el desarrollo de la sociedad*. Santiago de Chile: Universitária, 1970.

Holloway, Margaret, Louis Bailey, Lisa Dikomitis, Nicholas J. Evans, Andrew Goodhead, Miroslava Hukelova, Yvonne Inall, Malcolm Lillie, and Liz Nicol. *Remember Me: The Changing Face of Memorialisation: Final Report*. Hull: University of Hull, 2019. Retrieved 27 July 2022 from https://remembermeproject.files.wordpress.com/2020/04/remember-me-overarching-report-e-version-final.pdf.

Hoskins, Andrew. "Memory of the Multitude: The End of Collective Memory." In *Digital Memory Studies: Media Pasts in Transition*, edited by Andrew Hoskins, 85–109. New York: Routledge, 2018.
Huyssen, Andreas. *Present Pasts: Urban Palimpsests and the Politics of Memory*. Stanford: Stanford University Press, 2003.
———. "Natural Rights, Cultural Rights, and the Politics of Memory." *Hemispheric Institute E-Misférica*. Retrieved 27 July 2022 from https://hemi.nyu.edu/hemi/en/e-misferica-62/huyssen.
Jelin, Elizabeth. *Los trabajos de La memória: Colección memorias de la represion* [The works of memory: Memories of repression collection]. Espanha: Siglo XXI de Espana, 2002.
Lambert, Joe. *Digital Storytelling: Capturing Lives, Creating Community*. New York: Routledge, 2013.
Mbembe, Achille. *Crítica da Razão Negra* [Critique of Black reason]. São Paulo: n-1 edições, 2018.
Mello, C. J., and J. O. Peña. "Tecnologia social: a experiência da Fundação Banco do Brasil na dissemifnação e reaplicação de soluções sociais efetivas" [Social technology: The experience of Fundação Banco do Brasil in the dissemination and reapplication of effective social solutions]. In *Tecnologia social: uma estratégia para o desenvolvimento* [Social technology: A strategy for development], edited by Daniel Seidl and Sandra Santos Cabral. Rio de Janeiro: Fundação Banco do Brasil, 2004.
Merrill, Samuel, Shanti Sumartojo, Angharad Closs Stephens, and Martin Coward. "Togetherness after Terror: The More or Less Digital Commemorative Public Atmospheres of the Manchester Arena Bombing's First Anniversary." *Environment and Planning D: Society and Space* 38, no. 3 (2020): 546–66.
Philips, Ruth. *Museum Pieces: Toward the Indigenization of Canadian Museums*. Montreal: McGill-Queen's University Press, 2012.
Pink, Sarah. *Doing Sensory Ethnography*. London: SAGE Publications, 2009.
Puig de la Bellacasa, Maria. "'Nothing Comes without Its World': Thinking with Care." *The Sociological Review* 60 (2012): 197–216.
Smith, Laurajane, and Emma Waterton. "Constrained by Commonsense: The Authorized Heritage Discourse in Contemporary Debates." In *The Oxford Handbook of Public Archaeology*, edited by Robin Skeates, Carol McDavid, and John Carman, 153–71. Oxford: Oxford University Press, 2012.
Sodaro, Amy. *Exhibiting Atrocity: Memorial Museums and the Politics of Past Violence*. New Brunswick, NJ: Rutgers University Press, 2018.
Slim, Hugo, and Paul Thompson. *Listening for a Change: Oral Testimony and Development*. London: Panos Publications, 1993.
Thompson, Paul. *The Voice of the Past: Oral History*. New York: Oxford University Press, 2017.
Turion, Célio. *Ponto de Cultura: o Brasil de baixo para cima*. São Paulo: Anita Garibaldi, 2010.
Vickery, Jonathan. "Cultural Rights and Cultural Policy: Identifying the Cultural Policy Implications of Culture as a Human Right." *Journal of Law, Social Justice & Global Development* 22, no. 1 (2019): 128–51.
Worcman, Karen. "We're All Curators: Collaborative Curatorship as a New Museum Experience." *THEMA: La revue des Musées de la civilisation* 4 (2016): 125–30.
Worcman, Karen, and Joanne Garde-Hansen. *Social Memory Technology: Theory, Practice, Action*. New York: Routledge, 2016.
Worcman, Karen, Rogério Silva, and Sarah Faleiros, eds. *Brasil Memória em Rede: um novo jeito de conhecer o país* [Brazil memory net: Another way of knowing the country]. São Paulo: Museu da Pessoa: Itajaí: Editora Casa Aberta, 2010.
Worcman, Karen and Vasquez Pereira, Jesus. *História Falada*. São Paulo: Museu da Pessoa, 2006.

Chapter 8

BEYOND A HUMAN RIGHT TO MEMORY

Anna Reading

In many cultures, memory is articulated not only within people's minds and bodies and extended through collective culture but also through ancestral and non-ancestral spirits relating to animals and the natural non-human world.[1] In post-conflict societies such "spirits can be carriers or triggers of individual and collective memories of the violence."[2] This chapter shows how so much of our discussions of a right to memory are deeply rooted in modern Western thought based on vexed hierarchies that sequester off all that is non-human, including other living species and the natural environment of the earth, mountains, water, and air. What if we expand ideas of a right to memory to consider a greater cosmology for memory; after all, the Universe remembers gravitational waves and other planets are understood to remember their past lives through traces and signatures that remember ancient microbial lifeforms.[3] Does Mars not have a right to memory?

This is not such an outlandish proposition if we consider that the Earth Justice movement has sought to reframe legislation and its judicial practices beyond the anthropomorphic to develop laws for environmental personhood that reflect the rights of the non-human and recognizes rivers and mountains as living beings.[4] Even so, such jurisprudence is not such a radical departure, rather, it is simply the formalization and extension of what human cultures already acknowledge in practice through stories and songs of rock sites as beings or rites of memory for the non-human, from pet cemeteries to the ordination of trees.[5]

This chapter explores the implications of living indigenous knowledge practices and the Earth Justice movement for more-than-human memory and what, in turn, this means for conceptualizing and understanding a right to memory. What might we be required to rethink, analytically and methodologically, in terms of a right to memory, once we include the natural world and the wider universe? In this volume, thus far, a right to memory has been concerned with debates within a paradigm that places human memory at its heart, neglecting more-than-human pasts, including those not directly related to the history of human beings. This chapter seeks to broaden our discussion by using an environmental justice framework, drawing light from work within environmental humanities and the sciences, as well as new materialism and indigenous humanities. First, I briefly explore work within memory studies on planetary memory and natural memory before critiquing and extending the previous chapters in this volume to develop a right to memory that is beyond and more-than-human.

Context: Planetary and Natural Memory

Memory beyond the human is increasingly discussed within emergent memory studies research that draws on environmental humanities. A key concern is how nature and climate change are being remembered within literature and other art forms.[6] Rick Crownshaw, for example, examines how the Anthropocene as a geological epoch is "legible in the geological record that is being left by humanity's collective geophysical agency," which is then remembered through the "atmosphere, lithosphere, biosphere, and hydrosphere" and how, in turn, this is expressed through literary memory.[7] Relatedly, Clara de Massol de Rebetz explores planetary memory of climate change and human activities on "non-human life forms" and "non-biological matter":

> legible through human archives but also through non-human traces of extinction—flood lines and drowned islands, extinct species and future fossils, CO_2 levels in the atmosphere and plastic particles contaminating bodies and landscapes. Planetary memory is accessible through what is destroyed and what remains, what has been inscribed in the air, into the rocks, the soils, the bodies of living things and deep into the oceans.[8]

De Massol de Rebetz also analyzes forms of human commemoration of more-than-human lives at the time of the sixth mass extinction.[9] Drawing on Ursula Heise's concept of "eco-cosmopolitanism," she examines the example of Remembrance Day for Lost Species. People gather around the world every year on 30 November to mourn extinct species through the enactment of funeral ceremonies. Her work provokes the question of whether and how lost species should have the "right" to be remembered, with perhaps public memory institutions playing a major role in environmental awareness and sustainable environment.[10]

Yet, despite research within memory studies that extends our understanding of memory into natural and planetary memory, there is a lacuna—with no work to date that addresses a right to memory beyond the human.

Rethinking Memory Rights beyond the Human

In the previous chapters of this volume, any discussion of memory rights for more-than-human life forms and non-biological matter have been notably absent. Yet, reflecting on these preceding chapters and reading beyond them can also—as we shall see—point to some elements we might include within emergent conceptual thinking for memory rights beyond the human. Jay Winter in this volume writes, "The duty to remember is a family matter." Our top priority, he argues, is the "intimate responsibility" of remembering family members after death. For Winter, exemplars involve human dramas, for instance, the problem faced by Sophocles' Antigone in burying her brother Polyneices. Doing so violated Creon's decree to bury her brother without respect. She rails that, although to remember her brother may end her own life and offend the king, to not remember him would be to commit a greater wrong and offend the gods. Remembrance is a sacred act, argues Winter, and when Antigone remembers her brother, she confirms her humanity. Winter's chapter reveals the deep anthropomorphic bias within our conceptions of a right to memory. Memory rights are considered solely a human domain with jurisprudence and rights to protect and preserve what makes us distinct from other species, i.e., "our humanity." Winter segues into a discussion of the impossibility of remembering so many during World War I, World War II, and the Holocaust. From these three, he charts the emergence of the human rights movement after 1945 "working to establish a new balance between the state, the individual and civil society was an act of remembrance then, and it remains so today." He shows how the UN Declaration of Human Rights emerged from the mass slaughter of total war in 1914–18 and the subsequent mass murder of Nazi genocide. Seventy years on, the climate emergency means that, as a matter of great urgency, human beings are required to think about the sixth mass extinction and planetary ecocide. This requires what climate emergency activist Greta Thunberg has described as "cathedral thinking. We must lay the foundation while we may not know exactly how to build the ceiling."[11] In terms of memory, it means including more-than-human memory rights. These are and will be the new grammar of commemoration and justice in order to limit what humans can do to other species and Mother

Earth. While the Declaration of Human Rights was based on preserving humanity after the shock of genocide, the Universal Declaration of Earth Rights implicates a far wider and deeper world of more-than-human memory, which is or will be our response to the crimes of ecocide.

We can further extend and clarify this idea by building on Lea David's distinction in this volume between a right to remember, defined as "an individual's right to self-determination" and a duty to remember that refers to "a collective moral imperative [that] has a long trajectory and is directly connected to human rights abuses."

In going beyond human memory rights we should also make the distinction between the non-human person's right to self-determination and to a collective obligation to remember rights abuses of the more-than-human in the form of ecocide. There may be a duty to remember, for example, an extinct species or a dried-up river system because they are non-human persons whose rights have been violated, as suggested in projects such Remembrance Day for Lost Species.[12] Are humans doing this because we think that we can been redeemed if we do? Or is it that we have a duty to remember the Black Rhino and the Xerces Blue Butterfly because we think doing so will prevent further mass extinctions and contribute to a better, more sustainable world? The organization Greenpeace, for example, on its website in 2021 featured the article "18 Animals that Became Extinct in the Last Century" stating that providing a memory of them and why they became extinct acts a "stark warning."[13]

Importantly, though, Lea David in this volume argues that in human terms this distinction between a duty and a right is deeply entrenched in neoliberalism, with an implicit assumption regarding the economic value of human suffering that then produces new inequalities. The notions of "duty to remember" and the "right to memory," she argues, rely heavily on the neoliberal logic of the monetization of human rights abuses. This insight chimes in with observations by environmentalists for a non-economic rationale for the standing of nature. In 1972, Christopher Stone's essay "Should Trees Have Standing" revealed how existing laws considered nature beyond the human being as without rights.[14] He argued that while we could argue for the value of trees in economic terms, we might think of trees as having standing or value in their own right. Building on this, Roderick Nash, in "The Rights of Nature," argued that throughout history many disenfranchised groups including slaves and women have subsequently been accorded rights based on equal value.[15] Nash argued that a similar body of rights needs to include nature.

In this regard, Aleksandra Gliszczyńska-Grabias and Grażyna Baranowska's argument in this volume that some communities dominate memory may be read outward as a basis for extending memory rights beyond the human:

Every community and its story—sometimes kept for centuries and often distorted to build the community's identity in the least painful way—has a natural tendency to portray itself in a positive way. Of course, this tendency is also typical of individuals, but in the communal and collective dimension, it can become a socially dangerous phenomenon, positioned close to nationalism, messianism, and xenophobia.

Importantly, "community" here is assumed to be a collective dimension of humanity positioned through an anthropocentrism and speciesism in which anything that is not human is deemed to be of lesser value when it comes to rights, including the right to memory. Once we acknowledge this bias, a right to memory may begin to be reformulated from a biocentric viewpoint in which politically, economically, socially, and ethically all living things have equal value. Could we extend this even further and take an eco-centric viewpoint that accords value to the whole of nature?[16] If we do not do this then our discussions of a right to memory relies on a precept that involves a dangerous intellectual amnesia in which we forget that "our human social systems are inseparably fused with the larger Earth Community, namely our planet and all its species and ecosystems."[17] Instead, as with wider jurisprudence and discussions of rights, I content that in the twenty-first century "our systems of governance and law must equate with this wider context to ensure that the blinkered pursuit of human wellbeing is not at the expense of the integrity of the Earth."[18]

Rebecca Kook's discussion of democratic inclusions and the domestication of remembrance in this volume is also anthropomorphically framed, assuming that human memory both individual and collective are at the center. Drawing on research on a Holocaust remembrance initiative at the grassroots level in Israel, Kook focuses on what she calls a right to memory "on the ground," articulated through local initiatives. Although Kook's work only considers human memory rights, nonetheless, if we build on this in discussions of more-than-human memory rights, it points to the importance of including community and on-the-ground eco-initiatives as ways of remembering and preserving the memories of non-human subjects.

Relatedly, Karen Worcman and Joanne Garde-Hansen's chapter in this volume reminds us how important it is that "every social group" should be able to "select, produce, and analyze" the past in accordance with its own cultural values when performing memory work. The term "social group" here refers to a human social group. How might every ecological group or community be allowed to produce its own history and memories within its own set of values? A key premise in their work is the idea of "thinking-with," which provokes the question of how to think or feel with non-human persons and biota, as well as how to think-feel with non-biological matter. James Canton's *The Oak Papers*, derived from sitting beneath an eight-hundred-year-old oak tree over the course of a year, offers some clues. He suggests that through "corporeal connection," we can produce "a powerful feeling of remembrance in the simple act of touching an old oak. It is bodily remembrance through time."[19] A related approach is posited by Nan Shepherd in her biography of a mountain in which she describes "its weather, its airs and lights, its singing burns, its haunted dells, its pinnacles and tarns, its birds and flowers, its snows, its long blue distances."[20] To write the memory of the mountain requires a different way of discovering and learning in which "the sense must be trained and disciplined" and the body "trained to move with the right harmonies . . . One of the most compelling is quiescence."[21]

While this might help us epistemologically develop new methods for "thinking-feeling-with" rights beyond the human, an ontological basis for existence and with it more-than-human rights can be extended from Thomas Berry's "Origin, Differentiation and the Role of Rights."[22] For Berry, "The Universe is composed of subjects to be communed with, not of objects to be exploited"; and "The natural world on planet Earth gets its rights from the same source that humans get their rights, from the Universe that brought them into being."[23] As subjects, each component of the Universe is capable of having rights. Berry argues that all members of our earth community possess rights since "Rights originate where existence originates."[24] To this we then might add that a right to memory originates where existence originates. Berry maintains that all components of the Earth community have three rights: "the right to be, the right to habitat or a place to be, and the right to fulfil its role in the ever-renewing processes of the Earth community."[25] Memory, I would suggest, is an integral part of these three rights: memories for the human and more-than-human require being, as well as what we might call placing or being in place, as well as processes of renewal through change. Importantly, Berry argues that although rights are universally applicable, they are variable according to species: "All rights in living forms are species specific and limited. Birds have bird rights. Insects have insect rights. Humans have human rights. Difference in rights is qualitative, not quantitative. The rights of an insect would be of no value to a tree or a fish."[26]

Do we then, by extension, conceive of a right to memory for biota that is also species specific? Do birds have bird memory rights and a tree have tree memory rights? And, as Berry notes in relation to human rights, do these species-specific rights then act with rather than negate or obliterate the rights of other species?

The ground-breaking "Wild Law: A Manifesto for Earth Justice" that added a spiritual and moral dimension to what had been a legal and historic discussion about the rights of nature has since led to laws enacted at the local, national, and international levels that accord both rights and citizenship to other living species as well as more-than-human biota such as water, air, and minerals. For example, in 2008, Ecuador recognized the Rights of Nature in its Constitution. In 2011, it upheld the rights of the Vilcabamba River to not be polluted or ruined by human activity. One of the most significant international mnemonic acts recognizing the rights of nature has been the UN General Assembly's creation of International Mother Earth Day in 2009, which commemorates all life on Earth and the Earth as a living being.[27] Since then, the UN has sought the adoption of nine resolutions on Harmony with Nature to use a non-anthropocentric approach "in which the fundamental basis for right and wrong action concerning the environment is grounded not solely in human concerns."[28] At its sixty-sixth session, the UN passed a Resolution entitled "The Future We Want," which includes a specific concern with cultural heritage and traditional knowledge. Article J reads:

> (j) Enhance the welfare of indigenous peoples and their communities, other local and traditional communities, and ethnic minorities, recognizing and supporting their identity, culture and interests, and *avoid endangering their cultural heritage, practices and traditional knowledge*, preserving and respecting non-market approaches that contribute to the eradication of poverty. [Emphasis added][29]

This recognition of indigenous knowledge and heritage as integral to the future provides an important epistemological basis for how to conceive of a right to memory that includes the more-than-human. In this regard we might also extend Noam Tirosh and Amit Schejter's vision presented in their chapter, in which Amartya Sen's capabilities approach places well-being as integral to a just society, "enabling people to be what they value being." Their approach places human welfare at its center, but what if we were to extend this to the welfare of the whole planet and its ecosystem? Tirosh and Schejter argue that memory rights concerns provide the means of remembering through different media. In the case of memory rights for the wider planet, this may then well include ancient and new ways to read the world: it may include eco-translators and eco-advocates playing a crucial role to remember the wider planet's history and past and contribution to the future.

Conclusion

This volume began with the development of a right to memory that emerged out of the human rights regime after World War II, which sought "[to limit] not only what states can do against other states but also what states can do against their own citizens." Seventy years on, the Earth Justice movement is effectively arguing for what we might call a new grammar of commemoration with an even longer-range project of remembrance that seeks to limit what humans can do against other species and the planet. Various declarations of non-human rights are emerging as both a commemorative project and what we might term "future memory" in an age of mass extinction through ecocide, with the mass killing and destruction of non-human beings that occur every day without burial or memory. Going beyond the human means that we preserve the living Earth so that we can have a right to memory in the future.

Part of the recognition and understanding of a right to memory beyond that which is human will include learning and using new paradigms. We need to frame our thoughts in ways that are non-anthropomorphic, that disrupt millennia of education centered in human species narcissism that trains us to think, live, and accept catastrophic ecocide. Part of a right to memory in this case involves eliciting non-human viewpoints to be remembered and included, which will require both ancient and new methods and approaches. Jonathan Keats, experimental philosopher and artist, appointed slime molds as visiting professors to Hampshire College to create what he termed a "plasmodium consortium." The slime molds were consulted about a number of human problems that included mapping the cosmos and international border policies. These protists with no brain but with diverse cellular forms are, he claims, able to offer a more objective viewpoint on human problems, particularly when it comes to mapping because of their capacity to learn, habituate, and remember routes.[30] Understanding a right to memory beyond the human will mean appointing and entrusting non-humans to places of knowledge as well as dismantling the human egocentric, hierarchical approaches to power and knowledge. To the indigenous world view, human beings are the youngest, newest planetary arrivals in comparison with the rest of the planet. Plants developed long before humans, developing the heritable knowledge to make food from sunlight and water, generously making enough for their own sustenance and providing for the rest of the earth community.[31] A right to more-than-human memory requires us to learn both humility and animacy. "Our toddlers speak of plants and animals as if they were people [but] When we tell them that the tree is not a who, but an it, we . . . can take up the chain saw."[32] Learning new ways to analyze and read can, as Christopher Schliephake shows in relation to Greek texts such as *Pausanius*, reveal a "complex material web composed of water, soil, animals and land."[33] While this might involve spiritual or animist paradigms it could also utilize the insights of materialist history and in so doing open up the way for more-than-human voices, turning: "a static and monumental archive of cultural memory into dynamic and open imaginative spaces that allows us to analyze how ancient environments and their (textual and material) narratives have shaped, time and again, our understanding of humanities place in the world."[34]

Reading outwards from these debates on a right to memory we are able to remember that the right to memory for our planet is imperative. What, after all, will all these rights for human remembering be for if there is no planet to speak of? We might struggle over how and what humans should remember; we might go to war over our different versions of human histories; we might shout about the importance of our experiences as victims; we might bewail lost national identities and legislate to protect our indigenous heritage. But what is all this for if we have forgotten the most important rights of all, the memories of our shared living home, Earth, our unique planet.

Any understanding of a right to memory for the twenty-first century can be drawn from multiple projects that have already begun at local, national, and international levels to recognize that all living beings have pasts and histories worth preserving and sharing, as do all non-biological forms and abiota that to many indigenous knowledge holders and scientists animate the deep past. If we destroy a mountain to extract gold or rare Earth minerals, we destroy more than our natural heritage, we destroy a living being with a history, a world. Giving mountains rights, including the right to be remembered and the duty to remember them is only returning what was taken away. Recognizing rivers as persons gives us and the river the right to remember how their living water brings us life. Thinking beyond the narrow confines of a human right to memory means we grow into a future of being more than humankind.

Anna Reading (known as Amza), PhD, is Professor of Culture and Creative Industries at Kings College, University of London, UK and Honorary Visiting Professor at Western Sydney University, Australia. She is the author of *Polish Women, Solidarity and Feminism* (Springer, 1992), *The Social Inheritance of the Holocaust: Gender, Culture and Memory* (Springer, 2002), and *Gender and Memory in the Globlital Age* (Palgrave Macmillan, 2016) and co-edited *Cultural Memories of Nonviolent Struggles* (Palgrave Macmillan, 2015) and *Save as . . . Digital Memories* (Palgrave 2009). She jointly edits the journal *Media, Culture, and Society* and has written seven plays performed in the UK, Finland, India, Poland, United States, and Ireland.

Notes

With deep gratitude to Hilly Fields and the River Ravensbourne, London.
1. The origin story of Judeo-Christianity within Genesis is often read as a narrative to remember human expulsion from the Garden of Eden, marking the beginning of human separation and dominion over all that is not human. See Jones, *Losing Eden*. However, it is possible to reread ancient texts to include "the many non-human voices to which

writing bids us turn," as Christopher Schleiphake argues in "From Storied to Porous Landscapes."
2. Igreja, "Memories of Violence," 33–38, as well as Igreja at el, "Gamba Spirits, Gender Relations and Healing," and Stoller, *Embodying Colonial Memories*.
3. See Sutter, "The Universe Remembers Gravitational Waves." Much of the debate around whether the Universe remembers centers around black holes. While physicists such as Stephen Hawking have argued that they destroy everything they swallow, Leonard Susskind has argued that nothing is ever lost: the event horizon of black holes conserves the information of everything that goes into a black hole from a planet to a book. See Susskind, *The Black Hole War*. It is after all this premise that underpins NASA landing Perseverance—a robot—in a 45 km crater in Mars's northern hemisphere carved by a river 3.5 billion years ago "seeking the signs of past life." Quoted from Dacey, "Searching for Signs of Past Life on Mars."
4. See Roy, "New Zealand River Granted Same Legal Rights"; Safi, "Ganges and Yamuna Rivers Granted Same Legal Rights"; and Greene, "The First Successful Case of the Rights of Nature" and "Colombian Supreme Court Recognizes Rights." See also, CELDF, "Rights of Nature: Timeline"; and for New Zealand laws providing environmental personhood, see the Te Urewera Act 2014 and Te Awa Tupua (Whanganui River Claims Settlement) Act 2017. The "Te Anga Putakerongo mo Nga Maunga o Taranaki, Poujai me Kaitake," ("Record of Understanding for Mount Taranaki, Pouakai and the Kaitake Ranges") incorporates the peaks as a living, indivisible whole, to be referred to by their Tupuna names, including Taranaki, Pouakai and Kaitake and encompasses all of the physical and metaphysical elements of Nga Maunga from the peaks through to all of the surrounding environs.
5. Animal companions have long been remembered within human cultures leading to the development of formal pet cemeteries as well as commercial forms of remembrance. See Wolfelt, *When Your Pet Dies*, as well as Joyner, "Seven Beautiful Ways to Remember Pets," Baumgartner, "Re-Membering Pets"; and Withange, "Story of Tree Ordination."
6. See Craps and Crownshaw, "Rising Tide of Climate Change Fiction."
7. See Crownshaw, "Climate Change Fiction and the Future of Memory."
8. de Massol de Rebetz "The Anthropocene Memorial."
9. de Massol de Rebetz, "Remembrance Day."
10. Gustafsson and Ijla, "Museums: An Incubator."
11. Thunberg, *No One Is Too Small*, 67.
12. de Massol de Rebetz, "Remembrance Day."
13. "18 Animals that Became Extinct in the Last Century."
14. Stone, *Should Trees Have Standing*.
15. Nash, *The Rights of Nature*. See also Boyd, *The Rights of Nature*.
16. While dominion over nature is inherent within much of Judeo-Christianity (with exceptions such as Quakerism) other religions take a more biocentric stance, including Islam and Hinduism. In Hindu belief, the human soul can be reincarnated into non-human forms, and trees also have their own tree deity. The interrelatedness of all life is also an essential belief of Buddhism.
17. Wild Law Wilderness, 21 April 2004.
18. Wild Law Wilderness, 21 April 2004.
19. Canton, *Oak Papers*.
20. Shepherd, *Living Mountain*, 90.
21. Shepherd, *Living Mountain*, 90.
22. Berry, "Origin, Differentiation and the Role of Rights."
23. Berry, "Origin, Differentiation and the Role of Rights."

24. Berry, "Origin, Differentiation and the Role of Rights."
25. Berry, "Origin, Differentiation and the Role of Rights."
26. Berry, "Origin, Differentiation and the Role of Rights."
27. See "When Mother Earth Sends Us a Message." *United Nations.* Retrieved 28 July 2022 from https://www.un.org/en/observances/earth-day. The UN has five related observances, including Mountain Day, Wildlife Day, Biodiversity Day, Environment Day, and Water Day. The subsequent *2010 Submission for Consideration of the Universal Declaration on the Rights of Mother Earth* states in Article 1, "Mother Earth (1) Mother Earth is a living being." Article 5 states that "Mother Earth and all beings are entitled to all the inherent rights recognized in this Declaration without distinction of any kind, such as may be made between organic and inorganic beings, species, origin, use to human beings, or any other status" (6). Just as human beings have human rights, all other beings also have rights specific to their species or kind and appropriate for their role and function within the communities within which they exist.
28. See "UN Harmony with Nature." Retrieved 28 July 2022 from http://www.harmony withnatureun.org/. For a list, see "UN Documents on Harmony with Nature." Retrieved 28 July 2022 from http://www.harmonywithnatureun.org/unDocs/.
29. UN, "Future We Want."
30. Sterling, "Latest Jonathan Keats Intervention."
31. Kimmerer, *Braiding Sweetgrass*, 346.
32. Kimmerer, *Braiding Sweetgrass*, 57.
33. Schliephake, "From Storied to Porous Landscapes." He cites Raymond Williams' idea of "proper materialist history" that does not separate "nature and man." Williams, *Culture and Materialism*, 111.
34. Williams, *Culture and Materialism*, 111.

Bibliography

"18 Animals that Became Extinct in the Last Century." *Greenpeace*, 10 September 2020. Retrieved 25 February 2021 from https://www.greenpeace.org.uk/news/18-animals-that-went-extinct-in-the-last-century/?source=GA&subsource=GOFRNAOAGA034J&gclid =Cj0KCQiAst2BBhDJARIsAGo2ldX2sR_cL4cQ6JLL_tYpZrEOBvqMHVEKPah_Jk9Fr iZPmVHIkXbuJ1AaAns3EALw_wcB.

Baumgartner, Barbara. "Re-Membering Pets: Documenting the Meaning of People's Relationships with These Family Members." *Explorations: An E-Journal of Narrative Practice Issue* 2 (2010): 50–71.

Berry, Thomas. "Origin, Differentiation and the Role of Rights." *The Institute for Education Studies*, 11 January 2001. Retrieved 26 February 2021 from http://www.ties-edu.org/wp-content/uploads/2018/09/Thomas-Berry-rights.pdf.

Bond, Lucy Ben de Bruyn, and Jessica Rapson. *Planetary Memory*. Abingdon: RoutledgeAnon, 2010.

Boyd, David R. *The Rights of Nature: A Legal Revolution that Could Save the World*. Toronto: ECW Press, 2017.

Canton, James. *The Oak Papers*. New York: Harper One, 2020.

CELDF. "Rights of Nature: Timeline." Retrieved 6 September 2022 from https://celdf.org/rights-of-nature/timeline/

"Colombian Supreme Court Recognizes Rights of the Amazon River Ecosystem." *IUCN News*. 20 April 2018. Retrieved 3 February 2021 from https://www.iucn.org/news/world-commission-environmental-law/201804/colombian-supreme-court-recognizes-rights-amazon-river-ecosystem.

Craps, Stef, and Rick Crownshaw. "The Rising Tide of Climate Change Fiction." *Studies in the Novel* 50, no. 1 (2018): 1–8.

Crownshaw, Rick. "Climate Change Fiction and the Future of Memory: Speculating on Nathaniel Rich's *Odds against Tomorrow*." *Resilience: A Journal of the Environmental Humanities* 4, no. 2 (2017): 127–46.

Dacey, James. "Searching for Signs of Past Life on Mars with NASA's Perseverance Rover." *Physics World*, 10 February 2021. Retrieved 24 February 2021 from https://physicsworld.com/a/searching-for-signs-of-past-life-on-mars-with-nasas-perseverance-rover/.

de Massol de Rebetz, Clara. "The Anthropocene Memorial: Recording Climate Change on the Banks of the River Potomac River in Washington DC." *Sanglap: Journal of Literary and Cultural Enquiry* 5, no. 2 (2019): 1–15.

de Massol de Rebetz, Clara. "Remembrance Day for Lost Species: Remembering and Mourning Extinction in the Anthropocene." *Memory Studies* 13, no. 5 (2020): 875–88.

En-Act. *Wild Law Workshop*. 21st April 2004–24th April (2004). Retrieved 7 July 2022 from Internet Archive Wayback Machine: https://web.archive.org/web/20071007023233/http://www.peoplesearthdecade.org/events/calendar.php?event_id=285.

Greene. Natalia. "The First Successful Case of the Rights of Nature Implementation in Ecuador." *Global Alliance for the Rights of Nature*. Retrieved 22 April 2021 from http://therightsofnature.org/first-ron-case-ecuador.

Gustafsson, Christer, and Akram Ijla. "Museums: An Incubator for Sustainable Social Development and Environmental Protection." *International Journal of Development and Sustainability* 5, no. 9 (2016): 446–62.

Igreja, Victor. "Memories of Violence, Cultural Transformations of Cannibals, and Indigenous State-Building in Post-Conflict Mozambique." *Comparative Studies in Society and History*, vol. 56, no. 3, 2014, pp. 774–802.

Igreja, Victor et al. "Gamba Spirits, Gender Relations, and Healing in Post-Civil War Gorongosa, Mozambique." *The Journal of the Royal Anthropological Institute*, vol. 14, no. 2, 2008, pp. 353–71.

Jones, Lucy. *Losing Eden: Why Our Minds Need the Wild*. London: Penguin Random House Books, 2020.

Joyner, Lisa. "Seven Beautiful Ways to Remember Your Dog after They Have Died: From Handmade Quilts to Memory Boxes." *Country Living*, 14 August 2019. Retrieved 28 July 2022 from https://www.countryliving.com/uk/wildlife/pets/a28684081/dog-remembrance-ideas/.

Kimmerer, Robin Wall. *Braiding Sweetgrass; Indigenous Wisdom, Scientific Knowledge and the Teachings of Plants*. Minneapolis, MN: Milkweed Editions, 2013.

Nash, Roderick. *The Rights of Nature: A History of Environmental Ethics*. Madison: University of Wisconsin Press, 1990.

Roy, Eleanor Ainge. "New Zealand River Granted Same Legal Rights as Human Being." *The Guardian*, 16 March 2017. Retrieved 3 February 2021 from https://www.theguardian.com/world/2017/mar/16/new-zealand-river-granted-same-legal-rights-as-human-being.

Safi, Michael. "Ganges and Yamuna Rivers Granted Same Legal Rights as Human Beings." *The Guardian*, 21 March 2017. Retrieved 3 March 2021 from https://www.theguardian.com/world/2017/mar/21/ganges-and-yamuna-rivers-granted-same-legal-rights-as-human-beings.

Schliephake, Christopher. "From Storied to Porous Landscapes: Antiquity, the Environmental Humanities and the Case of Long-Term Histories." *Gaia* 29, no. 4 (2020): 230–34.
Shepherd, Nan. *The Living Mountain*. Edinburgh: Canongate, 2008. First published in 1977.
Sterling. Bruce. "The Latest Jonathan Keats Intervention." *Wired*, 5 July 2017. Retrieved 1 March 2021 from https://www.wired.com/beyond-the-beyond/2017/05/latest-jonathan-keats-intervention/.
Stoller, Paul. "Embodying Colonial Memories." *American Anthropologist*, vol. 96, no. 3, 1994, pp. 634–48.
Stone, Christopher. *Should Trees Have Standing: Law, Morality, and the Environment*, 3rd edn. Oxford: Oxford University Press, 2010.
Susskind, Leonard. *The Black Hole War: My Battle with Stephen Hawking to Make the World Safe for Quantum Mechanics*. New York: Back Bay Books, 2009.
Sutter, Paul. "The Universe Remembers Gravitational Waves: And We Can Find Them." *Space.com*, 6 December 2019. Retrieved 24 February 2021 from https://www.space.com/gravitational-waves-memory-space-time.html.
"Te Anga Putakerongo mo Nga Maunga o Taranaki, Pouajai me Kaitake" [Record of Understanding for Mount Taranaki, Pouakai and the Kaitake Ranges]. *New Zealand Government*, 20 December 2017. Retrieved 28 July 2022 from https://www.govt.nz/assets/Documents/OTS/Taranaki-Maunga/Taranaki-Maunga-Te-Anga-Putakerongo-Record-of-Understanding-20-December-2017.pdf.
"Te Awa Tupua (Whanganui River Claims Settlement) Act 2017." *New Zealand Legislation*. 20 March 2017. Retrieved 3 March 2021 from https://www.legislation.govt.nz/act/public/2017/0007/latest/whole.html.
"Te Urewere Act 2014." *New Zealand Legislation*. 25 July 2014. Retrieved 3 March 2021 from https://www.legislation.govt.nz/act/public/2014/0051/latest/whole.html.
Thunberg, Greta. *No One Is Too Small to Make a Difference*. London: Penguin Books, 2019.
UN (United Nations) General Assembly. Resolution adopted by the General Assembly on 27 July 2012 – *The Future We Want*. Retrieved 6 September 2022 from http://www.un.org/ga/search/view_doc.asp?symbol=A/RES/66/288&Lang=E.
Williams, Raymond. *Culture and Materialism*. London: Verso, 2005.
Withange, Hemanth. "The Story of Tree Ordination." *Friends of the Earth International*. Retrieved 25 February 2021 from https://www.foei.org/news/the-story-of-tree-ordination-in-sri-lanka.
Wolfelt, Alan D. *When Your Pet Dies: A Guide to Mourning, Remembering and Healing*. Fort Collins, CO: Companion Books, 2004.

Conclusion

Although this book began its journey in a crowded conference room in Madrid in 2019, the idea of a right to memory, as this book shows, is much longer and broader as well as being highly complex. A right to memory we argue is a socio-political mechanism that extends across questions of law, media, ethics, and history, and connects human rights with justice and empowerment for the weaker members of society. Our objective with this book has been to show the importance of thinking about memory in terms of rights discourses particularly in light of the ways anti-liberal movements and leaders mobilize history and memory to sediment discrimination and generate further inequalities both symbolic and structural.

In the field of memory studies, however, a right to memory has scarcely been examined. Nonetheless, it has been explored to a limited extent in fields such as archival science, media and communication, and political science which can be brought into the field of memory studies and which this book then has played a role in doing.

We hope that we have engaged our readers—who may be memory activists, academics, or those working in archives, museums, the media, or the law—to the key theoretical terms and questions raised by debate, as well as providing some practical and on the ground problems and solutions. Each chapter has sought to illuminate the topic and take forward the debate in a number of ways.

Jay Winter in "Antigone's Shadow: Human Rights, Memory, and the Two World Wars" focused on whether we have a duty to remember and to what extent this duty then provides a blueprint for wider discussions regarding a right to memory.

Anna Reading in "Framing Memory Rights in International Law" explored how international law frames memory rights. While her taxonomy is not to be considered definitive and indeed may, as any taxonomy does, serve to exclude as well as include, nonetheless, the chapter sought to provide a framework for current and future discussions of how a right to memory is discursively articulated at the international level.

Lea David in "The 'Duty to Remember' and the 'Right to Memory': Memory Politics and Neoliberal Logic" warned us against the conflation of a duty to remember with a right to memory, which she argued can lead to false beliefs about being able to protect humanity from future atrocities through commemoration alone.

Noam Tirosh and Amit Schejter in "Memory, Rights and Sen's 'Capabilities Approach'" made the case for the importance of centering media within our debates in terms of the ways this is integral to memory-making and hence memory rights. They build on Amartya Sen's "capabilities approach," which puts human well-being at the center of promoting a right to memory. Key to twenty-first-century thinking, they argue, is recognizing the role of digital media particularly in providing people with the capabilities they need to construct and tell stories about their past.

Rebecca Kook in "'The memory Belongs to No One and It Belongs to Everyone': An Analysis of a Grassroots Claim to the Right to Memory" provides a crucial reminder of the importance of grassroots claims to the right to memory. Focusing on an Israeli memory initiative called Zikaron Besalon (remembrance in the living room), the chapter examines how a right to memory can be materialized through grassroots mnemonic activities. Only if we include grassroots participation, she argues, can we really understand the relationship between democratic inclusion and a right to memory.

Aleksandra Gliszczyńska-Grabias and Grażyna Baranowska in "Using and Abusing Memory Laws in Search of 'Historical Truth': The Case of the 2018 Amendments to the Polish Institute of National Remembrance Act" focused on the relationships between historical truth and the ways memory laws can be used and abused in the case of Poland. They show how memory laws can sometimes be used to infringe memory rights and the right to truth in general and thus proving how crucial the right to memory can be when history is manipulated.

Karen Worcman and Joanne Garde-Hansen in "The Right to Produce Memory: Social Memory Technology as Cultural Work" focused on the example of the Museu da Pessoa (Museum of the person) in Sao Paolo, Brazil as an example in practice for an approach to realize digital memory rights for individuals and communities. They put forward the idea of social memory technology as a practical framework and technique for enabling the right to produce memory.

Anna Reading in the final chapter "Beyond a Human Right to Memory" turned the preceding arguments of the book on their head by asking why it is that we only consider human memory rights, given the impact of the climate emergency on other species. The chapter sought to decenter human memory asking about the right to memory of more-than-human beings. She showed how the rights of the more-than-human constitute the next stage of rights discourse and in so doing require a right to memory to be extended to remembering the rest of the planet before it is too late.

As with any edited collection, there will be biases and omissions, and what is not included is very often the starting point for the next stage of the debate. Although we attempted to include as wide a range of case studies and authors with different perspectives, we admit that particular areas of debate and empirical research are absent. Future work should consider, for example, case studies from other countries not included here particularly the African region, Australia, and China, as well as other countries from the Global South. There is also still room for more detailed work on countries in the Global North. Finally, building on Anna Reading's chapter on more-than-human memory rights there needs to be more work that considers non-Western and indigenous memory rights, which often take a different approach to knowledge-making and temporalities.

One commentator on recent memory law debates, William Holmes, notes that "memory laws range from the benign, to the bad and the ugly depending on their creators and enforcers." To that he adds that what is needed ultimately is not necessarily more laws, but rather outstanding public debate and historical research, along with public memory institutions that are free to provoke debate. He suggests that in relation to a right to memory, what is important is generating critical discussion around the topic: "the question, not the rule, is the answer."[1]

In this regard, we hope that this book in a modest way is part of this important public debate on a right to memory and that its arguments, theories, and case studies can be drawn on usefully by those in the academy but also those working to make laws nationally and internationally, as well as those working in regional and local public memory institutions.

Noam Tirosh is a senior lecturer in the department of Communication Studies at Ben-Gurion University of the Negev. His research focuses on the relationship between memory and media and their relation with democracy, justice, and human rights. He is the author of a score of journal articles and book chapters covering topics ranging from the European Right to be Forgotten to the memory rights of the Palestinian minority in Israel, refugees and asylum seekers, and Jews deported from Arab countries.

Anna Reading (known as Amza), PhD, is Professor of Culture and Creative Industries at Kings College, University of London, UK and Honorary Visiting Professor at Western Sydney University, Australia. She is the author of *Polish Women, Solidarity and Feminism* (Springer, 1992), *The Social Inheritance of the Holocaust: Gender, Culture and Memory* (Springer, 2002), and *Gender and Memory in the Globital Age* (Palgrave Macmillan, 2016) and co-edited *Cultural Memories of Nonviolent Struggles* (Palgrave Macmillan, 2015) and *Save as . . . Digital Memories* (Palgrave 2009). She jointly edits the journal *Media, Culture, and Society* and has written seven plays performed in the UK, Finland, India, Poland, United States, and Ireland.

Notes

1. Holmes, William. "Is It Time to Adopt Laws on Historical Memory in Britain?" *Human Rights Pulse*, 20 July 2020. Retrieved 23 July 2022 from https://www.humanrightspulse.com/mastercontentblog/is-it-time-to-adopt-laws-on-historical-memory-in-britain.

Index

activism, 67, 96–102
    climate emergency activism, 151
    human rights activism, 56, 60
    memory activism, 59, 95
agency, 46, 68, 150
American civil war (1861–1865), 3
archives, 43–44, 114, 121, 134–143

canon, 9, 34
capabilities approach, 76–79, 83–85, 155, 163
capitalism, 62, 142
Cassin, Rene, 20–29, 55
civil society, 19, 102, 138–9, 151
Cold War, 29, 43, 137
compensation, 61, 63, 76
connectivity, 36
Covid-19 pandemic, 36, 96, 143
crime(s), 24–27, 54, 56, 61, 63, 112, 115–124
    against humanity, 115, 118

Declaration on the Rights of Indigenous Peoples (2007), 6, 40, 45
democratization of memory, 2, 103, 136
disappeared persons, missing persons, 113, 120
duty to remember, 6–9, 17, 19, 29, 37, 53–69, 115, 151–2, 157, 162–3

Eastern Europe, 114–5, 123
ecocide, 151–2, 156
ethics of memory, 10, 53, 61, 94

forgetting, 10, 37, 54, 56–57, 79–82, 140
forgiveness, 53

freedom(s) and liberty, 10, 28, 77, 80, 84–85, 112–4
    fundamental, 106, 116
    negative form of, positive form of, 78
    of academic research, 116, 119
    of expression, of speech, 6, 37, 84, 115–6, 119, 122–4
    of memory, 58
    of opinion, 37, 115
    of press, of media, 83, 84
    to be what we value being, 80
    to mourn, 58
Freire, Paulo, 133, 139, 143

Geneva Conventions, 26
genocide, 8, 33, 37, 39, 44, 58, 93, 115–6, 119, 123–4, 151–2
globalization, 35, 94
Global North, 62, 135, 164
Global South, 135, 164

Havel, Vaclav, 10, 112, 123
healing, 47, 53–54, 98, 104
heritage, 8, 34, 37–41, 55, 135–6, 138, 143
    colonial, 133
    cultural, 38–40, 42, 44, 132, 155
    indigenous, 40, 44, 155, 157
    world, 40, 42–43, 45, 58
Holocaust, 9, 18–19, 25, 59, 61, 113, 151
    bill, 114, 118
    commemoration of the, 92–93, 96–106, 118, 153
    National Holocaust and Heroism Memorial Day (HHMD), 97
    negation, 114–9, 122–4
    Yad Vashem, 96–97

human rights
  activism, 56, 60
  European convention on (1950), 29, 116
  European court of (1958), 29, 116
  United Nations Commission of, 20, 28, 121
  Universal Declaration of (UDHR, 1948), 19–20, 25, 28–29, 36–38, 59
identity, 8, 33, 35, 39–40, 57, 67, 79–82, 85, 95, 106, 115, 155
  collective, 5, 79, 81, 93
  community's identity, 113, 153
  construction of, 6, 9–10
  cultural, 63
  digital, 6
  group, 79
  individual, 79, 84, 93
  Israeli, 105
  Jewish, 23
  national, 5, 33, 54, 58, 104, 113, 137
  online, 82
  politics of, 59, 61, 63, 65, 132, 136
  social, 104
Israeli-Palestinian conflict, 82–83

justice, 2, 4–5, 22, 25, 27, 35, 37, 44, 59–60, 66, 93–94, 122, 162
  environmental, 9–10, 149–151, 154–5
  European Court of, 6, 36, 57, 82
  historical, 59, 118
  natural, 22
  International Court of (Hague), 26
  social, 2, 5, 77, 98, 102
  transformative, 44
  transitional, 5, 37, 43–44, 53, 55, 60–61, 114

Kafka, Franz, 79–80

"last utopia", 1
law
  humanitarian, 25, 113, 121
  international, 7–9, 28, 33–47, 58, 113, 118, 122, 124, 162

marginalized populations, 62
media and communication, 4–10, 34, 37, 47, 58, 76–77, 80, 82–83, 85, 94, 141, 155, 162–3

  contemporary, 8, 80–86, 102
  digital, 2, 8, 76, 81, 134, 141, 163
  information and communication technologies ICT, 6, 60, 76, 78, 81, 84, 141
  mass media, 81, 84
  new media, 2, 57, 81–82
  policy and regulation, 60, 76–77, 82, 84–85
  social, 41, 94, 102–3, 119, 134, 142–3
  studies, 83, 102
memorials, 20, 22, 44, 66
memories
  counter-memories, 95
  individual, 80, 133
  national, 35, 39
  official, 123
  silenced, 2
minority, 55, 65, 95, 99, 117, 137, 142
  cultural, 95
  ethnic, 41, 60, 155
  political, 95
  racial, 60
  sexual, 60
mnemonic imagination, 79
monuments, 3, 38–39, 44, 54, 59, 114, 135
moral remembrance, 54, 58–62, 68
museums, 9, 38, 44, 54, 59, 96, 114, 132–4, 137–8, 141–3, 162–3

nationalism, 35, 39, 41, 113, 153
Nazism, 19, 23–29, 55, 61, 117, 119, 151
neoliberalism, 10, 62–65, 68, 152

occupation, 24, 27

pacifism, 22–25
patriotism, 23
political economy of remembering, 138
politics of recognition, 59, 136
post-conflict societies, 37, 44, 53, 64–66, 149
post-financial crisis, 138
privacy, 6, 57, 85, 136

racism, 3, 115, 138
refugees, 96, 99

right
  to be forgotten, 6, 36, 54, 57, 82, 86, 134
  to communicate, 6, 36, 82
Russia-Ukraine relationship, 115

self-determination, 65, 152
Sen, Amartia, 8, 10, 76–79, 83–84, 155, 163
Shakespeare's Hamlet, 9, 33
Sophocles' Antigone, 7, 9, 17–19, 28–29, 151
state sovereignty, 25, 28–29
storytelling, 38, 79, 140
survivors, 19, 25, 67, 96–97, 101

testimony, 5, 33, 96–97, 100–1
trauma, 53, 103–5, 136

truth and reconciliation commissions, 40, 44, 60, 94

UNESCO, 38, 45, 134,
United Nations, 6, 18, 20, 25, 27–28, 36, 44, 134

Western Europe, 114–5
witness, 47, 60
World War I, 17, 19–20, 23, 25, 28, 55, 151, 162
World War II, 7, 17–20, 25, 28–29, 36, 55–56, 59, 63, 92–93, 117, 119, 122–3, 151, 155, 162

Yizkor, 97, 23–24

Zikaron Basalon, 92, 95–106, 163

www.ingramcontent.com/pod-product-compliance
Lightning Source LLC
Chambersburg PA
CBHW070043040426
42333CB00041B/2179